Writer Tells All

INSIDER SECRETS TO GETTING
YOUR BOOK PUBLISHED

Robert Masello

AN OWL BOOK

Henry Holt and Company   New York

Henry Holt and Company, LLC
Publishers since 1866
115 West 18th Street
New York, New York 10011

Henry Holt® is a registered trademark of
Henry Holt and Company, LLC.

Published in Canada by Fitzhenry & Whiteside Ltd.,
195 Allstate Parkway, Markham, Ontario L3R 4T8.

Library of Congress Cataloging-in-Publication Data
Masello, Robert.
Writer tells all: insider secrets to getting your book
published / Robert Masello.—1st ed.
p.   cm.
"Owl book."
Includes index.
ISBN 0-8050-6551-2 (pb)
1. Authorship—Marketing.   I. Title.
PN161 .M38 2001   00-063229
070.5'2—dc21

Henry Holt books are available for special
promotions and premiums. For details contact:
Director, Special Markets.

First Edition 2001

Designed by Paula Russell Szafranski

Printed in the United States of America

1 3 5 7 9 10 8 6 4 2

For
my cousin Chuck Cohen,
the computer genius who saved my sanity

my editor, Liz Stein,
who let the secrets of the forbidden city be told

and

Jack "the Barracuda" Horner,
ruthless predator of the literary seas

The aim, if reached or not, makes great the life;
Try to be Shakespeare, leave the rest to fate!

—ROBERT BROWNING,
"BISHOP BLOUGRAM'S APOLOGY"

Contents

Part III: Celebrity

Part I

ART

Writing a book is a long, exhausting struggle, like a long bout of some painful illness. One would never undertake such a thing if one were not driven by some demon whom one can neither resist nor understand.

—George Orwell,
"Why I Write," *England Your England and Other Essays*

Mission Statement

What better place to begin a book about writing a book than at the very beginning of this one? It was late December, in the middle of the afternoon (just before my nap time), when I got the call from my literary agent in New York, who called to say, "Good news! We've got an offer—from Holt—for your new book proposal."

"We do?" I replied, with my customary confidence. "Really?"

"You're not going to get rich off this one, but it's respectable."

Now that I knew this was for real, I settled down enough to ask the agent a few of the usual questions, about the advance, the due date, the royalty rates, stuff like that.

"Don't worry about the details," the agent said, "I'll iron those out next week. Your job is to get off the phone and start writing."

We hung up, and I did what I usually do when I get a book deal. No, I didn't start writing. Taking care to step over the dog, I jumped up from my chair and, arms raised over my head, did a victory lap around my office. Total distance? About eight feet. But still, it serves.

When my wife got home, I told her the news, and we both did one more exhausting lap.

Then, as is always the case with these things, reality started to set in.

What had I done? Who was I to think I could write a book? What would I say? How could I say it in enough pages? What on earth had I gotten myself into?

Now, let me just say that I've been down this road many times before, so I know the landscape pretty well. Initial euphoria, immediately followed by doubt, fear, and trepidation. And then, hard on the heels of that, months of arduous and solitary work. There's nothing like getting a book deal to make you question your choice of vocation.

But in this particular instance, all of that *tsuris* (worry, for non-Yiddish speakers) *is* the point. It's *why* I'm writing this book in the first place—to explore and to explain the whole process of creating a book, from that first glimmer of a great idea all the way through to completion. The prospect of creating an entire novel, or a whole nonfiction book, is one of the most daunting I can think of. All you can see ahead of you is reams of blank paper waiting to be filled, and hours of solitude while you're locked in a lonely embrace with your computer screen. Outside your window, you'll hear the sounds of children playing in the sunshine, birds singing, ice-cream trucks tinkling their bells (I want to live where you live!), but you'll have to draw the blinds and stay inside, wrestling with your thoughts, your characters, your prose style. You'll wonder if this labor is ever going to be over, if you'll ever be able to walk into a bookstore and see your book there (preferably on a rack by the counter), if you'll ever be able to send a copy to that certain someone who turned you down for a date in high school. And all I can tell you is . . . eventually.

Writing a book is not a brief endeavor. In fact, it can be a pretty long haul. You will have long dark nights of the soul when you wonder whether your characters will ever cooperate and do what you want them to, days when you want to bang your head on the desk because the elegantly formulated thoughts inside your skull keep coming out a hopeless mishmash on paper, weekends when you are firmly convinced everybody else is at the beach and you're the only one alone in a room, stewing in your own juices. You'll stare bleary-eyed at the words you've just typed—Chapter Sixteen—and think, *Wouldn't it really make more sense to resurface the driveway right now? I mean, just how long can I keep putting that off?*

The challenge is to overcome those distractions and doubts, to keep your focus and plow ahead, because—and here you will just have to trust me for the time being—it's worth it in the end. In the end, you have a book—a finished book—with your name on it. With your ideas and your story, your words and your thoughts, inside of it. You've got something tangible to show for all your work and all your effort, something that no one can ever take away from you, something that exists, between two covers and in the Library of Congress, which proves you not only had something to say, but you had the courage, fortitude, and talent to say it. And that, my friend, is no mean accomplishment.

So where are we? We're at the beginning of the journey. You want to write a book—what kind I don't know, but it doesn't really matter yet—and I want to show you how to go about doing it. How to figure out just what your idea, or your story, really is. How to get started—formulating and outlining and planning your book. How to find an agent who will actually read and respond favorably to your material. How to get your manuscript, or proposal, to the right publisher. How to work with an editor—what to expect, and what to forget. How to navigate that entire complex publishing process, from contract to galleys. How to get your publishing house to get behind your book (strangely enough, they don't always do that) and promote it first to the stores, and then to the book-buying public. How to handle yourself on TV and radio talk shows, when your book becomes a media sensation and your life is no longer your own. How to open a numbered bank account in Grand Cayman where you can safely stash your royalties tax-free. (Okay, that last one isn't true. But the rest is.)

Oh, and one more thing. I'm a writer myself. Not an editor, not an agent, not a publisher. A writer. Just like you, I pull my hair out, one follicle at a time. Unlike the authors of other books you might just happen to come across, probably in the same section of the bookstore as you've found this one, I'm coming to you from the same chair you're sitting in right now. I know what it is to actually do the deed; I know what the hurdles are, and how to get over them. In this book, I'm going to level with you absolutely, and tell you just what you have to watch out for, what promises to disregard ("We'll be sending you on an international book tour, all expenses paid, on the company's Gulfstream 4!"), what methods you can use to bring your book the success and attention it no doubt deserves. I've already spoken to my brilliant, delightful, and supportive editor at this publishing house, and she's given me carte blanche to say whatever I want about the whole mystifying process of writing and publishing a book, whether it reflects well on the industry or not. So, sucker that I am, I'm going to take her at her word and do just that.

For me, this is either the beginning of a great adventure, or the end of my so-called career.

Confronting the Monster

Okay, this first thing I'm going to suggest that you do is either going to depress you no end, or lift your confidence level immeasurably. Let's hope it proves a booster.

Get out of your bathrobe, get dressed, and go to your local bookstore. A small, independent bookstore would be fine (if you can still find one), but what I'm really thinking of are those giant chain superstores.

What do you see when you get inside? Books—that's right. Acres and acres of books. Shelves as far as the eye can see. Racks and racks of new titles and old, in hardcover, trade paperback, mass market. Every year, something like fifty or sixty thousand new titles are published—that's in addition to all the titles that have come before and are still in print—and all of these books have got to fight for shelf space somewhere in this store. Even here, with seemingly unlimited space, with special areas devoted to everything from Astronomy to Architecture, Romance to Religion, History to Horror, there's only room for so many books. And as a result, some just won't make the cut.

Now you can take all this in a *negative* way. (My family has taken that tack for generations.) You can look at all these books, this overwhelming spectacle of competing titles, and you can say to yourself, *I quit. How am I ever going to think of anything that hasn't been written already? How will I come up with any story that will be able to hold its own against all the stories already in here? How can I ever expect to find any elbowroom for myself in* here, especially when Stephen King and Danielle Steel seem to have the whole first floor sewn up?

Or, you can take a more *positive* approach. You can look at all these books, all these shelves, all these sections, and say to yourself, *Wow—look at all the books that do get published! Look at all the authors who do find their way into print! Scads of them! And look at how uninspired a lot of this stuff is! I can do better than this! What was I so worried about?*

Now you're talking. What you've got to do is get past that monolithic, terrifying notion called A BOOK. Most of us who want to write books revere them. For years, we've studied them in school. We've relished them in private. We take one with us almost everywhere we go, on the train to work, on vacation, into the bed with us at night. We get engrossed in them. (A college girlfriend, frustrated that I wasn't giving her my undivided attention, once grabbed a book out of my hands and threw it out the dormitory window. "That was *Ulysses!*" I said. "You could have killed someone.") A book is a powerful, almost talismanic object for most of us, and writing one seems like the ultimate act of hubris.

But you've got to get over that. I yield to no one in my love for books, but that hasn't stopped me from writing them. So what if they're not classics? They're the best I can do, given my own talents and limitations, and in some instances, sometimes for whole pages at a time, they've been downright okay. When I wrote my first novel, I sent copies to my parents (divorced), then waited, and waited, to hear what they thought. Finally, I couldn't stand it anymore, and I called my mom and said, "What did you think?"

She took a second to find le mot juste, then said, "Leisurely, wasn't it?"

Hey, I'm no fool—I know a synonym for *boring* when I hear one.

Maybe, I thought, I'll do better with my father. When I asked him for his opinion, he hemmed and hawed for a minute, then came up with, "It's the kind of book your mother will like."

So okay, not everybody has to like every book you write.

But has that stopped me from continuing to write them? Absolutely not—just ask my therapist. You may or may not be able to please your parents, but don't tie yourself up in knots over it. Worry about pleasing yourself. Write the kind of book that *you* would enjoy reading. Write it the way you want to write it, the way you feel it has to be written, and hang the consequences (along with your critics). A book is among the most marvelous things around, but with very few exceptions—the Bible, the Koran, *Jonathan Livingston Seagull*—it's not holy.

Writing, however, can be. I'm not a religious man, but the act of writing does strike me as about as close to a communion with the soul as anything short of prayer. When you're writing, and I mean anything from a letter to a detective story, you're attuned to the voice inside you in a way you never are otherwise. You're listening to yourself, hearing words that are echoing only in your own heart and head, thoughts that you didn't even know you had until they found their way onto the paper or computer screen in front of you. Sometimes, I don't even know what I think about something—what I *really* think about something—until I've tried to write it down, and then it's as if another voice, another person were dictating the words, the scene, the attitude, and in the process revealing things I hadn't yet consciously recognized or understood. That doesn't happen all the time (most of the time I'm just struggling to say anything at all), but when it does it's pretty amazing.

There is, however, one thing that's needed if it's going to happen at all—and that one thing, which I dread as much as jury duty or a tax audit, is solitude. The fact that others dread it, too, and flee from it at every opportunity, is probably why we have what I now like to call the Starbucks School of Writing.

I was there just yesterday with my friend Bill.

Just to get a table, the last one free in the entire place, we had to clamber over twenty-seven backpacks littering the floor, step over nine computer cables, and borrow a chair that, until then, had been holding a stack of books, papers, and a Bread Loaf sweatshirt.

Bill and I had no sooner started talking than the guy at the next table looked up with a grimace and gestured at the laptop glowing on the table, right next to his empty coffee cup.

"Sorry, guys," he said, "but could you keep it down?"

Since I am nothing if not polite, I instinctively said, "Oh, sure—no problem."

A little embarrassed—had we been talking that loudly?—I took a sip from my coffee and looked around to see if any other table, farther away, had come free. None had. But then, like a cartoon lightbulb going off over my head, I had this astonishing thought.

I'm in a Starbucks! I'm not in a library! I'm allowed to talk in here!

Bill and I resumed our conversation—not at high volume, but within the easily audible range—and as expected, the guy looked up again, more peeved this time, and said, "Come on—I'm writing a novel here."

"Are you absolutely sure about that?" I said, with uncharacteristic courage. "Maybe it just looks like you're writing a novel there."

He appeared stunned.

"If you were really writing a novel," I explained, "you'd be home, behind a closed door, with no one around to observe you writing your novel."

"Well, then, what do you call this?" he said, turning his laptop so I could see the words on the screen.

"I call that typing. It's very closely related to writing."

Things could have gotten worse—the guy was clearly getting steamed and I was already wondering how I could make it to the door before shots were fired—when a Starbucks employee, God bless him, intervened.

"You know, you really can't just work in here all day," he said to the novelist manqué. "It's been a couple of hours, and we're getting kind of crowded."

"You've got to be kidding," the guy said, before pulling his stuff together, then punching a couple of buttons to turn off his laptop. "Forget it—I can go to The Coffee Bean and Tea Leaf across the street."

The Starbucks employee shrugged, and the guy left in a noisy huff.

"Thanks for coming to our rescue," I said to the employee.

"That's okay. He works in here all the time."

I'm sure he does, I thought. And now that the commotion was over, I could see others a lot like him, all around the place, hunkering down again over their laptops and notebooks, legal pads and journals. It reminded me of the little coffeehouses I used to go to in Greenwich Village, where the poets and songwriters used to hang out, scribbling furiously on paper napkins and place mats. And even then, I remember thinking, *This isn't writing that's going on here. This is a kind of performance art. The title ought to be, "Look at me—am I creative or what?"*

And even though you might not want to hear it, and Starbucks might not want to lose the revenues, I still think it's true.

Short of working as a morgue attendant on the night shift, writing has got to be the loneliest job in the world. And once you embark on a book, even if the embarkation *is* voluntary, you'll do anything you can to get away from it, to get back out into the world. You'll make up any excuse. You'll try telling yourself it's a nice day, and that there's a perfectly good bench in the park—not far from the boat pond—where you can sit outside and work in longhand.

Or what about that nearly deserted deli down the street, where they'll happily let you sit at a booth, nursing a piece of cheesecake, and write undisturbed for hours?

And what could be so bad, really, about a quick stop at that corner Starbucks—wouldn't a jolt of caffeine and sugar wind up *boosting* your productivity right about now?

There's no end to the stories you can tell yourself—and trust me, I know them all because I've *tried* them all. *Say, if I went to the movies this afternoon, that would fill me with so much guilt and self-loathing that when I got home, I'd write like the wind!* But stories, unfortunately, is what they are. If you want to write that book, you have to sit down, all by yourself, at a desk—or a table, I'll accept a table—and write it. It's as simple as that. And as hard.

Starbucks should be your reward, not your office.

Clearing the Hurdles

Now, if you're *looking* for obstacles to writing a book, things that will continuously trip you up, slow you down, and even bring you to a crashing halt, I've got a million of them. But there are three in particular on the track ahead, and if you ever expect to write a whole book, you're going to have to hurdle over every one.

The first hurdle, though you'll hate to have to think about them this way, is your friends. Well-meaning though they may be, they will get in your way every time. Because they're your friends, they will want you to come out and play. They will call you up all the time. They will have extra tickets to sporting events, plays, concerts. They'll want to fix you up with the perfect blind date, or drag you to a party, or just get together for a quick lunch. Where's the harm in that? A burger and fries, for goodness' sake! What—you're not planning to *eat* until you've finished your book?

But what they will never understand, so don't knock yourself out explaining, is that you're writing a book and you really have to stick with it. "Sure, you're writing a book," they'll say, "that's great! Let's go to the diner and talk about it!" And if you insist on staying put, or on taking a rain check for the party, the cup of coffee, the grand opening of the new mall, they will take offense. Maybe not the first time, but the second or third. I've got one very good friend, a creative type himself, but he never really gets it. I'll tell him I'm going underground, that I've got a new book to get written, but he'll still call me up for all kinds of things and get mad at me when I don't call him right back, or agree to go out. Sometimes, it's even occurred to me that he calls because he's not working himself, and on some subconscious level he wants to make sure that I'm not working, either. That is a low and reprehensible thought of mine . . . but it may have some truth to it.

What you've got to remember is that your friends will probably never understand what you've undertaken—and you cannot allow yourself to feel guilty about that. A lot of times I've felt so bad about not being as good a friend to someone as I should that I've given in and gone to some dreadful screening or pointless event just to keep the friendship alive. But it doesn't work that way; in fact, it works in quite the opposite fashion. When you're taken away from your higher calling, from what you know you should be doing, and want to be doing, to attend something that you weren't really all that interested in from the start, you only wind up resenting your friend for getting you into this, and nobody has a good time. You'd have both been better off if you'd stuck to your guns in the first place.

The same holds true for your family—in spades. You may be able to put your friends on hold, but your mother? Never. If I so much as *suggested* that you do that, I'd be consigned to the ninth ring of Hell for eternity. But your family will probably be just as obtuse as your pals. Let's face facts. In the eyes of the world, you're either at work—which means you're at an office, a factory, a prison yard, whatever—or you're at home. And if you're at home, you're not working. If you're at home, you can legally and legitimately be interrupted for anything from an urgent question—"Why can't you see stars during the daytime?"—to a routine chore, like emptying the dishwasher. What you have to convey is that certain times—such as the times when you are writing—are sacrosanct, and that you really are trying to accomplish something. You're writing a book behind those closed doors, not playing video games. (That is true, isn't it?)

The third big obstacle to writing your book is inanimate. It sits on your desk, silent most of the time, drawing no particular attention to itself. But in some ways, this thing is your most dangerous distraction of all—the telephone. Whenever you're stuck, whenever you're bored, lonely, depressed, anxious, it's sitting right there, whispering *Pick me up. Take a breather. Reach out and touch someone.* I've called my mother, my brothers, friends from high school. There have even been times when I was so desperate not to write that I've called up people I never really liked very much.

And occasionally, the darn thing rings. *Now isn't that an annoyance! How are you supposed to concentrate when you have to keep stopping to answer the phone?* Of course, this, I need hardly remind you, is exactly what answering machines were invented for. Let the machine get it. Let the machine take the whole message. You can listen in if you want to, but unless it's the lottery commission advising you where to show up to collect your winnings, just let this message, and all the others that come in, pile up. You can answer them all later—*after* you've finished your work for the day.

The Quota System

While it's true that writing a book isn't something that gets done overnight, or by grabbing a few minutes every other day, when you just happen to feel like it, it is something that you can do. Lots of people, as you know, already have. Why shouldn't you be one of them?

What it does take is a system, a method, a regular commitment to sitting down and getting some work done. That schedule can be anything you want. You can get up at three-thirty in the morning and work until six A.M. every day, then flop back into bed until your alarm goes off. You can take your lunch hour, eat for fifteen minutes, then spend the rest of the time writing. You can block out mornings on weekends and holidays. It's up to you. But until you get some kind of schedule, the chances that your book will be able to sustain itself, to keep the pace and the rhythm and the energy going long enough for it to reach fruition, are not good. There's an old rule of thumb among writers, and though I don't know if it's true, it sort of feels right. The rule says that for every day you're away from your book, it takes another day to find your way back into it again. From my own experience, that's about right. And it's especially true if the book we're talking about is fiction. That's a whole world you have to reenter, and it can easily take at least a day or two to get back into the scene, into your characters' heads, into the moment.

There's one funny thing, though, about getting on a schedule. Once you commit to it, once your mind (and your tush) get accustomed to the idea of sitting down and concentrating for a certain amount of time every day, your creative faculties start to attune themselves to that time. You'll find that on some level you've been preparing yourself for your work session, so that the minute you sit down you're ready to roll, ready to write, much more easily than you used to be. I know this sounds bogus, as if I'm just trying to con you into doing your homework, but it's true.

Now, having said all this, I live in fear of your asking me one simple question: what's my own schedule? Because, sad to say, I don't have one. (But I'm trying, really I am.)

Here's my excuse. Because I have to write for a lot of different places—publishing houses, magazines, newspapers, occasionally a TV show—my own schedule can be pretty erratic. If an editor calls to say that something needs to be set in type, or go to press, the next day, I can't very well tell him, "You'll just have to wait until I've worked on my novel for the day." Well, I guess I *could* say that, but it's doubtful I'd be getting any more work from that publication again. An inordinate amount of my time is spent fielding business calls (didn't I tell you the phone was your mortal enemy?) and just attending to the million and one things, none of them glamorous, that the life of a professional writer entails. To the extent that I can follow a schedule, I do. I get up kind of late, have coffee, walk the dog, have some more coffee, and unless there's something that really needs to be done, I start writing.

To be honest, and this is something that everybody has to decide for himself or herself, there are certain times of day when I'm just not as creative. Mornings, even afternoons, are okay for writing articles, essays, reviews, that sort of thing. But for sustained creative work, on a novel or a screenplay, for instance, the only time I really feel in tune with my muse is at night. After nine or ten o'clock. I don't think she's really awake until then, either. However, that's just me—I grew up in a household that kept really late hours; my mother and father would routinely start a game of Scrabble at midnight, my brothers and I would stay up late watching the Marx Brothers. It's only at night, when there's nothing but darkness pressing against my windows, when the phone has stopped ringing, the dog has conked out, and even my wife has turned out her light, that I feel as if my brain is finally bestirring itself.

How long will I work? That, too, depends on a lot of factors, but a couple of hours is about right. A lot of people who want to write a book think that you must have to sit there for six or seven hours at a stretch, but in almost every case, doing that would be pointless. Most of us have about two or three hours of good, concentrated writing in us at any one time, and after you've gotten it out, the well is dry and needs some time to replenish itself. Henry James called it "the well of unconscious cerebration," but I'm not sure my personal well is really that classy. Still, if you read interviews with writers, you'll find that all but the most prolific and ambitious of them work for just a few hours a day and spend the rest of the time storing up their thoughts and energy for their next bout with the keyboard or legal pad. In other words, stick to some kind of a schedule, but don't make it so onerous that you bail out in exhaustion after a week. In that respect, it's like picking an exercise regimen: make it too tough, and you'll quit, sore all over, before the month is out. Build slowly, and know when you've hit your threshold.

The other striking thing about most writers who talk about their work habits is that they almost always cite some kind of word quota that they strive for each day. Even the authors with long and successful careers behind them will admit that in the course of a day, they're lucky to get one or two usable pages; nearly every one of them would consider that amount to be a good day's haul. Philip Roth, as I recall, has said he's satisfied if he gets one page that he's happy with every day. The amazing thing is, if you just stick with it, even writing no more than a page or two a day, the pages eventually add up and before you know it, you've got a completed book. One page a day—roughly 250 words—will give you 365 pages by the end of the year, enough to make many manuscripts complete.

There is, perhaps, nothing more dispiriting, more enervating, than thinking of all the words, all the pages, all the work, that writing a book is going to constitute. If I allow myself to think about that when I'm getting started, about all the problems I'm going to encounter, the plot points where I'm going to get stuck, the sheer volume of the verbiage I'm going to have to produce, then I find myself paralyzed in my chair. It's like climbing a mountain—you don't want to stop and look up. The summit can look unreachable.

That's where some kind of quota system comes in handy; it gives you a reliable measure of your progress. Of course, I'd be lying to you if I didn't admit that my wife, Laurie, has come to dread that word "quota" like no other in the English language. As soon as she hears me start talking about it—as in, "I can't go out for lunch today, I haven't met my quota," or "I'll wash the car tomorrow—I haven't got my quota, yet," or "I know the sofa is on fire—I'll get to it as soon as I've finished my quota"—she knows that she's in for months of nearly monomaniacal behavior on my part.

She also knows that I've seriously begun my next book.

The quota is really just another way of setting a schedule, or timetable, for getting your book completed. Some days I feel really productive and I can sit at the keyboard for hours; other days, I can't wait to get free. But by setting an attainable goal—a certain number of words that I absolutely have to produce each day—I can gain a little flexibility. As soon as I've gotten, say, five hundred words—two pages—I'm officially off the hook. Some days it takes hours to get them, but on good days it doesn't. And the great thing about setting your quota unrealistically low, and five hundred words is pretty low, is simple: you're almost always able to meet it. Every day you can pat yourself on the back and say, "Well done, old bean, everything else you do today, should you decide to keep on working, is pure gravy." You know you've done something, made some progress toward your ultimate goal, and you can feel remarkably virtuous for doing anything more than that.

Is this ridiculous? Maybe. But it works for me, and frankly, some variation on it works for almost every writer I know. By breaking up the task of writing a book into easily manageable hunks—a few hours a day, a couple of pages at a time—you've made the great beast a lot less terrifying. You've chopped it up into digestible pieces. You're able to keep on track, and keep your sanity, while plodding dutifully ahead. Writing books really is a task for tortoises, not hares.

Your Worst Boss

In one of the most painful ironies of the writing life, you have now traded any bad boss you've ever had for the worst one of your life.

You.

No matter how bad that guy was at the burger shop where you worked after school, or that woman who pushed you around when you temped at the real-estate office, at least you got to go home at night and forget all about them.

When you're writing a book, the only boss you've got is you. The only person who probably cares if you ever even finish the darn thing is you. The only person who can get you there—across the finish line—is you.

And there's no escape. Get up in the morning and the first person you have to face is you. Go to bed at night and the last person you tuck in is you. And all the time in between, running errands, doing your job, fixing dinner, you're still with you, the boss—the only one who knows for sure whether or not you've done your writing, met your quota, stuck to your self-imposed schedule. It's awful.

That's why we have those wacky things like quotas and schedules—so we'll have something to show that internal boss to get him off our backs for a while. "Look, I've got three—count 'em, three—good pages today! Lay off already!"

Being your own boss means exercising self-discipline. If there's anything that separates book writers from almost every other kind of writer, it's this ability to stick to the plan, to see something through for the long haul. Short-story writers can knock out a tale in a couple of days if they feel like it. An essay or an article can take a journalist an afternoon. But unless you happen to be Georges Simenon, who was famous for banging out his Inspector Maigret novels in a week or so, a book requires that you take the long view. You won't be rewarded for your labors next week, or even next month, but you will be rewarded—and you've got to keep this in mind—one day. One day, you'll complete your manuscript. And the very fact that you've stayed with it for the entire course will bring you an even greater degree of satisfaction than the writing of merely a story or essay can ever do.

I once had a writing student who was working on a novel, one of those coming-of-age tales, based, I was quite sure, on her own recent college experiences. Every week she brought me a chapter, every week I gave her my comments and suggestions, and the next week we did the same. After four or five months, she had completed the book, which she was pretty happy with. Until she discovered, after sending it hither and yon, that no publisher was willing to take it on. As I tried to explain to her more than once, this book was not a failure just because she couldn't get it published. It was her first novel, her first serious attempt at fiction at all, and how many of those ever see print? What I tried to impress upon her was that she'd done it, she'd seen the thing through, and that fact alone separated her from almost all the other would-be novelists out there. So what if this time around she hadn't grabbed the brass ring? She'd learned a lot, just from the process, and the next time she'd stand a much better chance of finding her way into print. Most important of all, she'd proven to me, and to herself, that she had the stamina the job required.

I also urged her to reach a truce with her inner boss. Already she was wondering if she should throw herself into a different novel, only partially thought through, or give up the whole idea of writing and take a job at a friend's public-relations agency. Having managed my own career with only mixed results, I instinctively shy away from giving out career advice, but in this case I told her the one thing I did know: Relax. She'd been out of college about fourteen months, and already she was trying to decide which career choices had to be eliminated, which professional path had to be irreversibly embarked upon, what hopes and dreams had to be boxed up and put away for good. One of the marvelous things about writing is that you can do it anytime, at any point in your life, and nobody can stop you. You don't even need a computer; a legal pad and a pen will do. As long as your inner boss gives you permission, and a little time to yourself, you can always start right in.

Fact or Fiction

It never fails. In every class I teach, I ask the students—who, because these are often adult-education, or extension, classes, come in all ages—what kind of book each one of them is planning to write. In the last class I taught, a young guy came up during a break, bubbling with excitement, to tell me about his book. "I'm a lawyer," he started out, "and it's all about this case I worked on. So I've got to be careful, I know, that I don't get sued. I'm a lawyer—did I mention that?"

"Seven seconds ago."

"Right. Well, I want to write about this incredibly bizarre case, involving this rich old family in Pasadena and what really went on behind their closed doors."

"Okay," I said. "As long as you know you're going to have to be careful you don't break your lawyer-client confidentiality, and all that."

"Oh, that's not going to be a problem," he said. "It's a novel."

"My mistake. I thought you said it was going to be about the actual case and family."

"It is," he said, growing a little exasperated with my slow-wittedness. And then, even as I knew what he was about to say, as I waited in silent horror, he opened his mouth and out came, "It's going to be a nonfiction novel."

I've heard this one so frequently, I no longer shudder . . . even though a shudder is precisely what it deserves. I don't know why or where this confusion over the difference between novels and nonfiction arose, but it is so persistent that I feel we might as well take a minute or two right now to set things straight.

Yes, there are some famous books, most notably Truman Capote's *In Cold Blood*, that purported to blur the boundaries—and to some extent did—by using all sorts of fictional techniques to tell a true story. But regardless of what those authors, their publishers, or the book jackets might have said or suggested, those books are not novels. If they're true stories, populated by real people and recounting a sequence of real events, no matter how gussied up they are with conjecture, recreated dialogue, and internal monologues, they are nonfiction.

True stories. Fact. Equals nonfiction. And most editors, if they so much as *sense* that you are tampering with the evidence, muddying the waters of what you know with what you imagine, will take a great big detour around you and your project.

Now, a novel, on the other hand, is an imagined story. A tale made up by the writer. I was about to say "made up out of whole cloth," but that, I think, is where the confusion arises. Just because the novel you are planning to write may be inspired by, or loosely based upon, things that really happened to you or someone you know, that doesn't make your book nonfiction. You are drawing upon remembered elements—people, places, events—but you are filtering them through your imagination, you are changing them in such a way as to create something new, something artistically satisfying, something fictional. In *War and Peace*, Tolstoy wrote about the battle of Waterloo, but nobody's ever accused the book of being a nonfiction novel. Yes, Napoleon, a bona fide historical figure, makes an appearance, but it is in the service of a made-up story primarily centered around characters like Natasha Rostova and Pierre Bezukhov, among others. History serves as a dramatic backdrop to much of the action, but the book is a novel, nonetheless.

There is one thing I'm willing to concede, however, and that is the trouble that arises from the very term "nonfiction." What a weak, wobbly, self-negating word it is. Afraid to tell you what it is, it tells you instead what it is not. *I'm* not *fiction!* No wonder people get confused. It's like those medical tests which come back "positive" when the news is bad, and "negative" when the news is actually good. In the time it takes you to sort it out, you can have a heart attack.

The Pulitzer Prize winner Richard Rhodes, author of *A Hole in the World* and *The Making of the Atomic Bomb*, shares my distaste, but he's come up with a solution. In his own book *How to Write* (worth picking up just as soon as you've thoroughly absorbed every single word in this one) he suggests that we use the word "verity" to describe all the things that aren't fiction—essays, histories, textbooks, biographies, monographs, etc. His book, I see from checking the copyright page, was first published in 1995, and so far, I'm afraid, I've never heard anyone use the term "verity." I guess that tells us it hasn't exactly caught on. But if my vote counts for anything, I vote for verity. It may not be the perfect solution, but anything, as far as I'm concerned, would be better than "nonfiction."

But nonfiction, for the purposes of this book, will have to serve. However many people it continues to baffle, it's still the industry standard.

That said, and the distinction I now hope reasonably clear, you have a big decision to make. With a "nonfiction novel" no longer in the cards, you have to decide which side of the street you want to walk down—the novel side, where you make up some characters and a story for them to participate in, or the nonfiction side, where you tell a true, even if somewhat embellished, tale.

A lot of aspiring authors get stuck right here at the starting gate. They just can't make up their minds about what kind of book they really want to write; they've got too many ideas vying for their full attention, too many projects in one stage or another of mental development. And then, once they finally pick one and start to work on it, they abandon ship when it hits the first snag. That's the great, but insidiously harmful, thing about having a lot of ideas: as soon as one starts giving you trouble, you can decide it's not your fault—that *idea* itself was fatally flawed!—and now that you've had more time to think about it, wasn't that *other* idea a better one, anyway? Like most writers, I've got dozens of aborted, abandoned, and forgotten book ideas, languishing in boxes and drawers in my office. There's the novel I started about the Mayan archaeological expedition—that one went to maybe one hundred pages, before I saw a movie that I thought was too close to my plot and I decided to give up. Or then there's that New York thriller (seventy-five pages in the box) that I felt was moving off-track somehow, only I was too lazy to analyze and fix the problem. And what about the bittersweet memoir about growing up in the Midwest (a couple of dozen pages of notes)? In every case, I ran out of steam, because I wasn't committed enough to the idea, I got bored, I came across something else (a book, a movie, a TV show) that I thought explored too much of the same territory, whatever. Excuses come in more colors than a box of crayons. While it's easy to get excited about a book at the outset, it's much harder to stay that way as you encounter the myriad, and absolutely unavoidable, problems that crop up.

But maybe, just maybe, if you know these problems are coming, if you realize and accept that there will be delays, detours, and difficulties with any book you undertake, you won't be so quick to set one project aside and turn your attention to another; that one won't be trouble-free, either.

At some point, you're going to have to look over all the possible book candidates, and forsaking all the rest, at least for a while, say, "That's the one." If this sounds like a marriage proposal, it sort of is. With any luck, you won't have to write this one book for the rest of your life, unless you're Proust, but you will have to live with it on a daily and nightly basis for a period of months, or maybe even years. If you're not in love right now, when you're getting engaged, the relationship will never work. You've got to be head over heels in love with this idea, because if you're not, and the inevitable doldrums set in, you won't have the passion to plow through them and stay committed.

So how do you make your mind up? As a man who didn't even consider getting married until his late thirties, I'm probably the last person you should ask about commitment. But putting that aside (and I'm very happy with the choice I eventually did make), you've got to look inside yourself and really think, *What matters the most to me right now? What story do I really want to tell? Which is the one that I just can't stop thinking about?* Don't start worrying about the marketplace, the competition, the time it'll take to complete the book—there'll be plenty of sleepless nights to worry about that stuff later on. Right now, just focus on what you want to do, because—and it's really amazing how this works—the thing that you *most* want to do will turn out to be the thing you will do the best.

The Hydraulic Theory

And once you do know what you want to write, once you've made your decision, by all means keep it to yourself.

What? You mean not tell anybody?

I mean, not tell anybody.

Now this runs counter, I know, to most people's inclinations. Most of us can't wait to tell our friends, sweethearts, and family members about our brilliant inspiration, our surefire bestseller. But over the years, I've developed something I call the Hydraulic Theory of Literary Composition, in which I believe quite strongly. (In the scientific hierarchy, it is currently ranked somewhere between the Theory of Relativity and the invention of Pop-Tarts.)

Basically, it goes like this: the more you talk about a book, the less likely it is that you will ever write it.

A book, I have decided, is kind of like a steam engine: every time you talk about it, every time you start telling somebody about its various twists and turns, you let out some of the steam, and eventually the whole thing just slows to a halt, from which it generally never recovers.

I have this friend Max, who's had a reasonably successful career as a freelance journalist, but his aspiration has always been to write a huge, Robert Ludlum/Ken Follett-style thriller. Last week, he stopped by my place, and within about fifteen minutes Max had, as always, managed to turn the conversation to his novel. The same novel that we've been talking about, if memory serves, for about four years now.

"Did I tell you that I've decided Jeremy Blade"—his dashing protagonist—"is going to have worked for a covert ops organization, and that when he uncovers the nuclear smuggling operation, he calls on his old boss, who's kind of retired to the Virginia hunt country, to assemble a crew of retired Cold Warriors to help him out?"

"No, I'm not sure you did."

"Oh, then you also don't know what happens next. The thing is, a lot of these retired guys hold grudges against the CIA, the NSA, the FBI, and one of them in particular has a bone to pick with Jeremy, though Jeremy is unaware of that when he takes him on. When they get together in Tunisia . . ."

Somewhere in here, I must admit, I generally drift off, though it doesn't seem to faze Max; I don't think he notices, and if he does, I don't think he cares. He's just so happy to be telling his story one more time, to be seeing it unfold before his eyes as he tells it, as he embroiders the scenes and even does some of the dialogue, that he pays no attention. What he's doing is telling the story that, for one reason or another, he can never get around to writing. I have this terrible feeling that, in another four years, I'll still be hearing about the latest plot developments in his as yet unwritten Jeremy Blade thriller.

Whenever I get buttonholed at a party, or after a class, by a writer who starts giving me a blow-by-blow account of his or her plot, I know that's a book that will never see the light of day. All the energy of it, all the interest it holds, even for its author, is being expended in talking about it. The book is vanishing into thin air right before our eyes. Did you ever notice how published authors react on talk shows and interview segments when the interviewer asks them about their next book? It's as if they were asked "What's your kinkiest sexual fantasy?" Real writers instinctively know that they need to be wary, that they can diminish, even jinx, their best idea by going on about it to all and sundry. When they have to get off the interviewer's hook, authors on the talk-show circuit almost invariably offer some canned response, along the lines of "Well, I've just been noodling with something for a while," or "I have a few things in mind, I just haven't decided on one yet," before trying to change the subject altogether.

There's another danger, too, to airing your idea. It would be great if everyone you told it to reacted with a clap on your shoulder and a "Wow, that's the best idea I've ever heard! You must be a genius after all." But that's unlikely. Instead, you're likely to start getting their opinions. Suggestions. Even worse, their *help*: "Have you thought about telling it from the hamster's point of view?" "What if your protagonist *died* halfway through the book? That would really catch your readers off guard!" "Wouldn't the book be more salable if your hero was also a master of the martial arts?" You do not want to hear all this; you do not want all these voices, all these comments, all these helpful suggestions, clanging in your head—especially when you're still trying to hear your own voice clearly and without static. Good books don't get written by committees, or by conducting public polls.

And they don't get written by creative-writing classes, or writers' support groups, either. There's a temptation, and I know it well, to get out of your room, to socialize with other people, to try out some of your material, especially the stuff you've written that you think has turned out well, and which might earn you some applause. Lots of people do this, lots of people submit their works in progress to public scrutiny, but I still contend that, by and large, it's a bad idea. In college, I took several creative writing classes, and, my own work aside, I saw what I thought was a lot of psychic and artistic damage being inflicted. I saw fellow students whose work was skewered, with whatever fine intentions, by their classmates, and while some of these skewerings might even have been warranted, others were not. I saw good ideas battered beyond recognition, I saw strong initial impulses watered down until they were drivel, I saw distinctive voices taking on too many colorations from too many comments by too many people. I even saw a teacher take one student's idea, which in my opinion, was pretty fresh and clever, and reshape it until it was now just like ten other things I'd already read. The student in question was a young African-American guy, and his story had wedded an inner city background to a different kind of story altogether, but by the time the instructor was done with it, everything unusual had been taken out and what the guy was left with was yet another dreary account of one young man's struggle against gang life in the ghetto. Although the student seemed to be accepting of the teacher's changes, I swear that I'd seen him visibly deflate before my eyes. I wanted to stand up and scream, but decided that I should wait until the class was over.

Outside, in the hallway, I pulled him aside and told him that I much preferred the story the way he'd originally constructed it. Another student, who overheard, jumped in with her own, "Yes. Don't change it. Do it the way you wanted in the first place." The guy gave us kind of a weak smile and trudged off, now *totally* confused—the teacher, the *pro*, had told him one thing, and now a couple of classmates had told him another.

I'm not suggesting you have to tell no one, ever, anything about what you're writing. If someone's interested, you can say you're working on a book (there are far more shameful things you can admit to). You can even say a little bit about it—"It's a murder mystery, revolving around a paranoid writer who's always getting asked what he's working on"—but under most circumstances you should just leave it at that. Under what circumstances should you consider saying more? That would be if (a) the person you're talking to is an editor who's just admitted to having a huge budget, and no books to spend it on, or (b) if you're hopelessly stuck, or unsure of something in the book, and the person you're turning to is what I like to think of as your ideal reader.

Every writer should have one such reader.

Many writers, even the ones like me who prefer to work in private, have one person whose judgment they trust, and in whose hands they don't fear placing themselves and their work. A person they are confident will offer good objective advice, and do it with no personal animus. A lot of writers use their spouse or partner in this capacity, but personally, I'd never do that. What if my wife didn't like it? What if it caused her to lose what little respect she still had for me? What if she decided she should leave me for somebody who could write better? No, when it comes to my wife, I just want her to think that everything I write is inspired, and, if I'm ever crazy enough to *ask* her what she thinks, to say precisely that: "Everything you write is inspired, honey." If she walks into my office while I'm writing, I put my hands up in front of the computer screen to hide what's there.

While I was living in New York, I did have an ideal reader, my friend Linda, a writer who lived two blocks away. Actually, Linda and I were each other's ideal reader. She'd regularly show me her work, and no matter what I had to say about it—it was always good, it sometimes just needed some pruning—she'd listen carefully, ask intelligent questions, make notes and later changes. Occasionally, when I wasn't too utterly ashamed of it, I'd show her mine. But even then, I'd drop off the pages with her doorman and skulk back an hour or two later to get her reaction. I really valued Linda's opinion, she was the consummate craftsman, but I also knew that she'd give me even the worst news in a gentle, encouraging manner. She'd sit in her green wingback chair, with her legs folded under her, going through the text, while I'd squirm on her sofa— or on the floor, if she implied that whole pages had to go—trying not to whine so loudly that the neighbors banged on the wall. Linda knew not to become alarmed by my antics. And I knew that when I absolutely, positively, needed an objective and sympathetic reading, she was the one I could turn to. If you're writing a book and you don't yet have a Linda in your life, you should get one.

"Why Don't You Write One of Those Sidney Sheldon Books?"

Can I tell you just one more thing that can go wrong when you talk too much about the book you're writing? It happened to me the last time I was talking to my father about it. I was breaking my own rule, I know, but since the poor man cannot understand how I make a living at this game, I was foolishly trying to put his mind at rest.

Anyway, I'd no sooner given him my brief spiel than he took the cigar out of his mouth, looked at me with an expression that was equal parts puzzlement and sorrow, and said, "But why don't you write one of those Sidney Sheldon books? I see those books all over the place."

Subtext: *I never see yours anywhere.*

There were two things that galled me about that question. The first was the assumption that I wrote books that sold less well than Sidney Sheldon's do *on purpose*, that I was relentlessly pursuing some grand plan to spend my life in poverty and squalor. But even worse was the assumption that if I *chose* to, if I could just stop being so stubborn for once, I *could* sit down and write a Sidney Sheldon book.

"Well, Dad," I said, kicking myself for ever getting into any of this, "if anybody who felt like it could sit down and write a Sidney Sheldon book, we wouldn't need Sidney Sheldon, would we?"

"Now you're just being a smart alec."

This is how most of our colloquies end.

But by now I've heard every variation on this theme; I've had one friend or another advise me to write everything from a Dean Koontz book to a Danielle Steel. I've even had a manager I once hired tell me to stop writing the kind of novels I was writing at the time and "do a Tom Clancy book." One publishing professional alerted me to the fact that nonfiction adventure books, such as *Into Thin Air* and *The Perfect Storm*, were hot: "You should do one of those big, true-life, outdoor disaster stories about polar exploration or the Amazon jungle, or rock climbing in some remote mountains somewhere." I thought about it for a bit, but the most courageous expedition I'd personally been on was an overnight canoe trip in Wisconsin, when I was twelve. The camp counselor was really scary—he could make his eyeballs roll up into his head until they were completely white—but even with that, I felt the bestseller potential of this exploit was slight.

The danger here is not only in listening to these people; it's in forgetting something so simple, so basic, so plain, that it's easily discounted. The reason Sidney Sheldon is Sidney Sheldon isn't that he sells a lot of books. The reason his books *sell* is that he believes in the stories he tells, and he enjoys them. He is *invested* in those stories and those characters. He's not just writing them to make money (though I'm sure he has no objection to that). He's writing the best stories he knows how, the best way he can, and that's the reason he has succeeded. His books have connected with a huge audience that likes his tales and likes the way he tells them. And successful as he is, he could no sooner write a Tom Clancy book than Tom Clancy could write a Dean Koontz—or than I could write a Sidney Sheldon.

In any book, a kind of communion goes on between the author and the reader; the two of them are pretty much locked in a silent embrace, usually for a lot of hours. And if the author's heart isn't in it, if he's faking it, if he's just trying to imitate some formula in order to sell some books, the reader quickly figures it out. It's not like an announcement is made—ALERT: SLUMMING AUTHOR AT WORK!—but the reader somehow hears it all the same and winds up putting the book aside. It's the same feeling you'd get if somebody told you he or she loved you, and you knew in your heart that it wasn't true. If this was true love, you'd ask yourself, why are you still afraid to leave your wallet on the nightstand?

I have a friend Kevin, who's not a bad writer, but if he actually spent his time writing his own stuff, instead of trying to figure out what the secret formula is that other writers, from Anne Rice to Michael Crichton, have used, he'd have accomplished a whole lot more by now. Last month, after Mary Higgins Clark's monster deal with Simon & Schuster was announced, he called me up to crow, "I've figured it out! I know how her books work."

It was as if he'd just mastered the Superstring Theory of the universe. "That's great," I said. "Maybe you should call *Scientific American*."

"Laugh if you want," he said, "but I know how she builds those books now—she does this little trick with short chapters, for instance—and I'm going to write one myself. That's going to be my next project."

Never wanting to rain on anyone's parade, I wished him luck. And for the next month or two, he will probably be slaving away on his Mary Higgins Clark project—until he loses interest or discovers that he *isn't* Mary Higgins Clark—by which time he will have decided that there's an even simpler and more obvious formula to Clive Barker's books, and that he's going to write one of those instead.

Whatever you might think of the prose style of Sidney, Tom, Mary, or Clive, it's a style that they make work. And they're the only ones who can do it. Even if you knocked yourself out trying to analyze, digitalize, and finally replicate it, you still wouldn't be able to do it. So save yourself the trouble. Instead of wasting your time on cloning experiments, direct your efforts to finding your own voice and subject, and maybe someday you'll be joining these industry titans in the bestselling pantheon. Let other misguided writers try in vain to imitate you.

If you're not really sure what kind of book you should be trying to write, if you think you'd like to try your hand at everything from a biography of Herbert Hoover to an intricate whodunit, but you don't know where you should start your career, there's one easy way to help you decide. Look and see what's lying on your nightstand. (Disregard the *TV Guide*.)

The book that's there is probably the best indication you'll ever get about where your real interests lie. This is the book you've chosen to read for pleasure when you get into bed at night. And any book you attempt to write should be the kind of book that you yourself would pick up and read for pleasure. If it's not, if you're slumming—writing, for instance, a romance just because you think they sell—the cynicism behind your effort will surely surface and sink the project. Trust me on that.

I could quote that line from Joseph Campbell and say something about how you should always "follow your bliss," but frankly, it's always sounded a little doofy and New Age to me. But the idea, I guess, is fairly sound. Figure out what excites you personally, then translate it into your own work. Write the kind of book that you'd pick up in a bookstore and buy.

If I look at my own bedside table right now, what I see—aside from a pile of junk that includes everything from take-out menus to an expired passport—are books by Michael Frayn, Nick Hornby, and Martin Amis. I wish I could have told you I was reading Goethe's letters, or a study of nuclear fission, but I'm not. When it comes to reading for pure pleasure and relaxation, my tastes right now run to the comedic and satiric (and British, too, I guess). What can I say? Still, when it comes to deciding what kind of book I might like to write next, these bedside artifacts are as good an indicator as any I'm likely to get.

Only you know what's on your own bedside table, and only you can decide which road you want to take first. You can always take another road, any number of them in fact, later on. I mean, we're not talking about writing just one book here, are we? We're talking about launching a long and fruitful career. But the best way to start is to go where you already know your heart, and your natural inclinations, lie. No matter what comes of it, at least you'll have had some fun that way. What you want to do—oh, all right, already—is "follow your bliss."

Outlining Nonfiction

Laying out the foundation for a book—the organization, the tone, the material it will cover—is in many ways the hardest part of the process. Done right, the house you build on this foundation will stand securely and strong; done wrong, or not at all, and you'll be lucky to get out before the whole thing comes crashing down on your head.

For the moment, we'll start with nonfiction books. Nonfiction projects are easier to sell to a publisher, because publishers, in turn, find nonfiction books easier in many respects to sell to the public.

With a novel, a publisher never knows. The book could turn out to be a total dud, or the next national sensation. Unless Oprah anoints it, which is as good as money in the bank, it's always an open question whether the book will take off, or disappear overnight. Even the big brand-name novelists occasionally lay an egg for their publishers.

With nonfiction, the game is a little easier to figure out. A publisher can take a look at the topic you're proposing and compare it to other books on that general subject matter, and gather from that a pretty good idea of just how many potential readers there are out there. Let's say your book is called *Lentil Health*, and it's all about how we can improve our life and energy levels by eating a diet of nothing but lentil beans. The publisher, scratching his head and wondering if this is a good idea or not, can check to see if similar books have already been done, and if so, how well they sold.

But you should have done this same homework long before.

One of the first things you should do when you're putting together a nonfiction book project, long before you actually sit down and write the formal proposal, much less any of the manuscript, is to take a trip to the bookstore and browse through the appropriate section. Ask, in this instance, for the beans or legumes area, and after the helpful clerk has pointed you to the most remote section of the selling floor, where all bean-related titles are shelved, you can see if your idea is truly a fresh one. Let's see now, there's *Navy Bean Nights*, *The Garbanzo Gourmet*, *A Thousand and One Things to Do with Lima Beans*, but so far, so good—not a single competing lentil title. And *nothing* whatsoever making claims as extreme as the ones you're prepared to make in *Lentil Health*. Jot down the titles, copyright dates, publishing houses, and a brief description—for your eyes only—of what those other books covered. You might want any or all of this information later on.

Just to make sure you're on firm and unplowed ground, you should probably go to another bookstore or two. Check *their* bean books. Then go on the Internet, to Barnes&Noble.com or Amazon.com, and do a quick search to see if anything turns up. Make notes on any titles that come even close (it's additional data you might need when it comes time to do the proposal). And let's just say, for argument's sake, that one suspicious title does turn up: *Get Yourself a Good Lentil Plan*. It was published four years ago, it's listed as out of print, but Amazon can do a search and try to find a copy for you. By all means, have them do it. If some editor or agent happens to mention this book, you'll be able to say, with confidence, "I've read it, and I can give you three good reasons why it's out of print, but my book will never be."

All of this is ammunition that you will want to have in your arsenal—and the military metaphor, by the way, is not a mistake. Selling your nonfiction book is indeed a little like formulating a battle plan. You've got to think things through and be prepared for whatever hard questions get thrown at you. Some you can duck, but some you've got to meet head-on.

So far, however, we seem to be in the clear and making progress.

What have we learned already? We've learned that there's a certain small but defined, and probably ardent, audience for books about beans.

We've learned that although there are related titles, there aren't any books currently available extolling the singular virtues of the lentil. We know, in short, two of the most crucial things to selling a book proposal: one, that there's a potential audience out there, and two, that there's an unoccupied niche that your book is uniquely qualified to fill. This is all good news.

But what do you do with it? Do you shut yourself up in your room and start writing the book? Do you write a proposal? A letter to a publisher? Do you call an agent? Do you call a press conference?

Okay, let's take a deep breath. First of all, you've got to figure out exactly what it is you want to say, and how you want to say it. What exactly are you planning to do in your book? Is it going to be a first-person narrative about how, once you'd restricted your diet to lentils, your general health and well-being dramatically improved? Or is it meant to be an authoritative survey, with lots of studies and scientific evidence to make a case for the often overlooked bean? Is it a cookbook, a manual, a diatribe? Or maybe a little bit of all those things?

In one class I taught, I remember an older woman who showed me her proposal for a book she had entitled *My Bursitis*. I am not kidding. When I looked it over and suggested that she might want to call the book something like *All about Bursitis*, or *Bursitis and You*, she got prickly. "Why would I want to do that?" she said.

"Because a book should try to reach a somewhat larger public—in this case, for instance, other people who also suffer from bursitis."

"But it's not about their bursitis!" she complained. "It's about mine."

I understood. But that's what might have made it an essay for the *Bursitis Sufferers' Newsletter*, not a book.

Your book, whatever its subject, has got to appeal to a sufficiently large audience that it would be worth a publisher's while to bring it out and try to sell it to those people. "But what if it's my life story?" you might ask. "What if it's a memoir, like *Angela's Ashes*? Aren't those books just about one person's experiences?" True. A life story or memoir can appeal to a vast audience, not only through the artistry of its telling (and you don't get much better than Frank McCourt at that), but because the story it tells has a universal resonance. In their accounts of hardship and triumph, these books tell us, and teach us, a lot about ourselves, about how people can behave under conditions of overwhelming adversity. It's hard to know how a book focusing exclusively on your personal bout with bursitis (or fondness for lentils) could do the same. But I could be wrong; in the end, these things all boil down to a judgment call.

You've also got to decide, regardless of the approach you are determined to take, if there's enough material here for a book. A couple of times, I have sent off premature proposals to my agent in New York, and they've come back with "It's an article, not a book," scrawled on the front page. (The equivalent, I guess, of *My Bursitis*.) Is the approach you're taking, and the material you are planning to cover, going to fill enough pages to make a book? I never fail to be amazed at some of the titles I now see in the stores, books that do seem to be nothing more than *Taking a Really Great Shower*. Do we really need a book about this? Are there people so benighted, and grimy, that they need an entire book to instruct them in something so elementary? I'm sure you've seen those books, too, but don't let them persuade you that anything goes. Those books often have curious histories behind them—perhaps they were commissioned by an especially dim publisher, they're "by" a pseudo-celebrity or radio host, they've got a pre-order from the author himself, who plans to give a copy to each of his showerhead company's five thousand employees—whatever. If you're going to write a book, and especially if it's going to be your first, try to find a topic that merits a full-scale, book-length treatment.

Let's assume that, even after careful consideration, you've decided that *Lentil Health* still fills the bill. Time to move forward.

Which should you do first—an outline, or a proposal? Both are frightening ordeals, enough to make any writer slip a videotape into the VCR and sit back for a couple of hours of decompression.

But as you're going to have to include an outline of some sort in your proposal, I vote for starting with the outline and getting it out of the way. It's like eating your vegetables first . . . before you eat, in this case, the rest of your vegetables.

I'm sure you hate the very thought of outlining (and so do I, if it's any comfort); however, you've got to do it. And later on, when you're actually confronted with the task of writing a book you've sold, you'll be awfully glad that you have the outline to lean on. When you have those unavoidable moments of stark terror, moments when you wonder what you've gotten yourself into, you can look at the outline and say to yourself, *See? I used to think I knew what this book was about. And a publisher thought so, too. Maybe all I have to do is follow this very capable outline!*

An outline will help you remember what you'd planned to do in the first place. Even as I'm writing this book, I'm constantly referring back to the outline, and the mock table of contents, that I included in my proposal. Now, it's true, I keep coming across stuff that I find somewhat baffling—what did I mean when I said that I'd include a section on the "Six Secrets Every Writer Knows"? (What are they? I don't know. Why didn't I jot them down while I knew what they were?) But by and large, the outline still manages to keep me on track. It's a framework, rickety at times and subject to much change—but at least it's there, and I know that if I follow it reasonably faithfully, I'll cover most of the ground I meant to cover, in the order I meant to cover it in.

If it makes things any easier for you, let me add that nobody's looking over your shoulder here. The last time you wrote an outline, you were probably back in high school, and you were doing it for a teacher who was intent on making sure every A had a B, every 1 had a 2, every line was indented correctly, all that stuff. There is no grading here, and for the moment, your outline has to work—and make sense—only for you.

When I'm writing an outline for a nonfiction book (we will get to the peculiar problems of outlining novels in the next chapter), I try to put myself in the mind of the reader and try to figure out what the questions will be, and when they will occur. In other words, what does the reader need to know, and when? With this book, I've been able to use myself as that ideal reader because when I was writing my own first books, I had all the questions about publishing that you no doubt have now. A lot of the questions seemed awfully basic, sometimes so basic that I was embarrassed to ask them. In order to get an understanding of how the publishing world worked, I had to search all over the place—I combed through books and back issues of *Writer's Digest* magazines, I went to lectures and readings, classes and signings. Consequently, I'm sticking as close as I can in this book to that innocent reader—me then, you perhaps now—and trying to address each question, each problem, each area of interest as I remember it came up for me, and as it's probably coming up for you now.

And that, I think, is probably the simplest way to approach doing an outline for your own nonfiction book. Imagine someone who knows nothing, or not much, about your subject, and then lay it all out for him. This book, following the natural trajectory of a book from the first glimmerings of a bright idea to the eventual publication of the finished product, has been relatively simple to organize. But what if the book you want to write doesn't provide you with such an easy narrative device? What if it's something more nebulous, a look, say, at the influence and effect of sports on American life? That's a broad topic, a substantial one, and any book on the subject would have to have a pretty well developed and supported thesis. In fact, your thesis is probably where you would want to start with such a book. In a way, your thesis is where you want to start with *any* nonfiction book.

What are you trying to say? What is the point—or argument—you are trying to make in your book? If you can't get all of this clear in your own mind, then you will never be able to make it clear to your readers. Whatever your topic, it should be—indeed, it *must* be—clearly focused. The more trouble you have figuring out where to start your outline, the more likely it is that you haven't gotten your focus right just yet. At the beginning of your book, you want to be able to give the reader at least a glimpse of the landscape that is going to unfold before him. What, for instance, are you going to say about sports in American life? That it has encouraged a competitive ethic? That it has desensitized American men? That it has permeated the business climate in some salubrious or insidious way? Start your outline with a broad overview of what your book is going to be about, then take a good hard look at the points you plan to make. What sort of order do they naturally fall into? For example, you probably don't want to launch into a whole discussion of the football/baseball/basketball triumvirate without sketching in a little of the history and background of each sport. That right there might tell you to do three short chapters on the origin and evolution of each sport, before you bring them all together into a sort of comparison and contrast. The more you think about what it is you want to say, the more you'll discover there is a natural and even necessary order to the ideas and points you wish to make. Let your argument—or philosophy or view of the subject—dictate a framework for the book.

Once you start laying the book out, point by point, don't get hung up on the details. Let the river flow as freely as possible, because it will probably be following its natural course. Yes, you'll want to do research for the actual book—you'll want to get your facts right, your chronologies straight, your references correct—but for now, it's enough to know that you'll be able, eventually, to back up the assertions you're sketching in. For instance, in the outline you can simply say that sports make up a surprisingly large percentage of the gross national product, but you can pin down exactly what that latest figure is later (though *before* you send out your proposal; anything you go so far as to put in your proposal should be indisputably correct). What you want to do is trace an arc for the book, an overall plan that takes you, as if in a story, from a beginning to an end. All the major points and topics should be included in your outline, along with whatever you'll need to illustrate or back them up ("baseball and beer consumption increase in perfect tandem!"), but again, you don't have to knock yourself out filling in every jot and tittle. It's enough that you know where the jots and tittles are, and how you'll eventually be using them.

Take a few days, or a few weeks, if that's what it takes, to hammer your outline together. Don't worry at all about your prose style or jazzy chapter headings, or any of that. This is just an outline, remember, a skeleton on which the flesh will be grafted much later. And just because you put it together in some particular fashion right now, that doesn't mean you can't take it all apart or change it later on, which you can, of course; and somewhere along the line I can almost guarantee that you will. When you get to certain points in the actual writing of the book, you may have a much better, or different, idea altogether. But that's par for the course. It doesn't mean you did a bad outline; it means your book is showing signs of life and taking on a somewhat altered form of its own.

Now, if you want me to tell you how exactly to *record* this outline—on a legal pad, on index cards, in a computer file—then I'm going to have to say, do it any way you like. One friend of mine has a massive corkboard on his wall, and he tacks colored index cards all over it, then moves them around as the book takes shape. Another friend uses the automated index-card function on her computer program. Another swears by his yellow legal pads; he claims he can't think something through on a computer, he needs a pen in his hand and paper in his lap. I tend to scrawl things in longhand, too, until I realize that I've reached the point where I'm starting to amass enough stuff, and enough of it is becoming illegible, even to me, that it's time to sit down at the computer and type it up. Once I see it typed and printed out, I feel as if I've taken one more step toward making this project something real, something I'm actually going to try to make happen.

How long should your finished outline be? Not to get too Zen about it, but as long as it needs to be, no longer. Depending on the book and subject, your outline could run anywhere from a few pages to a couple of dozen. As I've said, it's just a game plan, not an elaborate play-by-play. For example, my outline for this book came to seven or eight single-spaced pages; that allowed me enough room to hit the high points, in sufficient detail, that I was satisfied they deserved to be there, but not so much that I lost sight of the overall structure and movement of the book. Personally, I feel if your outline is getting really long, then you're starting to do more than an outline—you're starting to write either the book itself, or the one thing that many writers find even more daunting than an outline: a proposal.

Proposing Nonfiction

The crazy thing about book proposals is, everybody knows how to write one, and no one does. (My, I am feeling Zen this morning.) When I was doing my reconnaissance for this book by checking the bookstore shelves, I must have come across half a dozen books devoted solely to telling writers how to write their proposals. I should probably tell you that I took the time to comb diligently through each one, but I haven't lied to you yet and I don't want to start now. I did "glance through" a few, but frankly, they put me to sleep, and when it comes to writing a nonfiction book proposal, the best and most succinct advice I ever got was from my second literary agent, a guy named John.

"Write me a letter," he said.

"Why?" I replied, since I was sitting right there in his office, complaining that I didn't know how to write my proposal.

"Just write 'Dear John' on the top of the page, and then write me a letter, as if all you're doing is telling me about this great book you're planning to write."

It couldn't be that simple, I thought, but when I got home and had finished washing the windows, vacuuming the carpets, and rearranging the hangers in all the closets, I sat down, wrote "Dear John" at the top of a page, and then started telling him about my book, just as if I were indeed writing a letter to a friend. And I'll be darned if it didn't work. Once I'd stopped thinking about mean and scary editors, about publishing boards and editorial meetings, about people and readers I didn't know but already imagined as being groundlessly hostile to my book, I was free simply to tell my story, to communicate my enthusiasm and interest in doing this book. It also freed up my prose style; instead of being constricted by what my unknown reader might think or might like, I just went with what *I* liked, writing the way I would if it was just a loose, casual letter to a friend. After all, that was the way the final book—if we ever got that far—was meant to sound, too, so the editors might as well know right now what my writing style, at its most unfettered, was like. (Incidentally, some agents who use this "letter method" submit the proposal to publishers without even removing the "Dear John" at the top; editors don't seem to mind it at all.)

When we were talking, in the last section, about writing your outline, I suggested that you keep your potential reader in mind at all times, and take him through the material step by step; I'd like to suggest you do the exact same thing with your proposal, only this time it's your future editor you should keep in mind. And editors have got a whole different mind-set.

Editors, like you, enjoy reading; that's what attracted them to this profession in the first place. They probably majored in English; they might even have tried their hand at writing now and again. But that was then and this is now, and any editor who's been in the business for longer than five minutes has undergone his or her own rude awakening —they have discovered that publishing is a business designed, like any other, to make money, and that only as long as they continue to make money for the company will they hang on to their private corner cubicle, with its narrow window, steel gray file cabinet, and easy access to the automatic coffeemaker across the hall. (For *good* perks, try Wall Street or Hollywood.) Unlike most businesspeople, editors enjoy the life of the mind. But like all the rest, they have to turn a profit.

As a result, when you're working on your proposal, you, too, have to keep your eye, at least to some extent, on filthy commerce. Your proposal, while it should of course be literate and well composed, must also be a kind of business plan. It must not only hold an editor's interest, but it must also whet his or her business appetite at the same time. You're not just asking the editor, and the publishing house where he works, to read your proposal and enjoy the experience; you're asking him to fork out money for it, to commit company funds to developing and bringing to market—not an easy endeavor—your project.

You're also asking him to take you on as his partner. The more comfortable you can make an editor feel in terms of your capabilities, the better your chances of selling the proposal to him. A book is a long-term project, and he's got to know that you understand your responsibilities in terms of the work ahead, along with the realities of the marketplace. Does he expect you to include a full-blown marketing plan in your proposal? No, that's *his* problem. But does he expect you to appreciate the fact that a marketing plan is going to have to be done, and that your book project is going to have to prove itself to be financially feasible and wise? Yes, he does.

So make things easy for him, and don't horse around. Make sure your proposal is as clearly, as neatly, as concisely presented as it can be. That does not mean you include fancy graphics or printed cover sheets. It does mean you respect the editor's time (in addition to being underpaid, he's also overworked) and get to the points you want to make as quickly and as logically as you can.

What I said earlier, about no one knowing exactly what a proposal should be, is true, but there are certain things any proposal has got to do. How you want to do it—in bulleted paragraphs, in longer essay form, with selected sections of the book itself—is up to you, and is largely determined by the nature of the project. But on the must-do list are the following:

First, you've got to grab the editor's attention. With a nonfiction project, you could do that in any number of ways. If it's an account of some expedition you took, you could start off with a harrowing description of how you found yourself hanging by a thin rope over a gorge in the Hindu Kush. If it's a book about some imminent technological revolution, you could describe how this coming wave is going to change the face of publishing (that ought to get an editor's attention). If it's that book about lentils, you could start with some amazing but little-known statistics about the huge average bean consumption among Americans. Whatever you do, you've got to make the editor sit up a little straighter in his or her chair, and keep reading.

That same agent who once advised me to start the proposal with a "Dear John" also advised me to "sell the sizzle, not the steak." A proposal isn't the finished book; it can't be. But it can, and it must, give a tantalizing *taste* of what the book is going to be. The opening of your proposal has got to waft something so delectable, so appetizing or gripping or surprising, across the editor's desk that he's compelled to turn the page. And then the next.

But not too many. A proposal that's too lengthy or dense runs the risk of turning off the editor; there may be so much steak in it that he gets full and doesn't feel like eating any more. That's not what you want. You want a hungry editor—an editor who wants more of what you're selling. To make what he's reading as digestible as possible, I like to break up the pages and the sections of the proposal into clearly demarcated chunks with headings, subheadings, bullets, etc. I want the editor's eye to course across the pages swiftly and easily, finding what he needs, knowing where to look. The object, really, is to make his experience of reading the proposal as enjoyable and interesting as it can be.

A good nonfiction proposal will not only lay out your idea in a few well-written pages but will then go on to show how you plan to develop and explore it. That's where that outline I made you do earlier will come in very handy. (Now do you forgive me?) Spruce it up a bit and you can include whole sections of it in the proposal; you may even be able to turn it into a quite viable table of contents. An editor who wonders if your idea will be able to sustain itself over the length of an entire book can look at this outline and see for himself that, yes, it can.

But because we're assuming here that this is your first book, or you're an unknown quantity to this editor, we have to figure that he'll still need to see something more than your pitch letter and table of contents; he'll need to see some actual prose—a chapter or two, maybe even three. What if it turned out that you could write a dynamite proposal, but the actual book was somehow beyond your powers? Unlikely as that is, an editor will still want to make sure. He has to make sure. Even though, for instance, I'd written a number of books before this one, the acquiring editor at Holt made me submit an additional fifteen or twenty pages of text along with the proposal before she ultimately bit. (Not that she was out of line! She is every writer's dream of an editor, okay?) The rest of the proposal came to ten single-spaced pages. (While any completed book manuscript you submit must be double-spaced to allow for easy reading and editing, a proposal may be single-spaced or double. Double-spaced, however, is generally preferred, as the editor of this very book reminded me after the fact. Oops.)

Just how much of a book should you write before starting to submit it? There's some leeway here. I suppose, if you're independently wealthy, and you feel compelled to write your book your way, come hell or high water, there's nothing to stop you from sitting down and writing the whole darn thing. But even if you did, you wouldn't be wise to submit the entire, completed book to editors or even agents. Nobody has the time to read the whole thing, not right off the bat. (The only possible exception might be a memoir, which is such a tricky proposition that no proposal can ever entirely convince your agent or editor that the book can be pulled off. It's all in the telling.)

Most editors, stressed-out to begin with, can only deal with the ingredients of a standard proposal—that letter your agent may have had you compose, your overview or outline of the contents of the book, a note on the competing titles out there, the sources you intend to draw on, a brief author bio, and a couple of sample chapters. That's about all any editor can wade through, and all any editor needs to make his or her decision. If an editor does need something more—clarification, elaboration, a specific question answered—he'll ask for it (which is a good sign—only an editor who's taken the bait will keep on nibbling at the hook).

For this book, I'll confess, the acquiring editor did make me go back and address, in even greater detail than I had in the proposal, the real or perceived competition that was already out there. While you have of course chosen very wisely by picking up this book, I don't deceive myself that you weren't tempted by other somewhat similar titles. Books about writing and publishing are proliferating at an alarming rate, and if I weren't part of the trend, I would heartily deplore it. My editor—oh, let's give her a name, it's Liz—wanted to be absolutely sure that my book was going to distinguish itself from all the others, that I had some unique approach or take that would appeal to people who wanted to write a book themselves. And fortunately, I was able to convince her that I did.

How, exactly? Well, in this case, I was able to persuade her that I was going to come at this topic from the point of view of the writer—the only point of view, as it happens, that I knew. I'm not what you might call a publishing professional—an agent, an editor, a publisher—and while there were several books out there written by such folks, I didn't see any books written by working writers like myself, books that concerned themselves with the actual process of writing and publishing of a novel or nonfiction book. It was enough of a niche for me to exploit, and the reason I was able to exploit it was that I had done the legwork I recommended to you earlier. I had seen what other books were out there, and I knew what they covered, and what they missed. To my way of thinking, there was a hole on the shelf—not a big one, but a hole nonetheless—and when Liz asked me about the competition, I was able to satisfy her that I'd acquainted myself with it, and I'd come away still convinced that there'd be a market for my book. To some degree, this assurance put her mind at rest and kept the hopes for my proposal alive.

The other asset I had, and in the nonfiction arena this cannot be underestimated, is that I had some putative authority when it came to my subject matter. I had indeed been writing books for a living for years. Editors like to see that you have some real and credible expertise on the subject you are proposing to write about. If it's physics made easy, then what are your degrees and where have you taught? If it's mountaineering, what have you climbed? If it's international terrorism, were you involved somehow with Interpol, the CIA, the Red Brigade? Or have you simply written investigative pieces on this subject before? Editors must be persuaded not only that your topic is a good one, but that you are the logical person to write it.

With that in mind, many nonfiction writers find it's best to team up with someone. Let's say your interest is in dinosaur digs out west. Yes, you could research and write a book about these discoveries all by yourself, but when it comes to selling a book on the subject, you might find it useful to have allied yourself with a respected paleontologist. It would give your project heft and weight and instant credibility. Not to mention that you'd have an authority on hand to make sure everything you say is right, or at least defensible.

If, in the end, you still decide to write the book entirely on your own, and get sole credit, you can consider including the paleontologist as someone who will provide, say, the scholarly foreword. That way you can still trade to some extent on his reputation, but at the same time do things your way. And the publisher will feel that the material in the book has still been, to some extent, vetted and vouched for. Everybody wins.

Finally, there's one more vital, if invisible, element to any and all proposals, and I couldn't move on without at least bringing it up. I've seen a number of proposals in my day, from students and friends, and in more cases than I care to admit, there was still one thing lacking. Even when the proposals were very professionally done, with clear exposition, well thought-out subheads, good sample chapters, everything I've already mentioned, they failed to communicate one essential, but mysterious, thing—and that one thing was enthusiasm. Some of them were so clinical, so detailed, so thorough, that when I turned the last page I felt as if I'd been reading a grant proposal, not a book proposal. I felt no electricity.

Now I presume that the book you're planning to pitch to publishers one day is something that you're excited about writing, that it's a project you really want to do. So by all means let that excitement come through; it's not unprofessional of you. Don't even worry about coming off as a little over the top; better that, any day, than muted. You need to make the editor who's reading your proposal feel your enthusiasm, your energy, your ardent desire. You've got to convince him that you're going to write this book, no matter what, and that nobody on the planet, frankly, could write it as well or as passionately as you're going to write it. Why, he'd be lucky to get it on his list! Nothing's as contagious as confidence and enthusiasm, and by the time the editor is done reading through your proposal, he should be feeling as eager to get the book rolling as you are!

Proposing Fiction

My first novel, I sold by accident.

I had just written a nonfiction book for a major New York publishing house, and the book had done okay, but not great. I felt that the publishers had done a less-than-stellar job of promoting it, and all I wanted now was to be free to sell my next book elsewhere and see if I couldn't do better.

But the major publisher had a clause in our contract that said they got first dibs (technically called "first right of refusal") on my next book, whatever it was. So, just to get this problem over with and behind me, I wrote three pages of a horror novel and gave them to my agent at the time, John, to send over.

"This is just three pages," he said, incredulously.

"Exactly," I said. "Let them turn it down, and then we can figure out what I really want to write next, and for what publisher."

Well, John sent the pages over, neatly folded in a white number 10 envelope, and about a week later he called me.

"I've got good news and bad news," he said. "You want the good first?"

"Sure."

"They like your three pages."

They what? My scheme was backfiring. *If this was the good news, what was the bad?*

"The bad news is," John continued, "I'm not sure if you know how to write a novel. Do you?"

That one I had to think about. I mean, I'd certainly *read* enough of them. *Moby-Dick*, *The Mill on the Floss*, *Goldfinger*. But could I write one?

A few days later, John and I had a meeting with a couple of editors at the publishing house in question; they told me they really liked my idea (as much of it as was communicated in the three irresistible pages), and we talked about where the rest of the story was going to go. Never one to stare a book deal in the mouth, even if it *was* with the same publisher that a week previous I'd been desperate to get away from, I spun out the rest of the hastily concocted tale—demonstrating, as I recommended in the previous section, *enthusiasm!*—and we left the room with the fundamentals of the deal in place.

On the street outside, John turned to me and said, "You had me convinced up there."

"Of what?"

"That you know what you're doing."

"Great. That makes one of us."

Now, I don't mean to complain. Even then I knew that this sort of thing never happens. (Today, it happens even less than that.) And of course I realized that there were a lot worse problems a writer could have than trying to figure out how to write his next, already-contracted-for book. I should be jubilant, I knew, but the doubts and fears were already starting to overwhelm me.

There's a good chance that you'll feel that way, too, when it comes to writing your first novel. (I might as well tell you right now that even on your second, third, or tenth novel, your doubts don't entirely go away.) But as I had done with the nonfiction books, I knew I had to construct an outline, a game plan; I didn't have to stick to it chapter and verse, and nobody else would ever even have to see it, but I would need it as a means of convincing myself, whenever I got stuck or lost, that there *was* a way out. There *was* a whole story here, and if I just followed the plot as it was laid out in the working outline, I'd eventually arrive at the other end with a completed book. Not necessarily a *great* completed book, but a completed one, nonetheless.

An outline for a novel is a lot more slippery than one for a nonfiction book. As we've discussed, a nonfiction book demands that you cover certain material, and to a large degree, that material itself dictates the order in which it's to be arranged; you can't go on about the king of Siam without saying a little bit first about Siam itself, where it is, that sort of thing. A novel, however, has no such boundaries; it can go anywhere, do anything, and be whatever you want it to be. It can be written in the past tense, present tense, or future tense, I guess, if you can figure out how to do that. You can use an omniscient point of view, a first-person point of view, or a third-person point of view. You can chop it up into lots of short chapters, several very long ones, or let it run on with no chapters at all, if that's what you feel like. This freedom, this wide-open field of endless possibilities, is what makes writing a novel so thrilling, exhilarating, and often, to be perfectly frank, terrifying. You can get stuck in a novel, right about halfway through, in a way you never get stuck when you're writing a nonfiction book.

That's why you need that outline—even if it's only for your own perusal, and even if it can never take the precise form of a nonfiction outline. You don't really have As and Bs and Cs here; you have twists and turns, flashbacks and (if you're very New Wave) flash forwards; you cut around in the action from this place to the next, from that character to this, maybe even changing the point of view as you go. You can outline a novel till the cows come home, but by the time you finish writing the book, you'll see that tons of what you outlined have gone right out the window. When I wrote the outline for that first novel, I firmly thought a guy named Peter was my protagonist, but when I actually wrote the book, his wife, Meg, turned out to be. It just goes to show you.

Even so, the outline is worth having. It's a rough road map, nailing down the major plot points, laying out the major scenes or turning points in your story, reminding you where to start, where to go (in general), and where you're hoping to wind up. A friend of mine was once crying on my shoulder because he was halfway through his novel and he felt as if he was completely lost.

"Did you do an outline?" I asked, and when he nodded yes, I said, "Well, what did your outline say happens next?"

That's when he looked even more mournful. "My outline says, 'They go out into the world and trouble ensues.'"

I could see his problem.

"What does it mean to go out into the world?" he wailed. "I wrote it and I don't even know. And what about the trouble that ensues? What *kind* of trouble?"

That's why the more detail you can put into your novel outline, the better off you'll be later on. You can always alter it, or even throw it out, but at least it's there if you need it. And trust me, on those dark nights when you feel as if you'll never be able to find your way out of the woods again, you'll be awfully glad you have it.

There was once a time, way back when I was starting out, when you could indeed sell a novel with a few chapters (the three-page thing was a total fluke) and a rough précis for the rest of the story. But those days, I'm afraid, are gone. Publishers are very wary, very cheap, and very bottom-line-oriented these days (with the exception, of course, of Holt, the fine, generous, and visionary publisher of this book). Unless you are a proven quantity—an Anne Rice, a Donald Westlake, an Elmore Leonard—they're going to want to see a finished manuscript from you, the whole shebang, from chapter one to the end. Even if what you've got is, as they say in Hollywood, very "high concept" (meaning it's big and simple and bold enough for your average producer to "get it" immediately), you're still going to be better off, in the long run, writing the whole thing and then trying to sell it, than you would be if you tried to take your high concept out into the marketplace in an incomplete state.

Once a book is done, no publisher can offer you less money than you deserve by arguing that you're asking him to bid on a pig in a poke. Nor can he claim that the ending didn't live up to the potential of the first few chapters and demand, as a result, that the deal be cancelled and your advance returned (which, incidentally, he would be entitled to do). No, a completed manuscript is what it is—it's all there—and if a publisher wants it, he can offer you every nickel that it's worth. Maybe, if you're lucky and your agent is good, even more.

. . .

Now for some glad tidings. Yes, you may have to submit an entire manuscript of your novel, but, on the plus side, that means your proposal can be brief indeed. In fact, it's hardly what you'd call a proposal at all; it's much more of a cover letter, really, introducing yourself to the editor or agent to whom you are submitting it, and mentioning any previous writing credits you might have, from an article in *Good Housekeeping* to a college fiction prize. As for the novel, give yourself a couple of paragraphs to offer a précis of the story and the kind of book it is ("a murder mystery in the tradition of Agatha Christie, but brought up to date and set on a small New England college campus"), but do not attempt to provide a full plot summary. Even *The Godfather* or *The Firm* would seem dull in a plot summary. If there's anything else that you think is relevant and that you'd like to add—the fact, for instance, that you actually served as a dean on a small New England campus for many years—this would be the time and the place to do it. Aside from that, your project has to stand on its own two feet.

Later on, we'll discuss the process of submission to agents and editors in greater detail—it's arguably the most crucial step in any publishing plan—but for now, with a full novel to write, you've got your work cut out for you.

Genre Snobbery

Among the many uncomfortable moments in my life, one of the most acute was participating in a group book-signing at a store in the San Fernando Valley. There were five or six of us at a long table near the entrance to the store, and each one of us had a stack of our new book in front of us. While I knew a couple of the other authors (local writers generally get to know one another after a while), the woman next to me, Eleanor something-or-other, I did not know. She was about forty, with long dark hair and a very serious demeanor. I introduced myself, and she took my hand as if I'd handed her a dead haddock.

"This is your new book?" I said, stating the obvious, as I took a copy from the top of her stack. It was a handsomely produced hardcover from Random House, with glowing reviews of the author's previous book on the back cover. "This looks very interesting," I said, with genuine conviction. "Congratulations."

"Thank you," she said, straightening in her chair and staring off into the middle distance. She did not glance at a copy of my own book—a lowly paperback original—and she didn't ask me anything about it, either. Nor, when all of the writers took a ten-minute break to schmooze in the back of the store, did she join us.

She was, as I then realized, a genre snob. She was the first of the breed that I had ever knowingly encountered, but she was not alone. There are scores of them out there.

As far as Eleanor was concerned, there's mainstream fiction, and then there's that genre junk, and never the twain shall meet.

Mainstream (which is where she clearly felt she was positioned) is upscale fiction, literary fiction, Updike and Doctorow, Toni Morrison and Joyce Carol Oates. Mainstream titles used to be published exclusively in hardback, but now they are sometimes issued in sophisticated, softcover, trade paperback editions. They still carry a kind of literary imprimatur, they get reviewed in newspapers, their authors teach at Bennington or Bread Loaf. Mainstream titles aspire, however modestly, to become part of the canon.

Genre books, on the other hand, usually have their very own section in the chain bookstores: sections with placards that read ROMANCE or MYSTERY or SCIENCE FICTION. They're usually published as mass-market originals, the kind of paperback you might also see in a shop at the airport or on a rack at the supermarket. Apart from Eleanor, all of the authors at that table had written genre books, and the genre in question (to make matters even more painful for our friend Ellie) was Horror. *Oh dear Lord, the shame!*

Now, I'm not proud of the fact that the novels I've written so far have fallen into the Horror genre (also called, depending on the store, the Supernatural, the Occult, or simply Thriller), but I'm not as embarrassed as perhaps I should be, either. (When people have asked me where they can find my novels, I tell them to ask the bookstore clerk where they put Stephen King, and then look two shelves down. If I'm there at all, that's where I'll be.) Genre novels are easy to sneer at, but they've also got a lot going for them, especially for newcomers to the writing trade.

Not the least of these advantages is the fact that publishers need them. There's a steady market in all of these categories (that's why the chain stores have standing sections devoted to them), and while publishers are waiting to find the next big thing—the novel that will get front-page coverage in every book review in the land—they still need to come up with enough regular titles every month to keep their editors busy, their pipeline filled, and their spots in the stores and on the racks occupied. Genre books perform all these functions admirably.

For you, they can serve as a way into the business. There's something a little less intimidating, less perplexing, about writing a so-called genre book than there is about a mainstream novel. If you're a fan of some kind, *any* kind, of category fiction, then you know what the conventions, the style, the feel of those books are. If you like historical romances, for instance, you know the sort of plucky heroine you should create, the authentic backgrounds against which you should set the action, the love affair on which she must embark, and the moody, mysterious lord whose heart she must somehow conquer. If it's Westerns, you know the scrubby, forlorn landscape, the rugged cowboys, the Native Americans (who used to be bad, but now are good), the barroom brawls and cattle drives and fights between ranchers and farmers for precious resources of land and water. In other words, you know the drill.

You also know the landmarks that must appear somewhere in the terrain. In any genre novel, there are landmarks—clearly visible features of the landscape, things you need to provide, regular features that any fan of the genre would miss if you failed to include them (such as a tastefully erotic, but never raunchy, consummation scene in a bodice ripper, or a final shoot-out in a Western). These features can be like beacons in the night, points that you can travel between, from one to the next, and thereby stay roughly on course throughout your book. When you're writing a genre novel, it's easier to tell when you've strayed too far afield; the book no longer sounds or feels like its cousins.

Now, that can be a good thing—maybe your book is breaking free of conventions, maybe you're about to bust the category wide open and emerge from it as the product leader. Dean Koontz and Elmore Leonard once labored in obscurity, their books consigned to the genre sections of the bookstore, until they gathered enough momentum, enough of a reader base, and enough of a reputation to win their own liberation and acclaim.

The only way to write a genre novel, or for that matter, the breakout book that manages to take you into mainstream country (I'm sure Anne Rice was told more than once that she should be content to tell her vampire tales as paperback originals) is to write your book as well as you can. If there's a danger to genre thinking, it's the notion of "good enough." "It's only a genre novel, a cheapie paperback—why should I knock myself out to make sure every word is perfect? I'll worry about that when I write my big, mainstream, breakout book!" Writing at anything less than your full power is the surest way of never *getting* to that breakout stage. Always, always, do your best work.

Writing a genre novel—or writing a novel and then finding out, when it comes time to sell it, that publishers are considering it a genre title that they'd like to bring out as a paperback original—is nothing to be ashamed of. The worst part of it is that your advance will probably be lower than you'd expected—$5,000 or $10,000 is the average range. But your goal, let's not forget, is to get published, more than once, and to build your career, and your reputation, in such a way that you and your work get bigger and better treatment each time out. When it comes time to sell a second, or third, book, the publisher takes careful note of the fact that you've done this before. Some people might tell you, as one Boston agent once told me, that this can backfire: "If publishing houses see that you've been writing mass-market, generic stuff, they won't look at you the same way. They won't take you seriously." And I suppose that's possible. It would certainly account for the fact that certain authors write their genre novels pseudonymously, in order to preserve their real names for their mainstream titles. But an editor who dismisses an author of mere genre novels on that ground alone wouldn't be looking at the bigger picture, would he?

Personally, if I'm an editor or a publisher, and a manuscript comes across my desk from a writer who has proven, under whatever publishing circumstances, that he or she can deliver a completed and publishable manuscript, then I'm favorably impressed. It doesn't make me think that the new manuscript or proposal in front of me is somehow tainted or second-rate. It makes me think that this writer is serious about his profession, that he's done this before, and that this time around, he will have utilized all the things he's learned from practicing his craft up until now. Maybe this book is the one that will make him a household name, and wouldn't I be smart, as an editor, to be the one who signs it up? (And while I'm at it, if I'm very smart, I also discreetly inquire about the rights to the author's backlist.)

Title Search

With profound apologies to Jane Austen, it is a truth universally acknowledged that a book in possession of a good subject must be in want of a title—and nobody, for that matter, knew that better than Austen herself. After *Sense and Sensibility* hit it big in 1811, two years later *Pride and Prejudice* came out (delayed by publishing vagaries, the latter was actually written first). But what she knew, long before Robert Ludlum and Michael Crichton, was the importance of establishing a brand-name title, a similar-sounding formula that would alert readers that what they were getting was more of what they already liked. Do you think it's coincidence that Ludlum's titles are almost always three words—*The Bourne Identity*, *The Rhinemann Exchange*, *The Aquitaine Progression*—or that Michael Crichton's are almost always very short, even a single word, such as *Airframe*, *Sphere*, *Disclosure*, *Congo*, *Timeline*? Titles are of vital importance, and anything that makes then stick—and even better, subtly ties them to other books in the author's oeuvre—is a big help.

Some of us, such as my friend Dave, are great at coming up with titles. Every time he writes a book, or a short story (and he writes a lot of them), he comes up with not one but usually two terrific titles for them. I really envy him. Even though I know full well the power that the right title can bestow on a book, and I give it my all, I still have to struggle to come up with even one satisfactory choice. (I take comfort, however, in the fact that even F. Scott Fitzgerald couldn't do it very well.

His original title for *The Great Gatsby*? Try *Trimalchio in West Egg*.) There are many points in the life of a book when it can be given its proper name—before you've written a word, when you're halfway through the manuscript, when you've finished the first draft—but the sooner you can arrive at a good title, the better. What you want to avoid is "catalog panic"—that frantic search for a title because your publisher has to print up the sales catalog *next week*, and unless you can come up with something, you won't be in it!

Among the many reasons for arriving at a good title sooner rather than later, one of them is paramount: a good title is like a bell you can ring every time you sit down at the keyboard, a bell whose sound will fill your head with the peculiar music, the tone and cadence and pitch that this book is meant to achieve. It's a touchstone, a reminder of what you're trying to accomplish here, and if it's a title you're pleased with, just saying it out loud will make you want to kick into gear and start writing some more of the book that will one day flaunt it. No matter how incomplete the book may be, a title gives it a certain legitimacy and heft. You're not simply writing a stack of pages, or even just "my book" —now you're writing something with a name on it. Now you're writing your own personal *For Whom the Bell Tolls*, *The Grapes of Wrath*, *The Scarlet Letter*. Memorable titles, like those, are evocative, they hint at themes of biblical weight or great mystery—*What is the scarlet letter?*—and they make us want to pick up the books to find out more.

Titling a novel is in some ways an artistic, intuitive process. You've got to come up with a few words that hint at, or sum up, or suggest something important about the book, even if that idea is never articulated, in so many words, in the text itself. Your title has to reel in readers (not to mention an agent and an editor), telling them just enough to stimulate their interest, and at the same time giving some indication of the kind of book that this is. If you title a book *Love's Wild Ride*, you have to understand that you're going to attract a largely (exclusively?) female audience, and at the same time, you're going to drive away pretty much everyone looking for a serious read. If, on the other hand, you call your book something like *The Mind-Body Problem* (and that's an actual title of a wonderful novel, so consider it taken), you're going to draw people intrigued by a sardonic, pseudophilosophical feel. If you call your book

Def-Con 5, you're going to get Tom Clancy's fans at least to pick it off the shelf. No matter when you actually sit down to come up with it, the title of your book can't be an afterthought or a throwaway; it's a critical component, and to an alarming degree it can make or break the book itself.

Sometimes, a title will just come to you. For one book I wrote, I couldn't decide on a title until I realized what I was saying every time someone asked me to describe the book. "Well, it's about my adventures in Hollywood," I'd say, "breaking into the TV business, and all that."

"Huh," I'd usually get in reply. "What made you think of writing a book like that?"

"Well, every time I tried to find a way into the business, someone would say to me, 'Don't you have a friend in the business? That's how you get jobs in TV.' And I didn't have a friend like that. I want this book to be the friend I couldn't find."

About the fifth time I had this discussion, it finally dawned on me that I was saying my own title without even knowing it—*A Friend in the Business*. That's what the book was meant to be: the friend in the business, the one who would explain everything and help you get in, the friend everybody wishes he or she had in Hollywood. If you're stuck for your own title, that's not the worst way to go about finding one. Sit down with a trusted friend or two, and with the caveat that the sole purpose of this exercise is to help you come up with a title (*not* an editorial direction), let them ask you about the book. Let them ask you what it's about, why you're writing it, what excites you about it. Listen very carefully to what you say in reply—especially whatever you say more than once. Is there a catchphrase that keeps coming up, is there one point you consistently make more than anything else? Are there a few words that seem to sum up the plot, or tenor, or gist of the book? My cousin Chuck was stuck for the title of one of his novels, and we found it only when I asked him what the name of his protagonist was.

"Nicky Silver," he said.

Five seconds later, we had *Silver Linings*, which also, luckily, fit the story.

For one novel I wrote, time was running out, and I had already gone through all the obvious sources. I had gone through my *Bartlett's*

Familiar Quotations, my *Oxford Dictionary of Quotations*, my concordance to Shakespeare, my *Classical Dictionary*, my collections of Romantic poetry, Victorian poetry, and memorable proverbs from around the world. Usually, when you're looking for a title and you want to find something that has that resonance, that scope and punch that you're looking for, you can find something in reference books like these. Words, phrases, and allusions that can stand just as they are or which, slightly altered, you can make your own. It's a tried-and-true technique, and it's worked quite nicely for such books as *Tender Is the Night*, *Death Be Not Proud*, *Of Mice and Men*, *The Sun Also Rises*, *Parting the Waters* . . . the list goes on and on.

This time it just wasn't working for me. I wanted a title that had some clout, some mystery . . . and a pedigree. But I was still coming up dry. That's when it hit me. Why couldn't I come up with a title I liked, something intriguing and evocative, and then give it my own pedigree?

In the book, there was an important and recurring image of a roiling black cloud, off in the distance. It was black and it made up the whole horizon. A black horizon, if you will. I liked that image, I liked those words, but I didn't want them to have come out of nowhere; I wanted them to have a provenance. Something classy. So I gave them one.

As an epigraph to lead off the book, I affixed the following quatrain: "In fields of light, a shadow plays / That men heed not, nor change their ways / Till Death's lean finger, jewel bedizened / Beckons them cross that black horizon." I called these lines a fragment of an anonymous eighteenth-century verse, and until this day, I have never confessed my chicanery to anyone. (Wait, that's not true—once, I actually received a call from a perplexed grad student somewhere, who thought he'd read all the known eighteenth-century verse there was, and who was making himself crazy trying to track this none-too-inspired fragment down. After swearing him to secrecy, I admitted my crime. He seemed greatly relieved—and not all that surprised.)

But when it comes to titling a nonfiction book, the process has certain peculiarities unknown to novels. With a nonfiction book, you get an important break in that you sort of have two cracks at the title. You get to choose something short and catchy to lead off with, and then you get to stick in a colon and, after it, add a short subtitle to explain what the book is really all about. (Although I privately refer to these titles as high colonics, this practice has failed to catch on industry-wide.) Take Anne Lamott's best-known book, for instance: *Bird by Bird* is the main title, and that's enough to make you wonder, *What's that mean, exactly?* Then her subtitle goes on to say, *Some Instructions on Writing and Life*, and you know that the book will have something to do with literary creativity. John Krakauer's book was called *Into Thin Air*—intriguing enough—but its subtitle, *An Account of the Mount Everest Disaster*, tells you exactly where you're going. You provide a nonfiction book with an informative and on-target subtitle for two reasons—first, to attract the right readers to your book, and second, to let the harried bookstore clerks know precisely where this book should be displayed and shelved in the store. (Despite its subtitle, I wonder to this day how many times *Bird by Bird* found its way into the Nature section?)

Even when you come up with a title you think is a perfect fit, be advised that you should have an alternate in the wings. Publishers often have their own priorities and opinions, and through no fault of your own, you might find that your title has been rejected. For over a year, I worked on a novel called *Arcadia*; I loved that title, it was even the name of the estate on which most of the action took place. But someone else got to it first, and I had to find something else. (Although titles as such cannot be copyrighted, you don't want to risk confusion in the bookstore.) So I chose *Before the Moon*, which was in a sense what Arcadia meant to the ancient Greeks—it referred to a time so long ago that even the heavenly bodies were unformed. I grew attached to that title, too, until the publisher said I couldn't use it because they had another book coming out that same season and it already had the word "moon" in its title.

"We can't both use the word 'moon?'" I asked. "I mean, our books are entirely different, they're not even going in the same areas of the stores."

"That's not the problem," the editor informed me. "The problem is, our sales reps will get them confused when they're out taking orders. Find something else."

So, reluctantly, I went back to my desk, and ultimately came up with a list of about a dozen titles for the book, and of course the editor picked the one that was my least favorite. (Okay, okay, the title they chose was *The Spirit Wood*—based on the fact that there were some haunted woods in the book—but after my third friend called to kid me and say, "The spirit would, but the body was unwilling?" I knew I'd made a terrible mistake.)

Publishers also listen to their marketing people, whose job it is to be aware of what's working out there and what's not. I once wrote a collection of light essays called *Why Didn't He Call Back?* with a subtitle, *And Other Mysteries of the Single Male*. At the time, I was writing a monthly column called "His" for *Mademoiselle*, and nearly half the letters I'd receive each month were asking me why some guy had said he'd call back and then hadn't. I thought it was the ideal title for the book, and so did my editor until somebody in the marketing department mentioned to her that a book with a similar title, published about eighteen months before, had not done well.

"I know all about that book," I said, when my editor told me about the problem. "I read it, it's not very good, and it's not even really about this stuff. It was a total misnomer."

"Either way," she said, "we shouldn't take the chance."

I knew what she was going to say next before she said it.

"Find something else."

This time, the publishing house rejected every title I suggested and ultimately alighted on their own—*What Do Men Want from Women?* a serviceable, if rather ordinary, title. Exactly *how* ordinary it was we wouldn't know until the book came out, right around the same time three other books with identical, or nearly identical, titles hit the stores; among the contenders was a new novel by a bestselling writer. Wherever I went on the promotional trail for a short time thereafter, I was invariably mistaken for this bestselling author—people would gush all over me and tell me how much they loved my novel! How funny it was! How touching! For a while, I'd correct them, explaining that my book wasn't the funny and touching one—mine was the one that simply had the same title. Then I stopped. Not only could I no longer bear to see their crestfallen faces, I also couldn't bear to see mine. I started graciously accepting their compliments—one guy bought me a drink in an airport bar—and if necessary, signing their copies of this other writer's book. On the one hand, yeah, it was painful—I was a fraud, a counterfeit, a usurper of another man's glory—but on the other, I've got to admit, it felt kind of nice to be so popular and well respected. The next best thing to writing a bestseller, I discovered, is getting the credit for one.

Muzzling the Three-Headed Dog

But before you can really get any book rolling, much less done, there's a fearsome beast with three heads, which you've somehow got to get past. When I'm feeling particularly high-falutin' about it, I think of this critter as Cerberus, after the ferocious three-headed dog of Greek mythology. When I'm not feeling that way, I think of it simply as those three carping voices in my head that I wish I could turn off. In this specific context, the dog, or whatever you want to call it, guards the gateway into any book, whether it's a novel or a travel guide, and barks so loudly and snarls so fiercely that many writers pick up their heels and run for it. I've been chased away myself more times than I care to count.

Each of the three heads represents a big problem, one that you have just got to come to terms with, because if you don't, your book will suffer for it. You'll be writing the whole thing while trying to look over your own shoulder—and that, I can tell you, is a surefire way to run smack into a tree.

The first head we'll call the censor. That's the nasty little voice that keeps whispering in your ear, "You can't say that. You'll hurt Harriet's feelings," or "Better not include that scene, Uncle Bud will know who you're talking about," or "Sex? You're going to include sex? Your mother's going to be reading this book!" The censor is the one that keeps pushing you away from your own experience, your own true feelings, in a futile attempt to render everything you write so neutral, so unrecognizable, so foreign to your own real perceptions that not a soul you know, living or dead, could possibly take offense.

The censor not only tries to remove all traces of life as you've lived it; if you're not careful, it tries to remove all traces of life as *anyone* has lived it. Yes, you've got to take precautions when you write; you've got to disguise or reimagine certain things so as not to expose or unduly injure other people. But you've got to be true to your book, too. In a novel, this is somewhat easier to do. You've always got the "It's-just-a-story!-I-made-it-all-up" defense. And one curious thing that I can tell you is, the people who you think will surely identify themselves as various unsavory characters and take offense, never do. The very fact that these characters are shown in a less than laudatory light means the people that they're modeled on will never even *imagine* that they could be the real-life counterparts.

The strange corollary to this rule, however, is that other people, who truly played no part in your fictional casting sessions, will, for whatever reason, find themselves in there—most notably in the heroic roles. I have one friend who's positive that I modeled one of my fictional protagonists—a strong, brave, beautiful artist—on her. It's not that my friend isn't all those things, too, but if I told her she'd never so much as crossed my mind while writing the book (frankly, in my head, I was picturing Sigourney Weaver), she'd be crushed. So why not let her go on thinking so?

Then, of course, there's what we might call the morality issue. The first time I wrote a truly lubricious sex scene in a novel, I wasn't worried about it when the book was just in typescript, and I wasn't worried about it when the manuscript came back from the copy editor. But when I saw the book in *galleys*, when I read those scenes (God forgive me, they even involved spanking) in cold hard type, just as anyone else reading the book would encounter them, I was mortified. *What if people didn't understand that it was my naughty character, and not me, that was into this stuff? What if the sex scenes came off as just plain silly, rather than wildly erotic?* And now, it really dawned on me that, yes, my mother, my father, my brothers would all be reading this stuff. How that fact had escaped me up until now was unclear; maybe it took seeing the typeset pages emerge into actual book form to bring it home to me, to impress upon me that this was indeed going to be a published book, with my name on it, and that people (even people I didn't know), were going to read it and possibly think that they now knew something pretty juicy about my own personal predilections for ping-pong paddles and corporal punishment.

Anyway, I panicked. I sent off an urgent fax to my editor's office, begging her to take out several sections, or at least trim them in ways I carefully laid out for her, before the book went to press. When I didn't have an answer within the hour, I called.

"What are you going on about?" she said, with some asperity. "It's a novel, and in this particular case, your main character is a Eurasian shipping tycoon. Who's going to think that's you?"

"I don't know, I don't care! *I'll* think it's me! We've got to change it!"

There was a silence on the line. Publishing houses hate it, you should understand right now, when you try to change things in galleys. That's the last stage before printing the book, and it can get expensive to reset the type. But I begged, I pleaded, and pretty much threw myself on their mercy.

"All right, already," the editor finally replied. "I'll take care of it."

My relief was overwhelming, my gratitude unfathomable, I got the best night's sleep I'd had since receiving the galleys. And this peace of mind lasted right up until the day, two months later, when they sent me my author's copies—and I saw that not one of my changes had been implemented. Everything—the sex, the spanking, the X-rated nightclub scene—was exactly as I had first written it. Not so much as a comma had been excised. For weeks, I was embarrassed to talk about the book at all with friends and family, but gradually even that embarrassment faded. For one thing, nobody seemed to care; for another, I'm not sure most of them got that far into the book. And now, all these years later, the book—big surprise—is safely out of print (though a friend did call to tell me that a rare first edition of it was being auctioned on eBay, where it eventually sold for a couple of dollars below the original cover price).

In a nonfiction book, however, the censor is even harder to defuse or circumvent. If what you're writing about is a neutral topic—the invention of gunpowder—then fine, don't sweat it. But if you're admitting right up front that this is a true story you're about to tell—a memoir, an exposé, an account of your cross-country car trip with your estranged spouse—then everybody in it, even when you take the trouble to change names and the occasional identifying detail, is presumably a real "somebody." With nonfiction, there's no hiding behind that "It's-only-a-made-up-story" defense. So you have to ask yourself, before you even start the book, how you are going to deal with this problem. Are you prepared to tell the truth, the whole truth, and nothing but the truth? Or are you going to try to walk a middle path, sparing those around you whenever you can and doing your best to put a favorable gloss on things? The decision is yours, I wouldn't presume to make it for you, but I would say that in a nonfiction enterprise, the censor could prove to be your most nettlesome enemy. That's why it's a good idea to make your peace with it at the outset, on whatever terms you wish. Decide what course you're going to take—letting it all hang out, or essentially taking a more diplomatic approach—and then stick to it. Discuss it, if you wish, with your mental health professional. But deciding, early on, what approach you plan to take will save you a lot of trouble, many delays, and possibly a lawsuit later on.

Even more dangerous than the censor—larger jaws, sharper teeth—is the critic, Cerberus's second head. Nothing, and I mean nothing, gets by this guy. He's in your face all the time, taking potshots at your prose style ("Have we missed any clichés so far?"), your syntax ("Isn't this the pluperfect tense, or am I the one who wasn't paying attention in eighth grade?"), your characters ("Does the word 'cardboard' mean anything to you?"), and your plotting ("Would she really put the bomb on the plane if she was planning to take the flight herself?"). The critic is omnipresent, omniscient, and impossible to turn off. Sometimes he even gets so far ahead of you that he starts writing scathing premature book reviews in your head ("An abomination of a book, whose author should be dragged through the streets by a team of oxen"). You get the idea: the critic is not always your friend.

And yet, you can't live entirely without him, either. Without some critical sense, some careful observation of what is winding up on the page, you'll be writing gibberish. Anytime you elect to write any words at all, you're selecting them from countless other choices. You're seeing how they work with what came before and judging how they'll go with what has to come next. You're listening to them in your head to see if they sound right, or if, instead, they're creating some unfortunate effect such as a verbal echo (repeating a word that you just used in the previous sentence). Your inner critic is helping you to make a million choices, and without his help your book would suffer.

So, what do you do? You reach some accommodation with him, just as you did with the censor. If something is making your critic really cringe, then stop and deal with it. Fix the problem then and there, even if it means tearing up that morning's work and starting all over. Sometimes, not fixing a serious problem when it first crops up can lead to all kinds of other problems down the line.

Good writers, professional writers, know when to pay attention to the critic; they know when he's got something legitimate to say, and they're not afraid to hear him out—no matter how painful it might be. I'll never forget the lesson I learned from my writer friend, Linda, who always took her craft for exactly that—her craft. At the time, she was working on an international thriller, but something was not feeling right. She kept working on it, moving the story along, keeping it twisting and turning, but she still felt that something was off-kilter. She asked me to give the manuscript a read and see what I thought. I read it, and what I thought was, she'd let her protagonist go to Switzerland on page ninety and the story jumped the tracks right there and didn't get back on them again for at least another hundred pages, when he returned to the States. But how could I say that? How could I tell her that all those pages felt to me like a detour?

I went over to her apartment with the manuscript in hand, we talked a little, and then she asked me what I thought. I was still beating around the bush when she said, "Come on, we both know something's wrong. Have you figured out what it is?"

"I think so," I said, reluctantly.

Linda waited.

"I think it's when he goes to Switzerland."

She nodded her head. "The book kind of goes into left field for a while there, doesn't it?"

I confirmed that it did. And before my very eyes, Linda removed the hundred-odd pages and tossed them into a seaman's chest she used as a coffee table. Not only that, she didn't seem devastated or defeated. Personally, I'd have been mortified, depressed, determined never to sully another page in this lifetime or the next. But Linda was okay. Was she *pleased* with having to surgically remove such a big hunk of the book? No, of course not. But she took the professional's attitude about it: on some level, a book, like a machine, has to work, and this one wasn't working. Now it might. And even though I'm still a big baby about my own work (if I ever ask for your opinion, I'm really only asking for praise), I was so impressed with her behavior that I try my best to behave the same way.

But if what you're getting from your inner critic isn't really strong opposition, if it's more like a kind of muffled complaint, a slight and vague sense of dissatisfaction, then tell the critic, "Yeah, I heard you, I won't forget, but I'll deal with it in the revise." Because it's important to keep two things in mind here. For one, you're always going to hear *something* from your critic; every time you have to make a judgment or choice about something in the book, he is going to weigh in, pro or con. And two, nothing you write will be completely and unalterably right the first time. Everything will need a rewrite. Everything. It doesn't make you a bad writer if you have to rewrite passages of the book later on; it makes you a diligent one. (If you must know, I just rewrote this section for the third time. And there's a strong possibility that I'll do it a fourth.)

Vital as the critical voice can be, a working writer has to know when to tune it down, or even turn it off—usually, when writing that extraordinarily difficult first draft. It's hard enough to charge ahead all the way to the end of a completed manuscript, but to do it with a nagging voice bending your ear the whole time, telling you to stop and redo something, change this, or improve that, is almost impossible. When the critic manages to take control, when his voice is louder in your head than your own, then it's time to take a break and tune him out. As my friend Linda puts it, how can you be expected to write with the same head you're being hit over?

• • •

And then there's that third obstacle—the slavering jaws of the perfectionist.

The first time I wrote a novel, I spent probably half the time on the three-page prologue, and the rest of the time in a panic, trying to complete the remainder of the book.

Not that the prologue wasn't, in the end, an example of what I can do at my finest.

But I was so worried about getting the book off on exactly the right foot, setting the mood, the tone, throwing in a little foreshadowing, a touch of class, a taste of the supernatural, that I could not stop playing with it. I had this notion that every time I sat down to write, I had to start reading the book from the very start again, and that then, when I got to the end of the material I'd already written, I'd just keep rolling along on the tide of the previous pages.

What happened, in actuality, was that I got stopped nearly every time somewhere in those opening pages. Was "gauzy" the right word? Maybe it should be "filmy"? No. Wasn't "transparent" what I really meant? Out would go one word, in would go another—until the next time I read through these pages and the same little waltz would have to be performed again.

Finally, it dawned on me that at the rate I was going, this book would probably be done about thirteen years after, according to even the most liberal actuarial tables, I was dead. So I forced myself to move ahead with the narrative.

What I was trying to do was make the thing perfect, from first to last. And while that may sound like a fairly laudable goal—shouldn't we all strive to make our work as good as it can be?—it is, in fact, a guaranteed way of never getting anything finished. And maybe, secretly, that's why we give in to it. Afraid of all the demons awaiting us down the road, all the pages we have yet to write, we focus instead on the tiny section of the book already done, already on the desk. At least *that* much is there; it's not going anywhere. And we can play with it as long as we like, pushing it this way and that, trying a little ornamentation, then stripping it away. Hours can pass, and we can get up from the desk feeling as if we've had a very productive day, when in fact all we've really got to show for it is two new commas and a couple of dependent clauses.

The perfectionist is really just the critic again, only this time he's dressed to the nines. He comes off as very sophisticated, very refined, and he claims to have only your best interests at heart. But it just ain't so. Until you thank him for his time and show him the door, you'll never get to the end of anything. And one way to say farewell without too much regret is to remind yourself that this good-bye is not forever. You can always welcome him back when you're done with a first, or perhaps a second, draft. That's when you'll have time to do nothing but polish your prose until every sentence shines like newly minted silver. You can keep that up, if you want to, until the day your final page proofs have to be returned to your publisher. The perfectionist, like the censor and the critic, has a definite role to perform—I live with the guy every working day of my life—but the ringmaster, the one who keeps all three of them under some sort of control, must ever and always be you. Someone once said that writers never really finish their books—they just abandon them (to their publishers). And that is certainly how it feels to me.

My Grandmother's Cadillac

Although my grandmother was a very lovable woman, she was not a very good driver. Back in the fifties, she had this immense light blue Cadillac, which was covered from front grill to tail fins with a million tiny dents, divots, scratches, bruises, and contusions. It looked as if somebody'd taken a ball peen hammer to it. It was never clear to me where all this damage was coming from until one night, when she was baby-sitting, she decided to take my brothers and me out to dinner.

We were pulling out of the driveway when the back bumper nicked the tree at the foot of the lawn. I thought about saying something, but she was my grandma, and I figured she knew as well as I did what had just happened. At the top of the street, she turned onto Ridge Road, her tires scraping against the high curb on one side, before she straightened out the car, with a kind of wobbly motion, and headed on toward our favorite restaurant, Mary's Cupboard. But it was dusk, the light was fading fast, and as we approached the restaurant parking lot, my grandmother said, quite off-handedly, "You know, I can't see a thing."

"You can see Mary's Cupboard, can't you?" I said, a little nervously. It was coming up fast on the other side of the busy street. In the backseat, my brothers braced themselves.

"Oh, after all these years I think I know where *that* is," she said with a smile, just before turning the car across two lanes of horn-blaring traffic, and into a chain-link fence that ran *around* the parking lot but didn't actually let you get inside it. For that, you had to use the entrance—about ten yards farther on.

Anyway, whenever I've come to the end of writing a first draft, particularly if the book is a novel, I think of my grandmother's Cadillac. Like the car, this draft is usually a large, ungainly thing, with a lot of dents and dings and scratches all over it. But it does run, it's intact, and if I go back and work on it for a while, I can hammer out, or seal over, most of the rough spots. And that, I have come to learn, is pretty much how first drafts are supposed to look.

Novels, especially. A nonfiction book generally comes closer to the finished mark the first time through; it's just the nature of the beast. But a novel, a form that is as malleable as it is idiosyncratic, can sustain a lot of damage just getting to the end of its first draft. What keeps a lot of people from getting there is that they keep stopping to repair the minor damage as it is incurred, instead of just plowing ahead and getting to the restaurant, as it were. You're certainly entitled to fix it up as you go—some writers can't move forward unless they're sure every word they've already done is perfect—but most writers need to keep up their momentum, they need to forge ahead no matter what and stagger across the finish line. Then, when they're rested up, they can look back and see what needs to be repaired.

When it comes to writing fiction, I think this kind of "forced march" attitude is particularly helpful. Novels can get bogged down so easily, and writers can so easily get lost, bewildered, or depressed. Often, it's only when you've made yourself get to the end of something that you can see what you've really got. I have one friend who writes detailed outlines of sixty or seventy pages for his novels before he starts, and while I admire his industry, that same method would never work for me. First of all, I hate outlining, and if I wrote a seventy-page outline, with all the details filled in, from plot points to snippets of dialogue, I know I'd never get the energy to then go back and write the story all over again. I'd be bored, weary, and asleep at the wheel. (I've already had the unpleasant chore of turning a novel I wrote into a screenplay, and even that felt as if my brain had taken a hit of Novocain.)

I'd also miss the serendipity, the surprise, the unexpected unfoldings that occur when you build a novel from a sketch, rather than from a thoroughly detailed blueprint. I won't say that *all* the best things in my novels came from unforeseen twists and turns, ideas that sprang out of nowhere but seemed, when I was writing them, to be exactly right . . . but I will say that a lot of them did. Not only did the protagonist of that first novel turn out to be somebody else, but in the next novel I wrote, a minor character—the hero's mother—who had appeared only once or twice in my outline, suddenly kept showing up in the story, moving things along, adding drama to every scene, until I no longer knew how on earth I had ever planned to tell this story *without* her constant intervention. In fact, when the editor read the finished manuscript, one of her first comments was how much she relished the character of the mother and looked forward to her appearances in the book.

Novels, I think, are among those things that you can plan or schematize or diagram forever, but once you get going, they take on a life of their own. I would almost go so far as to say that if they don't, you're doing something wrong. If what you're writing isn't occasionally taking you by surprise, if it isn't making you laugh or gasp or get a little teary, then all you're doing is connecting the dots, and the book may very well read that way. A novel that's really alive, that has a pulse of its own, grows in some mysterious and organic way; it's as if it takes from you, the writer, whatever it needs to flourish and become complete. On those very rare occasions when I open one of my old novels (and these *are* rare, because there's nothing I dislike more than reading my own prose), I'm often quite surprised. Not, mind you, by the audacious genius of the prose (if I thought that, I'd open them more often), but by a setting, an exchange of dialogue, a peripheral character, that I didn't know I had in me, and that even now, in some fundamental way, I do not recognize. *Where did that come from? How did I know that? Why did I think that?* When you're writing a novel, you're in touch with places in your psyche that you didn't know were there, places that, if you went consciously looking for them now, you'd never find. Places, it's quite possible, that were accessible only for the duration of the time you were writing that particular book, and are now, like a well in the desert swallowed by a sandstorm, concealed again for good.

I'm sure you've heard that old Creative Writing class saw, "Write what you know." And while there's much to be said for writing only about what you know first-hand from your own daily routine—taking the bus to work, drinking cold coffee at your desk, taking two weeks' vacation every summer—if I hear this mantra incanted one more time, my ears will bleed. For every person who's been creatively freed up by this notion, there are ten who get stifled. I'm sure I'm not the first person to suggest this, but as far as I'm concerned, you should "write what you *don't* know." So what if you haven't been to tenth-century Rome? If it grabs you, write about it. So what if you're not an international jewel thief living it up on the Riviera—if that's your fantasy, write it. If I only wrote about what I know (which is largely summed up by sitting alone at a desk, writing) I don't know who'd shoot himself first—me or my hapless reader.

Part II

COMMERCE
AND CRAFT

"Why don't you write books people can read?"
—NORA JOYCE TO HER HUSBAND, JAMES JOYCE

Bagging an Agent

My first literary agent still owes me twenty dollars.

I was writing for a lot of New York magazines at the time, and I guess my name was starting to surface here and there. One day I got a call from this agent—we'll call her Maxine—and she said, "I love your articles! And I'm dying to meet you! Do you have an agent?"

"No, I don't," I said, though, strangely enough, it had just recently begun to dawn on me that I might need one. Maybe Maxine—a junior agent, but situated at a prominent agency—might be the one I was looking for. I already knew her timing was good.

"Meet me tonight at Wilson's, on First Avenue," she said, "and let's talk."

Needless to say, I was plenty excited—*An agent! Who had called me!*—and I got to Wilson's, a popular restaurant and bar, half an hour before I was due there.

Maxine, an excitable young woman with brown hair that literally bounced when she spoke, got there about twenty minutes late, but we had a nice time talking, and I couldn't get over the fact that there was someone out there—a comparative stranger—who actually thought I had prospects. Even my own family hadn't gone that far. Anyway, Maxine could hardly contain herself, she had so many plans for me.

"First, we renegotiate your column contract so that you get at least twice what you're getting now. Then we do a book deal, based on the column, and then we talk to newspapers. If the column appeared in newspapers once or twice a week, instead of only monthly in a magazine, you'd pick up a much bigger audience. I don't need to tell you now that would translate into book sales. Then, the next thing we do is . . ."

She was off and running, and all I could do after a while was sit there and listen to my glorious future unfold. *I was going to be famous! I was going to be rich! I was going to have a date on any Saturday night that I wanted one!* Maxine had laid it all out for me, and it looked so great I could hardly wait to get started.

Then the check came, Maxine grabbed it, fished through her wallet, and said, "Oh, geez, I forgot to hit the bank. Could you lend me a twenty to cover this and the cab ride home?"

"Sure, no problem," I said, figuring what was twenty—which I'd surely get back, anyway—compared to the millions that had just been spread at my feet?

Maxine and I parted outside, and how was I to know, waving to her as the cab pulled away from the curb, that I would never again lay eyes on her?

I didn't call her the next day (I didn't want to look too eager) but I did the next one. She told me she was on another line and she'd call me right back. She did not.

A couple of days later, I called again, and got a machine. I left a message.

A week after that, I left another.

You know the rest of the story. I didn't get my twenty bucks back, I didn't get a raise for my magazine column, I didn't get a newspaper deal. . . . But I did get my feet wet. I knew enough to know that I needed a real agent now—if only to protect me from crazies like Maxine—and I went looking for one on my own.

But why do you—why does anyone—need an agent? Isn't it enough to write your book and simply send it out to Simon & Schuster or Random House, then wait by the phone until they call to make an offer? Ah, would it were so. Maybe at one time, years ago, you really could trust that method to work out for you: you could toss your manuscript *over the transom*, as it was commonly referred to, and count on some inquiring young mind at the publishing house to find it, read it, and champion its virtues around the house until somebody sat up and took notice.

But these days, there isn't a transom to throw it over, even if you tried, and those inquiring young minds are already up to their elbows in work. The way into most publishing offices is a lot trickier than it used to be, and if you're going to get inside, you have to know a few things about the business.

First of all, as I've said, it *is* a business, which means that the editors hunched over their littered desks don't have a lot of time to spare; they've got work to do, and dollars to generate. Even if you knew which ones to call—and editors have their own individual interests and specialties—it's highly doubtful they'd pick up the phone, or give you much time on it if they did. If you sent in an unsolicited manuscript, they'd probably just mail it back unread. It's nothing personal; at most publishing houses these days, it's company policy. The dreadful specter of future litigation hangs over them just as it does over Hollywood studios, and as a result, publishers are skittish about reading unsolicited material. What if a writer claims that his idea or manuscript was pirated in-house and decides to file suit?

Since editors and publishers don't have the time and energy to guard the gates themselves these days, they have assigned that job, for all intents and purposes, to agents. Let the agents read through all the unsolicited material out there and separate the wheat from the chaff, let the agents figure out what's publishable and what's not, and better yet, let the agents decide where to send the appropriate stuff. It's like an automatic sorting system, and apart from the fact that a good agent gets his clients more money for their books, it doesn't cost the publishing houses anything to maintain it.

How all this affects you, the writer, is probably fairly clear. It means that unless you've got a friend or relative working inside a publishing company, your best way in—perhaps your *only* way in—is going to be by using an agent. Even if there's something in your rebel spirit that says, *I don't need an agent to sell my work, no one can do that better than I can*, please get over it. When you're an established fixture on the bestseller list, *then* you can think about negotiating differently; for now, you need an agent.

• • •

Where and how do you find one? I wish I could tell you this is easy, but it's not. That should be some comfort to you while you're writing your craven letters and nervously placing your phone calls. What makes the job especially hard is that you're not just looking for any old agent who will take you on (though most of us are so grateful to the first one who *will* that we're prepared to sign away anything, from our life to our sacred honor). You're looking for an agent who will truly understand your work and know how to go about selling it. When you're shopping for an agent, you're not looking for a friend, an editor, a surrogate parent (though some agents have been known to serve as all three)—you're looking for a sales-person, an aggressive and connected go-getter who is going to make sure your book goes to all the right places, all the right editors, and fetches the maximum price. If that sounds cold-blooded, it's supposed to.

The most common and practical method for finding an agent is to consult one of those lists in the *Literary Market Place* or the annual *Guide to Literary Agents*, published by Writers Digest Books and available in most bookstores and libraries. You'll find dozens and dozens of names there of agents from New York City to Tuscaloosa, who will accept and read material from unknown writers. And you could certainly do worse than to pick a few names, agents who seem open to the kind of material you're trying to sell, and send them a query letter. What do you say in it? Just introduce yourself briefly—"I'm a writer living in Nashville, sup-porting myself at present as a steel guitar player"—and describe the work you'd like to submit—"a completed novel of 450 pages about a country and western star and his professional, and romantic, entangle-ments on the road." You can admit that you plucked this agent's name from one of the guides, no harm in that, and if you're querying a couple of other agents at the same time, you can admit that, too. It's perfectly kosher. Close your letter by asking if the agent would be willing to read all, or a portion of, the manuscript. Type "Sincerely," sign it, and you're done. Average waiting time before (and if) you get a reply? Two weeks to two months.

Now, a lot of writers can't stand to wait around, and they decide to speed things along by sending not just a query letter but the whole manuscript, or a mighty big piece of it. And that's certainly not illegal, nor unheard of. But agents who don't know you from Adam can get overwhelmed, I think, by the sight of a thick mailer filled with pages, or a bursting shoe box tied with a string. Many, in fact, make it a practice never to read entire, unsolicited manuscripts; in the agent guides and listings, they may even say what they will consider (such as a letter, one sample chapter, etc.). My own gut feeling, if I were starting out, would be to send just a letter first, and maybe follow it up with a call two or three weeks later, if I hadn't heard anything. A letter, one slim page in a simple white envelope, is pretty unthreatening, and perfectly professional. And no matter how busy the agent is, too busy in many cases to open up and deal with a big hunk of text, he or she will not be too busy to glance over a short, but pithy, letter. At least in theory.

An even better way to get an agent is to get a referral. Do you have any friends who are writers who would be willing to share with you the names of their agents? Don't be surprised if they're not; writers can get very defensive, and very secretive, about their agents, perhaps because they had to go to so much trouble to land them in the first place. But if you can find a friend who's willing to let you use his or her name to contact the agent, then by all means do it. If your friend says you may not, under any circumstances, use his or her name as a reference, then that's unfortunate. But of course you can still go right ahead and contact that agent. You just can't say that a friend referred you—and that would be true, anyway, because if you haven't already dropped that no-good, so-called friend of yours, you should.

Another way to get an agent is to trap one when he or she is in the wild. Agents lecture and appear on panels all the time, at bookstores, on college campuses, at library meetings open to the public. At writers' conferences, they're actually trolling for new clients. At all these events, they're essentially defenseless, with no secretaries, no answering machines, no intercoms to defend them. Go to one of these panels or colloquiums, introduce yourself afterward or during a break, and ask if you can send something in for the agent's opinion. With people around, and you standing right there, he can hardly say no; it would give the lie to all the blather he'd just been spewing about how open to new talent the business is.

Finally, there's a method that I personally strongly endorse; in fact, until I heard somebody else on that *Booknotes* show on C-Span describing it, I thought it was solely my invention. Either way, I think it works as well as or better than any other method at landing an agent. So here's what you do. Go to the bookstore and find two or three or four books that are as close as possible to the one you're trying to sell, then look in the acknowledgments section. Authors are grateful, one might almost say groveling, creatures, and they usually thank everyone from their mother to their dentist. (This is also a clever marketing gambit, the idea being that nobody can resist buying a copy or two of a book in which they are personally acknowledged.) Anyway, somewhere in there (though more so in nonfiction books than novels), you will often find the name of the agent, whose address you can then look up in *Literary Market Place*.

But what if the agent's name isn't included in the acknowledgments? Then check and see if the name of the editor is. Even if it isn't, the name of the publishing house surely is, and that's good enough. Call the publishing house or the editor's office, and once you've got a live, sentient human being on the line, say how much you enjoyed the book they published—they're always glad to hear that—before adding that you would like to know the name of the agent who represented the author on that project. This is not terribly privileged information, and chances are you will get it without too much trouble. Armed with this knowledge, you're going to be able to knock the socks off nearly any agent.

Your letter to the agent begins, "I am a big fan of *Elavil Nights*, and since I know that you successfully represented the author of that book, I thought you might be willing to take a look at my own novel, *Halcion Days*, which shares with it a darkly comic approach to the perils of anti-depressant use." It almost doesn't matter where you go from here; you've already done your job. You've separated your query from ninety-nine others on the pile. You've shown that you can do your homework, that you've taken an intelligent and resourceful approach to the business, and, best of all, you've made this agent aware that he or she has been specifically chosen, not culled at random from some general list. Any agent will find this sufficiently flattering at least to reply to you, and unless he's now categorically opposed to pharmaceutical fiction, he'll undoubtedly agree to read what you've got.

Among the advantages to using this targeted method of finding an agent is that you don't have to worry about whether or not the agent is familiar with the market for books like yours; you already know that he is. And presumably, he knows the players—the editors, the publishing houses—that would be interested in your manuscript. At one time, years ago, agents could probably be a lot like country doctors and do a little of everything. But in today's increasingly fragmented marketplace, agents, too, are becoming specialists. Some specialize in women's fiction, some in horror and sci-fi, others in tomes on public policy and social history. One of my first agents, John, was happy to sell a couple of general-interest nonfiction books for me—that's what he specialized in—but when I started writing novels, he had to take me aside and ask, "Is this what you're planning to do—write novels for a while?"

"Yes, I think it is," I had to admit.

He shook his head. "Then, in that case, you'd probably be better off with another agent. I don't read novels, and I'm not sure I'm the best guy to sell 'em for you."

While I was stricken at the time—I thought this was just John's way of giving me the brush-off—I later realized it was not. He was just leveling with me. But going out to look for another agent, I did have one advantage over most other writers: I already had a book or two to my credit, and because I lived and worked in New York, I had plenty of friends in publishing, all of whom I now asked for agent recommendations. Then, equipped with these referrals, I sent out letters, and within a few weeks I had answers from several agents who were willing to meet with me and discuss what I wanted to do with my putative career. (I've always liked a line that I believe the writer Richard Ford said: "Writers don't have careers—they have lives." It would certainly account for my own lack of a professional trajectory.)

Anyway, I met with one agent who was very attractive, very glamorous, and whose client list read like something out of *People* magazine. Her desk, credenza, and the otherwise stark white walls of her office were all adorned with photos of her celebrity clients, in matching silver frames. Most of them were movie stars who'd "written" their autobiographies, or socialites who'd "written" potboilers, or politicians who'd "written" their philosophical summations. I felt, with a sure and quiet confidence, that my photo would never in a million years make it into one of those silver frames mounted on that wall. Nor, frankly, did I ever want to have to sit there again, and look up at all those empty, fraudulent faces.

The next agent I met with, whom we'll call Geraldine, was the opposite. She'd no sooner have handled a movie star than raw manure, but I went to see her because a publisher, a guy I knew well, spoke quite badly of her. "Avoid Geraldine at all costs," he said. "She's a total nightmare."

Already I was intrigued. "How so?"

"I published a book by one of her clients last fall, and she was a major pain the whole time. She was always bugging me about the pub date, the cover art, the publicity schedule; she even called me, *after* the book was published, to complain about the quality of the paper stock. Can you believe that?"

I could. And it made me want to meet this woman all the more. As far as I was concerned, she sounded like the model agent, one who was unflagging in her efforts to get the optimum for her books and her authors. Her office was in an old brownstone at the top of a steep flight of steps. Inside, the rooms were furnished with rocking chairs, worn Oriental carpets, exposed brick walls. Now *this* was more like it. I felt as if I'd found a home. And I really did like Geraldine, a middle-aged woman with a no-nonsense perm, wearing a long, loose denim skirt and sipping a mug of herbal tea. But again, as I learned more about her client list and the kind of books she was enthused over, I started to have my doubts. If she had a client on her list who *wasn't* an anarchist, a revolutionary, or a convicted felon, I couldn't find him. This seemingly mild-mannered woman had what appeared to be a taste for mayhem, controversy, and politics of the most radical stripe. I just didn't know how I'd ever find the courage to tell her not only that I'd never done hard time, but that I wanted my next book to be a comic tale of dating in New York.

I went home and was thinking it over when the phone rang, and though I didn't know it when I picked it up, I was about to make the acquaintance of my next, and chosen, agent.

"Robert?" an officious young voice asked. "Please hold for Helen Stern."

Helen Stern? I couldn't believe it. Although I've made up this name, the person was real—and she was the biggest fish in the pond, the one I'd written to without ever figuring that I'd hear back at all. It was like applying to Harvard with a C average.

When she got on the line, she was all that her name suggested—she was brisk, efficient, to the point. I felt like a new recruit who'd just met the master sergeant. Not only that, she'd already inducted me into her platoon.

"I spoke to Neil," she said, referring to the editor of my last book, "and the sales figures were pretty good. He's willing to do another deal, for a little bit more than the last time, but I think if we look around we can find another house that'll make a bid and give us some leverage with Neil."

I was stunned. She'd already spoken to Neil? She was already operating on my behalf? I was already her client? Somehow, I guess I managed to mumble some thanks, and Helen said something about our meeting in person sometime, and then she was off on another call. Mature professional that I am, I lay on my bedroom floor for the next fifteen minutes, letting my heart slow down and my breathing return to normal.

Then I called my friend the publisher, the same one who'd bad-mouthed Geraldine, and told him what had just happened with Helen Stern. "What should I do?" I said.

"What should you do? Nothing. If Helen Stern calls you, you should just shut up and let her be your agent. She's the best there is."

"She is, isn't she?" I said, only now starting to feel the full effect of my coup. "I should just relax and be happy."

"Absolutely," he said, before adding, "as long as you're sure this wasn't some kind of a prank. You really do believe that was Helen Stern on the phone, right?"

"Yes," I said, doubt washing over me like a tidal wave. What if it *was* a prank? But it couldn't be; she knew too much, all about Neil, the new proposal, etc. It had to be Helen Stern. "It was definitely Helen Stern," I concluded.

"Well, then, congratulations," he said. "From now on, your books are going to be way too expensive for me to take on."

Thus began my long odyssey with the agent I retain to this day, though she has become such a big cheese I usually deal with one of her immediate subordinates (a talented and intelligent bunch themselves). But I do know, just from watching Helen at work all these years, what made her such a success, and what separated her from all the other agents out there hustling their wares. Not only has she never asked to borrow twenty bucks from me, she's shown me, over the course of time, what you should look for in an agent.

The Perfect Agent

Above all else, your agent is your advocate. She's the one who will take you and your work out into the world, and upon whose efforts your very livelihood depends. That's how important she is.

What Helen showed me, right off the bat, was that a good agent doesn't let the grass grow under her feet; in fact, her feet barely touch the ground, she's moving so fast. I didn't know how rare that was until I started working in Hollywood, years later, where I dealt with a dozen different TV and movie agents whose idea of doing their job was to sit around and wait for me, the client, to go out and find another assignment from which they could then rake off their commission—for doing absolutely nothing. Helen beat out all the other agents and won me as a client because she had simply taken the initiative and acted.

If I hear one complaint more than any other from my writer friends, it's that their agent takes so long to get back to them, and that's one problem, I must say, that never comes up with Helen. If anything, she sometimes gets back to me *too* fast.

After you send an idea, a proposal, or even a partial manuscript to your agent, you feel as if you've accomplished something. You look forward to sitting around for a week or two, wondering just how blown away she'll be by the magnificence of your prose and the brilliance of your conception. You lull yourself to sleep at night with visions of million-dollar deals and movie options. You imagine that she's already frantically juggling bids and offers.

But with Helen, all of that happy fantasizing can grind to a halt the very next day when she calls to say, "I don't get it. Try something else."

Whew. Now that can be pretty hard to take, all those freshly baked dreams crumbling to dust. There have been times when I've had to catch my breath. *What, I have to find another idea? I only get about one a year!* But all in all, I think I prefer it to the slow torture many of my friends appear to go through. Once your agent gives you an answer, even if it's not the one you were hoping to hear, you can at least make some informed decisions. If you see her point or accept her verdict, however painful that may be, you can move on to something else, where your chances of making a sale are measurably better.

Or, if you really want to, you can stick with the idea she didn't like—after all, *you* liked it—and even try to convince her that you can make it work. Maybe you can address her doubts and dispel them. Even agents, as they will be the first to admit, make mistakes.

Unless your publishing trajectory is going to be spectacularly swift and easy, you must accept the fact that your agent is going to have to give you bad news now and then. She's going to have to tell you that your new book idea isn't a marketable one in the present publishing climate, or that three editors have just passed on your latest proposal. Helen faxes me a copy of the rejection letters as they come in, which, I know, is a good idea, as it allows me to see who's turning me down and why. But that still doesn't make it any fun. (And I do wish she'd warn me first. I hate it when my wife fishes them out of the fax tray before I do, and then hands them to me pretending that she hasn't read them, especially the ones where Helen has scrawled something across the top like "Don't worry about it—he thought John Grisham had no talent, either!")

Yes, your agent may be a necessary tool, the hammer with which you plan to batter down the publishing doors, but sometimes, it's true, she'll leave you feeling as if you've just banged your own thumb.

That's one reason it's so important that you trust your agent's instincts and judgment. It's very easy, too easy, to get reflexively defensive about your work—it's hard to write, hard to put yourself out there and risk rejection, and it's hard to hear that some faceless editor or publishing house has not instantly embraced your work. It's also a knee-jerk reaction to blame the messenger; you can find yourself getting mad at your agent for submitting your work to such unresponsive, dim-witted places. *What was she thinking, going to such an undistinguished house? Doesn't she know what gold she's holding in her hand? Maybe she just doesn't have the clout I need.* I've got a couple of friends who change agents the way you change shirts, and it's usually because they've come to think the agent doesn't know how to sell their stuff. But unfortunately, the next agent usually fares no better.

Whether you stick with one agent or jump all over the place, the sad fact of the matter is, the agent will probably be more of a constant in your publishing life than your editor will be. Editors change jobs all the time; they get fired, promoted, they quit the business to find themselves, start a family, go back to grad school. On the project I worked on just before this one, the book was bought by an editor in chief who then passed me on, for actual editing, to a young editor I'd never met. That editor called me once to introduce herself, then left the company; she was replaced by another editor who lived in another city altogether and worked for the company from her home; again, I did not meet her, but she did her work (quite capably, I might add) and mailed me the results. By the time I'd made the minimal changes she requested, I was instructed to turn them in to yet another editor back at the company headquarters, who'd just been promoted from the ranks. To this day, though we have spoken on the phone often, I've never clapped eyes on this editor, either.

Writers were once wedded to certain editors, and the two of them did book after book together. Ernest Hemingway, F. Scott Fitzgerald, Marjorie Kinnan Rawlings all relied upon the acute editorial judgment and unfailing sensitivity of their legendary editor, Maxwell Perkins. (Fitzgerald even relied upon him for the occasional loan.) Author-editor relationships like that can still happen today—indeed, some writers doggedly follow their editors from house to house—but it can get complicated; many times, the editor may leave, but the author is contractually bound to the publishing house for one or more books to come. If you're lucky, the same editor who acquired, and edited, your book will stick around long enough to be there on the day the first printed copies come off the press.

Your agent, on the other hand, is almost guaranteed to be there.

To a large extent, agents do what editors used to do—they work with and nurture a writer through several books, over a period of years. If the agent is doing her job, she's looking at the big picture for you, plotting what books you will do next, where you will take them, how you'll steadily build your reputation and your audience. She's not only trying to figure out how to get you the next month's rent; she trying to figure out how you'll one day be able to buy a home.

Now I know that sounds like a big responsibility—and it is—but it's also the reason so few agents really excel at what they do. A lot of them, I'm sorry to say, just get your ticket punched once, and then they're off chasing some other deal for some other client. A good agent stays on the case—and on your case, too, making sure you keep the work coming.

That doesn't mean, however, that they do the work for you. Some writers seem to think that their agents should come up with their ideas for them. They want their agents to tell them exactly what will sell, and for the most money. Some agents actually do some of that; my old agent John was very good at coming up with nonfiction book ideas, and he would freely offer them to his clients. But again, that's not the norm. The vast majority of the time, the duty falls squarely on your shoulders alone. Your agent may turn out to be your first reader, she may be your sounding board, she may be a good place to air your notion for the first time, but the actual work, the day-to-day stuff, is still yours to do. The agent can offer some guidance, some pointers, but she's not likely to get down in the trenches with you and start digging. If she enjoyed doing that, she'd have been a writer.

Nor is your agent going to be your close friend. Yes, yes, writers often thank their agents in their acknowledgments as if they were the best and oldest of pals, and it's possible, I suppose, that that's true, sometimes. But not often. Writers who go looking for an agent who can be their buddy are looking for the wrong thing. You don't want a buddy; you've already got plenty of those. What you want is a business partner, someone who will do the part of the publishing job that almost every writer on earth, myself included, is incapable of doing. And that's negotiating.

When I was growing up and earning some spending money around the neighborhood by mowing lawns and shoveling snow, my mother used to tell me to finish the job first, and then when the customer said, "How much do I owe you?" to answer "Whatever you think is fair."

Do I need to tell you what a terrible idea that was? For every decent human being who thought ten dollars was fair, there were three who thought two dollars was enough to cover it. But that, unfortunately, remained my negotiating stance long into my adult life. *Whatever you think is fair*. It's a miracle I'm even alive today.

It's an agent's job to protect you, on the one hand, from predatory publishers, and on the other, from yourself. Writers are way too easy to please, and way too anxious to see their work in print; so anxious that they'll generally agree to just about anything in order to see it happen. Many writers consider it a *favor* to be published at all. I'd say that was appalling if it weren't for the fact that, way down deep, I often feel the same way. It's not healthy, it's not right, but it's there.

Remember that saccharine line from *Jerry Maguire*, when Tom Cruise says to Renee Zellweger, "You complete me"? Well, that in a way *is* what you're looking for in your agent—you're looking for someone who will fill in the part of the equation that you lack. The part that knows how to wheel and deal, the part that can retain an objective and businesslike stance even when it's your most personal work that's under discussion. You're looking for someone who thinks that *you're* the one doing the *publishers* a favor by offering them the chance—they should be so lucky!—to publish your book. That's not the easiest attitude to pull off—there are very few writers who can manage it—but agents can do it with their eyes closed.

They can also handle the adversarial stuff, which will inevitably arise. *What adversarial stuff?* you might ask. *I intend to get along beautifully with my publishing house, and work happily with any editor they choose to assign to the book.*

And well you may. I'm sure your behavior will be impeccable throughout. But the strange thing is, you and your publishing house, though you're ostensibly entering into this transaction as partners, also have some divergent interests, especially in the initial stages. Most of this divergence, not surprisingly, has to do with dough. You want as much of it as possible, and they want to part with as little of it as they can. From just such differences do conflicts emerge.

But in any and all conflicts of interest that come up, your goal should always be to stay clear of the bloodshed. Above the fray and out of the line of fire. That, more than any other reason I can offer, is why you need an agent. During the contractual negotiation, there are dozens of points, from royalty rates to cover approval, that have to be bargained over, and sometimes the bargaining can get pretty heated. For you, that kind of to-ing and fro-ing could prove a nightmare, poisoning your professional relationship with the editor you have to work with over the coming months or years. But for an agent, who's not going to be working with that editor the way you will, it's just another negotiation. Time and again, I would hear from editors who had to deal with the fearsome Helen, "Your agent is killing me! You can't imagine how difficult and demanding she is to deal with!"

And I'd say, "Gosh, I am so sorry. I have no idea what's gotten into her. I'll give her a call and tell her to back off."

And then I would indeed call Helen, but only to say, "You go, girl! They're on the ropes and reeling!"

Good agents also know, instinctively, which battles can be won, and which ones aren't worth fighting. No contractual negotiation, for instance, is ever an out-and-out victory for one side; they're all compromises, in which the author wins a few (a slightly higher advance, for instance) and loses a few (some foreign rights). Even though I've done a fair number of book deals before this one, I still wouldn't consider myself capable of winning the right concessions, or of ironing out all those little wrinkles in a contract that do not work to my advantage. A contract contains lots of small print . . . but print, however small, can contain lots of sly, conniving stuff; an agent should be able to smell the sneaky clauses from a mile away and get them cleanly excised.

Nor does the war end there. You never know at what point in the publishing process or over what issue trouble will arise. But take it from me, some problem *will* crop up. On one book I did, a reference book yet, the galleys came back with no page numbers! Helen read the publisher the riot act.

On another, a book was published (so it was already too late to fix) with no copy—no words, that is—on the back cover; it was just a blank, with nothing to entice, or even explain to, a reader what this book was about. The publisher assured us the mistake would be corrected in the second edition—as if the book would ever get there. (It did not.) All my agent could do was fume, along with me.

On a third, the editor had cut his list in half, and my book was one of the casualties. John was my agent then, and it was his job to make sure the book wasn't abandoned by the publishing house altogether. Since I was in shock at the time, John actually accompanied me to the editor's office, and while I sat there mute, my hands as cold as ice, John enlisted the editor's help in getting the book transferred from his imprint to another at the same house. Since the first imprint was classier, I lost some cachet, and since I now had to get on that second imprint's sched-ule, I lost some time, but I didn't lose the deal completely. John took care of everything in a calm and professional manner, and I actually uttered not one word the whole time; I sat there like a stone, and when John stood up and shook hands with the editor, I, too, stood up and allowed John to steer me out of the room. The next thing I knew, we were sitting in a deli down the street, and John was ordering me a bowl of matzoh ball soup. By the time it came, I could talk again.

For the record, John ran his own small literary agency, with just one other agent under him.

Helen, on the other hand, is now one of the principal players at a massive literary and talent agency, where she has swiftly risen through the ranks (though she was always, even from induction, a commissioned officer).

In other words, and here's why I'm bringing this up at all, I've been represented by a small agency—what is sometimes called a "boutique"—and by a big, monolithic one. And since I am often asked, Is it better to go with a small agency, where you can get individual attention, or a large one, with presumably more clout and name recognition? here's what I think.

It doesn't much matter.

At a small agency, you can get to know everyone, from the receptionist to the other agents; theoretically your agent will have less corporate-type busywork and maybe even fewer clients to distract her from furthering your career. She may even have a greater vested interest in your success, since she's sharing none, or less, of the revenue she generates from your work with a larger corporate entity.

The downside? It's always possible that this agency *isn't* well known and packs no punch in publishing circles. Ask the agent, and ask around, to find out who their other clients are—both the stars, and the meat-and-potatoes authors. (Starting out, and take no offense, you will probably be a meat or a potato.)

At a big agency, you can, again in theory, benefit from an impressive, powerful presence; if your name is on their team roster, then you're clearly a player to be reckoned with. Their envelopes get opened, their submissions get read, their agents get respect, and in turn, so do you. But the downside here could be that you get lost, or feel that way. With a fleet of clients bringing in megabucks, the agency can lose track of your small craft, and without their even being aware of it, while you're waving your hands frantically for help, you can sink with all hands on board.

To be perfectly fair, all these things, the pro *and* the con, can happen at a big agency, or a small one. Big agencies can have lousy agents, who will do a lousy job for you, and small agencies can have great agents, who will work like beavers on your behalf. Or vice versa. The bottom line is, it isn't the agency itself that counts nearly as much as it is the individual agent.

One thing, however, I do believe holds true across the board: most literary agents, and most of the ones you want, *are* in New York City. Personally, I've never had one that wasn't. That doesn't mean there aren't worthy agents in other places—places, for instance, that might be closer to where you live—Dallas, Chicago, San Diego. And when you're starting out, an agent in your own town can be very helpful; she can work with you in person on your proposal or your manuscript; she can hold your hand, literally, in times of crisis, such as when the feverish bidding for your novel exceeds the million-dollar mark. She can accept your latest draft over a cup of coffee at the local diner, thereby saving you a trip to the post office. And with the technological revolution, she can work more effectively than ever before with e-mails and attachments, faxes and voice mails, to keep in touch with editors and what they're looking for, back in the publishing capital of New York.

But what she doesn't have is all the access, all the firsthand inside info, that comes from living and working in Manhattan, where the lion's share of the publishing business is still located. She may know the names of the right editors, but she may not know them personally. She isn't going to the publication parties and panels where the schmoozing is done and the contacts made. A great deal of publishing, as with any business, is done outside the office, at social gatherings and industry events. New York–based agents, I believe, still have the edge in that respect; they can have their ear to the ground, and their finger on the pulse of publishing, more effectively than an agent anywhere else can. Proximity, as with virtually anything you name, confers a certain advantage.

Finally, there is the question of what you, the author, will pay for these services, whether they are rendered in New York, New Orleans, or Newton, Massachusetts. At a couple of the very large agencies, notably ICM and William Morris, the literary agents will take 10 percent of the proceeds from your sales and all the monies that accrue therefrom (such as your foreign rights sales, your royalties, your movie options, etc.).

At almost every other agency these days, the commission will be 15 percent.

Some agents will charge you for things like photocopying costs, postage, phone bills, etc., and some will simply keep track of those expenses and deduct them from any future sales the two of you make. Either way, I find that practice a little dubious, because it is so ripe for abuse—you, the writer, must accept the agent's word on all these putative costs ("I knew the right editor for your book was staying in Paris at the Georges Cinq, so I checked in to the room right next door! Wasn't that clever of me?"), which puts you in an unnecessarily awkward position. Do you just roll over and accept whatever the agent says she incurred in the way of expenses, or do you try to conduct an informal audit, asking just who that long-distance call was to, or why the photocopying costs came in at so many cents per page? It's asking you, the writer—already the most vulnerable and possibly gullible member of the publishing equation—once again to silently acquiesce, or to attempt to show a canny business sense you probably don't have. (I know that I don't have it.) I also feel that the agent, usually taking 15 percent of the pot, is already being adequately compensated, and she should absorb whatever minimal costs she runs up while doing business on your behalf. (Don't most businesses pay their own overhead?) Still, this is an argument I've never won, and it's a practice that's now fairly common. (Helen, incidentally, does not charge for such things. One more reason I love her.)

Either way, you should know what you're getting into when you sign on with any agent, and that means, possibly for the first time in your life, you're going to have to sit down like a grown-up and discuss such things as money, commissions, business plans, and so on. You have to find out what you're going to be charged for and what you're not, what level of compensation the agent is demanding (there are some who actually split the usual difference between 10 and 15 percent and come in at 12.5), what kind of approach the agent is going to use to market your work (wide and multiple submissions, individual pinpointed strikes), and who her other clients are (which is a good indication of her own strengths and interests). Uncomfortable as much of this may make you, it needs to be done and, trust me, agents do not take offense at your questions and concerns. They, above all, know this is a business arrangement and that it has to be treated as such.

There was a time when these arrangements were done verbally and sealed with a handshake. Even today, with my own agent, we simply work on selling each project as it comes up, and if it does sell, I receive a one-page letter after the fact affirming that Helen was the agent on it and that she's entitled to her percentage of the proceeds. Although the ground rules stay the same, it's as if we were working, essentially, on a per-book basis. But that's less the norm these days than is a contract, or agency agreement, for a set period of time, signed and sealed before you and your new agent get under way together.

Frightening as these agency agreements can appear, and I've seen one that ran to a dozen closely typed pages, they do serve an important purpose—they lay out in black and white, and sometimes exhaustive detail, everything that you and the agent can expect from each other. That way, nobody later on can claim to have been misled. How long a period of time do these contracts generally run for? That, too, can vary. If, for instance, you approach an agent with your completed novel, one that she decides she would like to represent, then the contract may run for only a year—that's time enough for her to send it out, for several rounds if she needs to, to get it sold. If your book is only partially completed, or perhaps just in the proposal stage, then most agents will want you to sign a two-year agreement—it could easily take that long to get the project into the right, commercially appealing state. (If you think that sounds like a long time, you have to understand that many writers, unlike you, actually dawdle. Often, agents find that they have to nudge, prod, or even lash their clients along.)

There'll also be some provision in most contracts for an extension, or automatic renewal, of the initial contract term—which seldom poses a problem. If things are going well, you'll both be happy to keep working together. If things are not going well—your book, for instance, is remaining stubbornly unsold—then both of you may be all too willing to go your own ways.

Most writers are fairly timid souls who, like me, quake at signing a car rental agreement, but you really shouldn't twist yourself into a pretzel over this. (Save that for the publishing contract.) What you don't understand in the agency agreement, ask about. What you don't like, suggest be changed. Most agents are pretty reasonable people, and they want to work with you at least as much as you want to work with them. Remember, a writer can always write, but an agent can't be an agent unless she's got material to sell—your material.

What especially gets my dander up, from the writer's point of view, is a cheesy little item generally known as a reading fee. Some agencies offer this service to would-be clients, charging them an up-front fee to read and evaluate the salability of their material. But isn't that what they were supposed to do for free? Isn't that what agents do—find salable material and sell it? The obvious question becomes, Are they trying to make money as real literary agents, or as an unofficial, high-volume clearinghouse for unpublished writers? Are they really in business to sell books to publishers, or to fleece the poor and unfortunate who, so desperate for guidance, send in their manuscripts for a professional agent's editorial opinion (which, in and of and by itself, is perfectly worthless)? If it's an objective editorial judgment you want, or help with your work, enroll in a local writing class and get your feedback from the teacher. And if you encounter an agent who asks for a reading fee before considering your work, well, I'd say thanks but no thanks. An agent should make money when she sells your material, not when she reads it.

Submission and Acceptance

Once you have selected that one lucky agent from the legion who have been striving to represent you (and do be kind when you let the others down), it's time to formulate the rest of your game plan . . . and put it into action.

The first thing your agent will want to do is fine-tune your proposal or, if you happen to have finished the whole book, your manuscript. A lot of writers get impatient with this step—they're raring to go and want to start spending the money!—but it's foolish to act so hastily now that you risk sabotaging all the work you've already put in. If you've picked this agent, then put some faith in her judgment and listen to what she has to say, no matter how much more work it might entail. If you thwart her, or resist taking her advice, she could either lose interest in the project or simply send it out to publishers with less enthusiasm than she might have had if everything had been done according to her specifications.

Of course, if you really disagree with something she wants to do, or how she wants to present your book to publishers, then say so. But if the two of you remain at loggerheads, or continue not to see eye to eye, then you just might have to shop around some more and find someone else to represent you. You and your agent must be on pretty much the same wavelength; she has to understand you and your book, and you have to have confidence in her assessments. Presumably, that's how the two of you got together in the first place.

Often, an agent will want to beef up or embellish a proposal in some way. I've been asked to add everything from an updated résumé to three more chapters of text; in one case, I was advised to throw in a couple of paragraphs expatiating on the many TV and radio appearances I've done. It is a plain fact of the business these days that publishers favor writers who are comfortable and articulate in a radio studio or on a TV show. Novelists, it's true, have a hard time getting on the air at all (the show host might actually have had to read the book), so for them it's fairly unimportant. But a nonfiction author who also happens to be personable, presentable, and good at providing sound bites has a slight advantage, even at the selling stage. One publisher requested I come into the office before they made an offer, and although it was ostensibly to discuss the book, I knew darn well it was so they could check me out and satisfy themselves that I'd make a decent impression if they decided to put me out on a book tour.

Your agent should be aware of all these angles that you must play, and make sure that you've covered as many of them as possible before putting the stamps on your submission and mailing it out. Assuming that the two of you have now done everything possible to make your package irresistible—everything is neat, orderly, well organized—the next thing you have to do is figure out where to send it.

Now, this, more than anything, is the agent's call. It's her job to know who's looking for books like yours. Through her years in the business, she should have accumulated a sizeable knowledge of which houses are publishing what, which editors are responsive to what kinds of material, what the going rates are for projects like the one you're submitting. She should know what your best bets are.

That said, your input can again be valuable. Have you, for instance, attended a writers' conference where you met an editor at a particular house? If so, tell the agent about it. Did you see a show on *Bookspan TV* that featured an editor talking about her interest in books just like yours? Tell the agent. Have you noticed, because you read so many books in this category, that a certain publishing house or imprint seems to publish a lot of them? Tell her. Not long ago, I submitted a rather bizarre supernatural thriller to my agent and she admitted to me that although she liked what she read, she wasn't all that familiar with this highly specialized publishing terrain. Because I *am* familiar with it, I was happy to tell her what publishing companies seem to be most productive and successful with such books, and then she went ahead and submitted the proposal and sample text to those places. (Did we sell it? I was afraid you'd ask that. No. Even for the wackiest and least distinguished publishing companies I could think of, this book was too far out there. When we got about the tenth turndown suggesting that the proposed novel might make a better video game or comic book, I knew it was time to play a solemn requiem and put it to rest.)

Depending on the project, and your agent's instincts, your book will go out to anywhere from one to a dozen different houses, simultaneously. She'll let you know when it goes out, and to what places (or at least she should), and then there's frankly not much more that you personally can do, other than wait and worry. If you were ever thinking about making a trip home to visit your folks, this would be an ideal time.

How long should you plan on staying at the old homestead before you can expect to start hearing back from the publishers? Again, it could range from a week to whenever. I submitted a novel to an editor eight years ago, and even though she said she was halfway through it and really liked it and was planning to make an offer, I'm still waiting to hear. (I will admit that it doesn't look good.) Normally, it takes from two weeks to two months to get the word. Most agents today are reluctant to let their projects drift around out there indefinitely; the longer your book has been languishing in the marketplace, the less alluring it is likely to be. As a result, most agents send out their projects to a raft of publishers all at once, and notify them all, if they're planning to make an offer, that they must reply by the "closing date." The idea is to get the publishers excited and on the ball, to create a little buzz around the book and a sense of urgency. Get in on the action now, before it's too late!

In the case of a nonfiction proposal, the closing date is usually about two weeks away; that gives the editor enough time to read through the proposal, think it over, and check out the competing titles already in the stores. In the case of a novel, almost always submitted as a completed manuscript, the closing date is usually a little later, perhaps a month away. It takes more time for the editor, and probably several others at the publishing house, to read the entire text, then get together to confer and share their verdicts. A novel, from their perspective, is always a more iffy proposition.

Sometimes, as the passes—aka rejections—begin to come in, an agent will start submitting the project to other houses that had been further down her list. Other times, she'll wait until she hears from everyone in this first round before deciding on her next strategic maneuver.

But what was that I just said? Did I just utter the dreaded R word—as in *rejections*? Are there publishers, you may wonder, so blind, so benighted, as not to see the blockbuster potential of your book? Sadly, yes. I've never written a book that wasn't rejected somewhere, and I'd hazard to say that there isn't a professional writer out there, even the really big guns, who hasn't had a turndown or two or three. The first Harry Potter novel bounced all over the place before finally finding a publishing home, and a small advance. *A Confederacy of Dunces*, by John Kennedy O'Toole, was rejected so many times its author committed suicide before the book was published, posthumously, and went on to win the Pulitzer Prize. J. P. Donleavy's manuscript of *The Ginger Man* was turned down by more than thirty-five publishers before getting into print; recently, it was voted one of the hundred best novels of the century and has sold, to date, roughly ten million copies.

Books get rejected for all kinds of reasons that have nothing to do with their conception or execution, so don't take it personally. Sometimes, they're rejected because this particular house is cutting back on that type of book, or, conversely, because they've already got too many similar titles already in the pipeline. Sometimes, the project simply doesn't suit a particular editor's taste. Sometimes, the house likes the book, but its comparative market analysis—done by their sales staff—tells them it won't do well; the market's glutted, or just not big enough. Sometimes the publishing house is secretly on the block, and they don't want to sign up any more books until their new owner, whoever it is, takes over. You just never know exactly why your book was turned down, so don't wear yourself out trying to guess. Move on.

Why dwell on the negative? For now, let's assume a more pleasant scenario is unfolding; let's assume that your book is stirring up serious interest—of the buying kind—from more than one publisher. When a book is hot, one publisher may often step forward and make what is called a preempt—a cash-on-the-barrelhead, take-it-or-leave-it, now-or-never offer. These offers are generally pretty lucrative—they have to be, since their purpose is to sew up the project then and there. And you may be tempted to take it. Your agent may be, too. If the offer is good enough, go ahead. But a sizeable preempt is also a strong indication that there's likely to be lots of interest—and other potential buyers—out there. The publisher making the preempt is trying to avoid the very thing that you may really benefit from—and that is an auction.

Now, the minute I say the word, I know you're picturing one of those Sotheby's auctions that are sometimes broadcast on TV, with a crowd of millionaires holding up little numbered paddles and an electronic tote board recording all the offers and converting the foreign currencies into their U.S. equivalents. A book auction is really not much like that . . . unless your agent is a real showboat.

Recently, a friend of mine, whose writing credits up until now were pretty much limited to stereo and record reviews, wrote a short memoir about a family reunion down South. I didn't read it, so I have no idea of its quality, but his agent, a woman I'd never heard of, told him she was going to hold an auction for it. When my friend called me, he was ecstatic.

"We're renting a room at the Beverly Hills Hotel with a bunch of phone lines, and we're just going to sit there all day fielding the offers!"

Okay, okay, I'll admit that my first reaction was overwhelming envy. But when I got over it, I said, as convincingly as I could, "That's fantastic! I had no idea it was going so well. Who holds the floor bid on the book?"

"The what?"

"The floor bid. I mean, has one publisher has already made an offer that the others have to top?"

"Nope, not that I know of," my friend said. "The auction hasn't started, so there aren't any bids at all yet." He paused. "Should there be?"

"Well, not necessarily. But sometimes, one publisher has made a standing offer for, say, fifty thousand, and that's the floor bid. In return for the guarantee, that same publisher gets the right to top any other offer that comes in during the auction by, say, 5 or 10 percent, and still get the book."

"Huh. My agent didn't say anything about that." But then, brightening, "She did say we were going to hold on to all the movie rights and stuff like that."

"That's always a good idea," I said, though I was already beginning to have my doubts about this agent, and this incipient auction.

The day came, and my friend and his high-flying agent apparently did take a room at the Beverly Hills Hotel, and, from what I gather, they sat there from 6 A.M. to 3 P.M., Pacific time, waiting for the phone to ring. It did ring once, but it was just the front desk confirming that they would be taking the late check-out time. No offers came in, that day or any day since. I just hope, though I've never had the heart to ask him, that my friend didn't have to foot the room bill.

Auctions work well, but only when the book, and the agent, have managed to whip up a bit of a buying frenzy in advance. If, by the time the closing date has rolled around, the agent realizes that there are several potential buyers for the book, she can notify them all that they must submit their offers on, say, Friday morning, before noon. If two or three publishers make nearly identical offers, she can then move on to what's known as a "best bid" situation—they all have one more shot to make their best, and final, offer. There are a lot of permutations, a lot of ways an agent can play out this endgame—and play the publishers off against one another—but as long as she manages to get you the best deal out there, then she's done her job.

Much of the time, however, selling a book is not as dynamic and exciting as this. For most of us, it means a few weeks of anxious waiting . . . and hoping, whenever we come home, that the message light flashing on the answering machine will turn out to be our agent with a banner headline.

The great thing is, sometimes it is.

"We've got an offer" may be the four most beautiful words in the English language, and for most writers—myself included—what comes next hardly matters. Auctions are great, but one offer is all you really need. For the next several minutes, while my agent relays the terms of any initial offer to me, I am hearing and understanding almost nothing; I am simply basking in the glow of acceptance, wallowing in the warm pool of approval, absorbing through every pore the honey of good fortune. I could go on like this, but I'm making myself a little queasy.

Anyway, the point is, if you've done your work capably and well, this call will come one day. It's perhaps the most exciting and gratifying moment in the whole process, the moment when you see all the work you've done pay off, when you can start to envision—really envision, knowing that it's going to come true—*your book*, printed and bound and on sale in your local bookstore. I don't know any happier news that an author can get (though the word "bestseller" certainly presents a possibility).

That's why the rest of it makes such a small impression. When your agent calls you with the glad tidings, she will generally have a few things firmly in hand, such as the amount of the advance and several variables, such as the royalty rate and foreign rights, that remain to be haggled over. She may even have put the publishing house on hold, as it were, while she checks with the other houses that have yet to weigh in. As we've discussed, there is no better leverage that an agent can possess than a standing offer from one house when she has to call the others. As with anything else in this world, people want what somebody else has got, and nothing so whets their desire as the fact that they may lose something good to someone else. An agent understands this.

So chill out, and let her continue to do her job. My own inclination, whenever an agent has called to tell me we have an offer, has been to say, "Call them back! Right now! Grab it before they go away!" But wisely, my agents have had cooler heads, and they have prevailed. One thing that to some extent does distinguish the publishing industry from many others—most notably, Hollywood—is that even a verbal offer made over the phone, with no accompanying paperwork yet, is still a firm and credible offer. It means something, and the editor who made the offer will stand behind it. The editor also knows, generally without the agent even telling him so, that the agent is now going to call around to the other houses where the project was sent to see if there's a better offer out there. It doesn't mean that he'll leave his own offer on the table indefinitely, but it does mean that in most cases you've got a few days, maybe even a week or two, to accept or reject it.

Regardless of whatever happens from this point on, you've got a deal and your book has got a publisher. So celebrate.

Over the next few days, the agent will make sure all interested parties have been heard from, she'll gather any and all offers, and then she'll call you with the results. Sometimes one offer is so clearly the leader—lots more money, a better house, whatever—that all others fall by the way-side. Sometimes, the offers are so close together that you and your agent will want to confer about which one to take. It isn't always a matter of simply taking the highest advance; sometimes one house will be offering you a hardcover deal for $10,000, while another will be offering you $15,000 for a softcover trade paperback deal. Well, the softcover deal is for more money, but maybe the hardcover deal will yield you more in the long run, after the book gets some good reviews and gets reissued (by the same publisher, or one to whom the paperback rights were sold sep-arately) in a softcover format. There are a million questions like these, and it is my fervent prayer that you have to worry about each and every one of them someday.

But for now, let me address the one burning question, which I'm sure is lingering in the back of your mind, as it lingers in any writer's. Just how much money is your book likely to bring? I wish I could give you a simple answer to that. But I can't. A book can fetch virtually any sum imaginable, from something barely worth taking notice of to several mil-lion dollars. Admittedly, those are the extremes. What I *can* give you are some ballpark figures.

If this first book you've written is what might be called a genre novel—in other words, it's most likely to come out as a mass-market paperback—you will probably be offered anywhere from $1,500 to $15,000. If your novel is a mainstream kind of book, one that might come out in hardcover and pick up some good notices along the way, you might get anywhere from, say, $5,000 to $25,000. Of course, the right breakout novel, one that really seems to catch the zeitgeist or get the publishing world excited about it, can haul in a lot more than that— you hear about books like these, such as *Cold Mountain* or *The Deep End of the Ocean* in the news—but again, those are once-in-a-blue-moon sit-uations. A friend of mine, a woman who has already had a fairly long and distinguished publishing career, recently had her latest novel published to good reviews, everywhere from *Kirkus* (a weekly industry review) to *Time* magazine. When I saw the *Time* review, I called her up to congratulate her, and it was then that she confided, to my consternation, that she was still floundering financially.

"But your new book looks like it's really making a big impression."

"That's great. But the publisher paid me a grand total of $5,500 for it, I worked on it for three years, and unless I manage to get a big paperback sale, or a movie option, I've still got to find some temp work again."

Man, was this depressing. I tried to buck her up, and yes, there did turn out to be a paperback sale in her future; however, it wasn't a big enough one to keep her solvent for long. The movie studios sniffed around, but none ever made an offer. And my friend is back to teaching an occasional writing class and writing the odd book review.

No one ever said the life of the writer was for the faint of heart.

If yours is a nonfiction book, the price it will get is dependent upon a lot of things, most notably its subject matter. If it's all about how to tie the various sailors' knots, you'll probably get in the low range, $3,500 to $7,500. If your book is about a new way to communicate with dogs, you could be onto something—maybe $10,000 to $30,000. If your book is about a new way to communicate with your spouse or lover, and you can convincingly claim that it will eclipse the Mars and Venus books, the sky might be the limit. When it comes to sex and romance books, if you can position yourself as some kind of specialist, a university sociologist with access to some brand-new groundbreaking studies, or a psychotherapist with a celebrity clientele, that will boost the price even more.

I happen to know two sex-and-relationship therapists who both did books recently, and I also happen to know what they got for them because, since neither one of them can write a complete sentence, they both came to me to see if we could strike a deal. In each case, they'd be the expert, and I'd be the writer (or ghostwriter). The first one got $75,000 from her publisher, the second got around $50,000 (though both of them lied to me about what they'd actually received—I got the real numbers from their editors). I didn't write the book for either of them, in part because I hate the idea of being the unsung ghostwriter, and in larger part because neither one of them was prepared to part with more than a few thousand dollars of her advance. (That, you may discover, is a painfully curious thing about the writing business: many people who aren't writers at all manage to collect large sums of money, anyway—they are the putative authorities on one subject or another. But when it comes time for them to hire someone actually to *write* the book that will bear their name, they can't stand to share the cash.)

Since I'm assuming, however, that *you're* the only one writing the book we're talking about just now, we can also safely assume that you'll be keeping the cash, minus the agent's 10 or 15 percent, all to yourself. *Mazel tov*. Just don't count on collecting the money next week, or even, for that matter, next month. The contractual process, which must be completed before the money starts to get paid out, can take many weeks, or months, all on its own. I had actually finished writing my last book *in its entirety* before the publisher had gotten around to paying me the *first half* of the advance, which was due about eight months earlier. Since I was feeling ornery by that point, and didn't want to lose what little leverage I had, I told my agent to let the publisher know that even though the book was done, and sitting in the agent's office, that's where it would remain until that first, way overdue check had come through.

But we were talking about having your book *accepted* for publication, so let's not spoil this moment with any more talk of delays and legalities. We have the whole rest of the book to do that. For now, be happy that your book has been sold and you are soon to join the ranks of published authors. Maybe your publishing deal is a great one, and maybe it's just okay, but either way it's a deal—they don't just hand these out on the street corner—and getting it is a very real accomplishment. Take the next week or so to make yourself absolutely unbearable to your close friends and extended family.

Art of the Deal

There are some writers who get started on the rest of their book the moment they have accepted the publisher's offer. Those writers are called industrious.

There are some other writers who wait to get rolling until their contracts have arrived with every i dotted and every t crossed. Those writers are generally called late.

As I've said, this contractual process—getting a long and legal document to the point where everybody's satisfied and ready to sign on the dotted line—can take a while, so if you're planning to sit on your hands until it's all done, you're going to lose precious writing time. Once your agent has made the deal with the editor, the transaction is essentially done; small points remain to be ironed out, but it's nothing for you to worry about or fill your head with. You need to keep your head clear to do the work that's still ahead.

When it comes to the contract, your agent is the one who should really be getting her hands dirty. A publishing contract is usually anywhere from five to fifteen pages long, and it's filled with dense type and absolutely baffling language; I once had to determine on my own if a contract allowed me to sell foreign rights in the U.K., and although I am a college graduate, and I read the relevant, or what I thought were the relevant, clauses six times over, I still couldn't tell if I owned those rights or the publisher did.

Still, there are certain big issues that any writer will want to make sure are clearly noted and stipulated in the contract, and these are the issues that are usually hashed out early on in the negotiating stage. First and foremost among these is the size of the advance and how it will be paid out. Let us say, for argument's sake, that your agent has procured an offer of $30,000, and you have accepted it. That advance can be paid out in two parts, which is what you want, or in four parts, which is a common, but annoying, publishing practice these days. Here's how it goes, in each instance.

If your advance is going to be paid half and half, you will receive your first $15,000 on signing the completed contract. But even then, you should count on waiting a month or so for the check to arrive at your agent's office, and for her to then turn around and issue you another check, with her commission deducted. The remaining $15,000, again minus the agent's commission, will be paid to you upon, in the customary language, "delivery and acceptance" of the completed manuscript. As you may have noticed, the tricky part of that last phrase is the word "acceptance." A publisher can decide that, even though you've delivered right on time, the manuscript isn't yet in an acceptable state. In other words, you can be sent back to do minor, or even fairly major, revisions.

Then, when you've done them, and the manuscript has met with the publisher's approval (which means your editor at the house has given it the thumbs-up), you will have satisfied the acceptance part of that clause and you'll get the second half of your money.

If, instead, your contract calls for you to be paid in four stages, you'll get the first $7,500 on signing, the second $7,500 on showing something like half of the manuscript, the third installment upon delivery and acceptance of the completed book, and the fourth and final part upon its publication. Your official pub date can be anywhere from nine months, in some cases, to two years away; the average wait is eighteen months. Why so long? Because once the publishing house has your book in hand, they have to get it written up in their sales catalogs, the sales reps have to go out and take orders, the publishing house has to then figure out how many copies they should print, all sorts of stuff like that. And in the meantime, you'll still have plenty of work to do with the editor, and later, the copy editor. It's a long and complicated process, which we'll get into in the chapters to follow.

One thing that I get asked a lot, and that seems to terrify many writers, is the notion that they might have to pay back all or a part of their advance, if the book doesn't do well. Let me put your mind at rest on that score; even though it's called an advance—as if it were a loan that might have to be repaid one day—it's not. Your advance is yours to keep, unless (a) you are hopelessly late with the manuscript, (b) you don't deliver the manuscript at all, or (c) the manuscript is deemed utterly unacceptable by the publisher. You don't have to give back the advance—in whole or in part—if the book fails to find an audience out there. Again, for argument's sake, let's say the book is selling for $20 a copy, and you have a 10 percent royalty rate. That means you'll be earning a royalty of $2 per copy, or 10 percent of the cover price. Let's also say that the book has now sold 15,000 copies. That would mean you had "earned out," in the industry parlance; 15,000 copies, at $2 per copy, comes to $30,000—the same amount as your hypothetical advance. You would not have received any of these royalties; they're just numbers on a royalty statement. But what the numbers are telling you is that you have successfully reached the break-even point.

Now, the *next* time a copy is sold, making the total 15,001 copies, you would earn another $2, which, in the fullness of time, you *would* receive. And $2 for every copy thereafter. In most cases, there's even an escalator clause, which means that after your book has sold a certain number of copies, the royalty rate rises slightly, so that you might earn an extra 50¢ or $1 per copy.

But suppose the book does not earn out? Suppose it sells only 5,000 copies, bringing your royalty earnings to $10,000. Technically, you're now in the hole to the tune of $20,000. Scary thought, isn't it? But that's all it is—really. If I had to pay back all the unearned advance money I've received over the course of my illustrious career, I'd be in bankruptcy court from morning till night. For years, you will receive royalty statements, and each one of them will show an outstanding "unearned balance" of $20,000, or $19,850, or $18,410. Gradually, the number gets whittled down, and then at a certain point, when the book is no longer in print, and no more copies could literally be sold, the number stops changing. Not that the royalty statements stop coming. For at least six years after my first novel had gone out of print, I continued to get royalty statements from the publisher reminding me just how little of the meager advance had ever been recouped.

With all of these variables in play, how can you ever know how much to expect? And when to expect it? With the exception of the advance, royalties appear to be perhaps the most intriguing element of the contract for most writers—at least I know it's the second most inquired-about subject whenever I teach a publishing course. In one recent class, a well-dressed middle-aged woman, a vice president at a local bank here in L.A., led the charge by raising her hand and asking me, in all seriousness, when she could safely quit her job.

"Why would you want to do that?" I asked.

"So I can concentrate on writing my other books."

Now, since this was a class for beginners, I was stymied. "You mean, you've already written a book?"

"Three. They're all done," she announced, proudly. Then, tapping two fingers against her forehead, she added, "They're just up here for the time being."

Now I was starting to get the picture. "So what you're really asking me is . . ."

"How much money will the royalties come to, and how quickly are they paid? I wouldn't want to do anything until I knew exactly how much I could expect." She smiled at her classmates as she added, "I'm a banker. We always like to know *exactly* what's coming in."

Aside from the fact that she'd jumped the gun in a rather large way—calculating the royalties on a book, or trilogy, that hadn't yet been written, much less sold—there was, of course, no sensible way to answer that question.

So I answered it insensibly. "Royalties, you have to understand, are a lot like quarks. Theoretically, they exist, but that doesn't mean that we ever actually see them."

Not surprisingly, this reply did not suffice.

"Here's the problem," she said, adopting the voice she might use to explain to a busboy why her bank was not prepared to give him a million-dollar home loan. "I need to put a new roof on my house, and I have two kids, one of whom is already in private school. Before I quit the bank, I need to have some idea—a *good* idea—of how much money will be coming in from each book." She folded her hands on the desktop and, now that everything had been neatly laid out, waited patiently for me to cut out the nonsense and give her that hard dollar figure she was asking for.

Others in the class were also waiting.

"Royalties," I said, trying another tack, "are like a gift from God. An unexpected rain shower in the middle of a drought. An unforeseen windfall. They're wonderful—a miracle, a blessing, a mitzvah—but they are also completely unpredictable and you must never count on them. Even John Grisham never knows exactly what they'll come to."

All I could see were glum and distrustful faces.

"Okay, then," a guy in the back chimed in, "suppose that's true. Even if you won't tell us what this lady's royalties might come to"—and he said it as if he knew I knew, but just wasn't telling—"can you at least tell us *when* she'd get them?"

The banker smiled over at him, as if to say, *Thanks for helping me out here. This guy's a slippery little weasel, isn't he?*

"Twice a year," I said, "the publisher sends you a statement, usually in a 9 by 12 manila envelope, with the return address showing the publishing company's accounting office. If you're owed any money in royalties, there's a check stapled to the top of the statement inside. So if you can feel a staple through the envelope—and I've learned to do so—then you can be pretty confident that there's good news inside."

Now everyone was becoming slightly mollified; I was finally talking about the money coming in again. I made a mental note to myself, and not for the first time, to pacify a restive class with talk of money. The more money, the better. So I elaborated.

"As you know, there are three kinds of books"—because we'd already covered this in class—"the mass-market paperback, the trade paperback, and the hardcover, and the royalty rates for all three of those differ. In most contracts, the prevailing rate for each of those categories will be used. Some agents can get the publishers to raise them a bit, that's part of their job, but the boost will generally not amount to more than a percent or two. That said, if the book does well, that one or two percent raise can translate into a lot of dollars for you."

More smiles all around.

Sensing I had a winner, I continued. "If, say, your book is a classy hardcover biography of Nelson Mandela, then your royalty rates might go something like this: 10 percent on the first 5,000 copies sold, 12.5 percent on the next 5,000, and 15 percent thereafter."

"So if the book was selling for $30 a copy," the guy in back broke in, "I'd get $3 for every one of the first 5,000 copies that sell?"

"Yes, exactly." I thought he'd be happy, but he didn't look it. "Is it still unclear?"

"Nah, it's clear enough," he said, "it just doesn't sound like a very fair cut. I think I need a new agent." This got a laugh, which I took advantage of by forging ahead.

"If your book, on the other hand, is a trade paperback, one of those slightly oversized or undersized softcover books, then your royalty rates would probably start at roughly 6 or 7 percent, and escalate a smidgen— say, to 7.5—after the first 25,000 copies. These are the same rates, by the way, that you'd get if this paperback edition was coming on the heels of your hardcover run.

"And if your book is a mass-market original, one of those rack-sized paperbacks, your rate would probably be a straight 8 percent. If your agent's on the stick, she'll probably get you a boost to 10 percent after the first 150,000 copies. Any questions?"

There was a brief lull, before the banker lady said, almost as if she were still trying to figure out when she could quit her job, "And these royalties, they're paid to you, all of them, twice a year, as soon as the book sales have been tallied?"

I was afraid she'd ask that. "No, not exactly."

Rebellion again stirred in the classroom.

"Why not?"

"Because there are a couple of things the publisher generally charges against your royalties."

"Such as?"

"Such as indexing fees. Let's say your biography of Nelson Mandela is a very weighty and scholarly tome that requires a complete and thorough index. The cost of creating that index can run as high as $1,500— though most indexes are done for a lot less—and that expense is deducted from your royalties."

Judging from their expressions, most of the class felt this fee was unjust, and frankly, I've always felt that way myself. That's why, when the indexing question has come up with my own publishers, I've always said the book doesn't need one, and if it does, then I'll do it myself. Strangely enough, after I've volunteered (with my heart in my mouth the whole time), the question has always gone away—and the publishers have agreed that the book doesn't need an index, after all.

But the indexing fee, I knew, was nothing compared to the other big problem I was about to introduce. "There's one other thing, too, that will affect how and when the publisher pays out your royalties."

The silence was deafening, but with one eye on the quickest means of egress (the window), I plowed ahead.

"It's called the 'reserve for returns,' and you'll see it in any standard publishing contract. Basically, it means that your publisher can hold on to some of your royalties for as much as a year or two—"

There was a collective gasp, and a menacing rustle toward the rear of the room.

"—until they know exactly how many copies of your book have actually been sold."

"Don't they know that when the books are ordered and shipped to the stores?" the banker complained.

"No, not really," I had to admit. "Bookstores order the books on consignment, as it were, and they can ship them back, unsold, anytime. Maybe 40 percent of the books they order, they wind up shipping back to the publisher for credit. But sometimes they don't get around to doing it for months and months, and the publisher wants to make sure that they haven't already paid out royalties on books that it turns out weren't sold but were just sitting around on the shelves, or in the storage room, at a bookstore somewhere."

"You mean to tell me," the banker said, "that even with computers and all of that, publishers still can't tell for *two years* if a book's been sold or not?"

I shrugged. "So they say." Somehow, I had become the unofficial apologist for the publishing industry—and a system that has never made much more sense to me than it was making right now to my class.

"So how many copies of a book usually get sold?" asked the guy who earlier had gotten a laugh by saying he needed a new agent.

Delighted as I was to move on, he had just asked the other great and imponderable question. How many copies of your book will be sold? How many angels can dance on the head of a pin? It's a question to which there is no certain reply. Still, I felt I owed it to the class—and now to you—to offer up some very rough idea of what an average book sale might be.

A good, literary novel, published in hardcover, with a couple of good reviews behind it in major metropolitan newspapers, might be expected to sell 5,000 to 15,000 copies. If the book was made of very commercial stuff, or had become a significant seller, it would stand a pretty fair chance of being reissued in trade paperback or even mass market later on, where the sales figures would probably be even higher.

For trade paperback originals, a respectable sales figure would start at, maybe, 7,500 or 10,000 copies, and go up from there. If the book managed to clear 50,000 copies, it would be a coup for you and the publishing house.

In mass market, as expected, the numbers get much bigger. For a mass-market book to make an impression, it has to get out there in huge numbers; hundreds of thousands of copies have to flood the bookshops and airports, fill the shelves at chain stores, dominate the racks at supermarket checkouts and drugstores. Part of the reason is the competition—there are lots of other paperbacks out there, vying for the fickle eye of the airline traveler, about to grab something off the rack before boarding the plane—and part of the reason is that the window of opportunity, the period of time during which a paperback book must find its public or die, is dreadfully brief. The average paperback original will survive on the shelves, before being removed to make way for the next crop, for about three to five weeks.

The average *trade* paperback has a slightly longer shelf life, maybe four to six months.

And a hardcover can hang around for six months to a year.

Of course, if the books are selling well, they can go on indefinitely. Nobody wants to hobble a winner. But if they're doing poorly, or even just muddling along, the stores will have to make space for the new inventory; they can't afford to keep books on the shelves that aren't sell-ing. They'll pack up the remaining copies and send them back to the publisher, in order to make way for the next wave of potential best-sellers. If the publisher decides that there aren't likely to be many orders of the book anymore, they may elect to sell their overstock to a remain-der house, which will in turn sell the copies at a deep discount back to the stores and any other outlet that wants to carry them. (Only hard-covers and trade paperbacks get remaindered; with unsold mass-market paperbacks, the stores simply tear off the covers, return the covers to the publisher for credit, and pulp the rest of the book. In other words, when you see a paperback being sold without its cover, that's an illegal sale.) Authors at this stage are also given the opportunity to buy copies of their soon-to-be-remaindered books at a small percentage over the publisher's cost—usually, just a few dollars per copy. For me, this has always proved a good time to stock up. Otherwise, the next time you need a copy you may have to comb through the bargain bins—and that's never much fun.

The Sea of Legalese

I have a friend whom we shall call Alan. Now, Alan is a very talented writer, wonderfully well read, delightful company, but he is also his own worst enemy. By the time my friend is done with a book deal, his agent is ready to kill him, his editor no longer wants to do the project at all, his girlfriend has usually left him, and even his pet parrot has pulled the cover over its own cage.

Alan is by nature a meddler, and if you're looking for something to meddle in, there is perhaps nothing more tempting than a publishing contract. Spread before you, on a dozen extra-long pages or more, is a veritable sea of legalese, a densely typed, indecipherable tangle of paragraphs and subparagraphs, clauses, riders, and definitions that deftly manage to leave the things they're defining even more unclear than they were to begin with. It's like all that gobbledygook on the back of a credit card agreement—do you, does *anyone* you know, actually read through all that? (Alan does.)

And every time he manages to get a book deal (each time, may I add, with a different publisher), he and I have to have the same conversations. He'll call me up with, "Can you believe this? They want to retain all rights in Trinidad and Tobago! That could be a big market for me!" Or, "Wait'll you see this—the publisher wants the right to pick what month the book will be published in. What if it's January? January is a dead month!" Or, "No way can I sign this contract—when they print the book, they get to choose the type size, no matter what I say!"

In Alan's view, he is just being proactive. He's a writer who knows he has to look after the business angles at the same time that he's plying his literary craft. He wants to be fully aware of what's going on with each of his books, and he intends to make darn sure that every little thing that *can* go his way *does* go his way. He's a very hands-on kind of guy. And that's a laudable thing to be.

Up to a point.

There's also a point at which the returns are diminishing, or nonexistent. Every author should be familiar with, and stay on top of, the business end of his book. There's no way I would advise you to do otherwise. But any book deal is a negotiation, an elaborate dance of compromise in which you give way on one thing and the publisher, one hopes, gives way on another. Nobody gets everything he wants: if the publisher had his way, he'd get your book for nothing; if everything went your way, you'd get a seven-figure advance and a four-continent book tour. An author who wants to quibble, or even fight over, every inch of territory in the contract will not only wear himself out, he'll wear out his welcome at the publishing house, too. And once a house turns against you, it can spell trouble for your book. Suddenly, the promotional budget, which was probably miniscule to begin with, can disappear altogether. The print run can drop. The general level of enthusiasm and excitement at the house can evaporate. Before you know it, your partner in this venture—and don't lose sight of the fact that your publishing house is indeed your partner—can leave you high and dry.

Whenever I enter into a new book deal, I try to pick my battles, for battles there must be, very carefully. The big issues that we talked about in the previous section, such as the size of the advance and the royalty rate, are worth going to the mats over. Even a 1 percent hike in the royalty rate can translate into thousands of dollars for you down the line. But the average book contract has a million other issues to squabble about, and most of them don't really matter all that much. It's not that they should be ignored, it's just that they're the kind of thing best left to your agent to deal with. She knows what to look for, she knows what can be changed, and she knows what can't.

Most of the text in any publishing contract is what they call "boiler-plate." That just means it's the standard language in all the company's contracts; it's also the language and provisions that get the company nearly everything they want from the deal. Every publishing house has its own contract, but in an agent's eyes these contracts are more alike than they are different; they all seek to preserve the company's money and enhance its rights. They're also designed to stake the greatest claim possible on the property known as your book, and on any future revenue streams (audio rights, foreign editions, stuffed animals) that it may generate. The boilerplate is the company's wish list, as it were, and it's not always easy to get them to change anything in it. Still, it's your agent's job to try.

And then there are lots of other somewhat nebulous areas such as due dates and cover-art approval, where you and your agent will find there's a little more room to maneuver (in large measure *because* these areas are less crucial). Although I hate to belabor all this—contracts are chiefly for agents, publishers, and lawyers to dicker over—I think it would be wise for us to take a very brief walk through a standard contract just so you know what to look for, what to expect, and what not to be shocked by when your own first book deal is done.

Most contracts begin with very standard stuff, entering, for instance, the name of your book and a line or two of description so that everybody knows exactly what's being contracted for. For this book, we entered a working title because I hadn't yet come up with one I liked, and we described the book as "a practical, but lighthearted, book about writing books, whether novels or nonfiction, from a professional author's point of view." Doesn't exactly sing, does it? It doesn't matter. No one in the outside world will ever see it.

Then, there are usually a few paragraphs about the exclusive publication rights the author is granting to the publisher (it'll sound as if you're signing your life's work away, but don't worry, you're not), followed by a lot of warranties and indemnification clauses, the purposes of which are to protect the publisher in case your manuscript turns out to be libelous, plagiarized, or some other dastardly thing. So, just to be on the safe side, don't libel anyone and don't steal somebody else's book, or even a hunk of someone else's book, in order to make your own. But then, I know you're not the kind of person who would ever do that.

Next, you might come to a section called something like "Delivery of Manuscript and Corrections," where things like due dates, word counts, and such are entered into the blanks. With respect to your due date, there is, of course, no problem if what you're selling is an already completed manuscript. You've already met your deadline. You're done! But if it's not done, if what you're selling is a proposal and a few chapters, then you *do* have to sit down and have a very frank conversation with yourself. You have to figure out exactly how long it's going to take you to write the rest of your book. Only you know how fast, and how industriously, you can write. In most cases, you'll be expected to come up with a due date that's six months to a year away, but many books take significantly longer than that—a year and a half, two years. Figure out what you think is realistic, and then, if I may offer some advice here, tack on a couple of months more. That way, you take a little bit of the pressure off your head, especially the first time out, and you allow yourself a little leeway just in case something else comes up in your life that unexpectedly cuts into your writing time. There's even a possible bonus to be had if you do indeed get finished before that date. You can use the time to refine, polish, or simply ruminate upon the completed text—maybe even making it better. Or, if you want to show off instead, you can turn the book in early. No publisher ever objected to an author who got the book in before the deadline.

A publisher *can* take issue with an author who's late. Publishers have to take the long view. They have to know what books are in the pipeline, when they'll be coming out the other end, what list (spring, fall, whatever) the book will probably fall into. They start planning about a year in advance of the eventual publication date, and they don't like surprises. If I can point to one mistake a lot of my writer friends have consistently made over the years, in some cases to the serious detriment of their careers, it's this inability to meet their deadline. Somehow, they've gotten it into their heads that this is still like high school, where you could go to the teachers and tell them you'd contracted mono and that you needed to get an extension, just another week or two, to get your term paper turned in.

But this isn't high school anymore.

Yes, you can ask your publisher for more time—it happens with some regularity—but I wouldn't advise it. It just creates a perception of you, however subtle, as someone who does not meet responsibilities.

If, for some unforeseen reason, life does suddenly intrude upon your time—and there are a million legitimate problems, from an illness to a family crisis, that can do that—then call your agent right away to discuss it, so she in turn can talk to your editor or publisher. The more notice you can give her, the more notice she can give the publisher, and the less disruption the delay will cause down the line. Everybody knows that a book is not an overnight proposition; you can't contract for one on Tuesday and deliver it done on Wednesday. It's a long process, one that stretches over months or even years, and in the interim, stuff can happen. Your job is to do your best to meet your obligations, and, when you can't, to explain what's up and permit your publisher to make the necessary adjustments. They can, if you're going to be very late and they get ornery about it, terminate the deal and demand the advance money back. But if you're up-front and honest with them, in almost every instance they will simply amend the contract and give you a new due date. (Just don't miss that one, too.)

When it comes to that little clause about "word count," again you just have to ballpark it. For most nonfiction books, the word count will probably come in somewhere between seventy and a hundred thousand words; for most novels, seventy to eighty thousand words. In the old days, the only way you could figure out how many words you had was to count the typed pages and then multiply by 250, which was considered the average number of words on a typed page. If you're using an old Smith-Corona, I guess you can still do that. With a computer, the task is of course only a few keystrokes away; use your word processor's word-count function and find out in a second or two how far you've come, and how far you have yet to go, to meet the word count specified in the contract. Again, if you come in a little low, it's no big deal, and if you come in a little over, that's no problem, either. (Between us, this book is over the specified word count in the contract, and just to give you a benchmark, it's around 87,000 words. Surprising, isn't it—I know it feels so much longer.) If you're going to be way wide of the mark—if your book is going to run twenty or thirty thousand words longer than the publisher is expecting it to—then you might have a problem; a longer book is more expensive to print, it has to carry a higher cover price, and it might be harder to find readers willing to pay the extra money and put in the extra time. If you see a problem like this developing, you might want to let your agent, or editor, know.

The next thing you might hit in the contract is a few paragraphs about "Publication Date." Of course every author wants to see his book in the stores about five minutes after he types the last word, but that's just not the way it goes. Your contract will probably give the publisher anywhere from twelve to twenty-four months, after delivery and acceptance of the manuscript, to bring the book out. It will seem like an eternity. But that's par for the course, so don't twist yourself into a knot over it. And be glad of it, in a way—the publisher is using that time to copy-edit the book, typeset it, bind it, get some blurbs for the jacket, print up advance copies to send to reviewers, and so on. It's possible the book could be published more quickly, but it wouldn't necessarily be to your benefit.

Your advance may be entered into the contract next, but since we've already talked about that, I'll just add that below this you might see all kinds of provisions for publishing your book in other formats. In other words, if you've got a paperback deal, you might see something about bonuses or royalty rates for a hardcover edition. While these figures and rates are generally irrelevant, they're there just in case the publishing house changes its mind with respect to the publishing plan for your book. Let's say that between the time you commit to write the book and the final manuscript is ready to be printed, you become a movie star. (It could happen.) That might change everything, and the publishing house just wants to make it clear that they have the option, for a certain sum and under certain conditions, to alter or expand upon the deal.

You'll also see a lot of figures, on the subsequent page or two, having to do with royalties from the licensing and sale of subsidiary rights; in the column on the right side of the page (in most instances) you'll see what percentage of the monies you as the author will retain from the sale of each of those rights. Every deal is different, and every agent will work harder to get some things than others, but by and large, the author's share from the sale of each of these separate rights will be 50 percent or more. Just to give you an idea of what some of these rights are, we'll start with what's called "first serial."

"First serial" rights refer to the magazine rights, sold by either the agent or the publisher, to print a piece of the as-yet-unpublished book. If your book is excerpted in *Vanity Fair* or *The New Yorker*, this can be worth $10,000 or more; in most cases, it's worth quite a bit less. (I've sold first serial rights for anywhere from $750 to $2,500.) But aside from the money—and for these rights the author keeps 90 percent of the take—it's a great way to get advance word of the book out there, and to start finding your audience.

"Second serial" rights, which always go to the publisher, refer to a piece of the book being printed *after* it's been published. Worth less than first serial (and you keep 50 percent), they're still gravy.

Then there are all kinds of foreign and translation rights, which, depending on the kind of book you've written, can add up. Don't sneeze at these rights. I've written books that I thought had no hope of being translated and reprinted in some foreign land—they'd hardly sold any copies right here in America—but sell they did, for kroner and lire and rubles and whatever they use in South Korea. In each instance, I got 75 or 80 percent of the total.

For "Reprint" rights, which the publisher retains, you'll get half of the money that comes in. If, say, you've written a hardcover mystery that's sold well, the publisher might license a paperback edition to a mass-market house.

"Book club" rights, which used to be pretty important, are a lot less so now, in the age of the Internet. Unless your book winds up as a Main Selection of the Book-of-the-Month Club, these rights will probably go for a couple of thousand dollars or less, of which you'll keep half. (I think we got a thousand for the last book club rights I sold.)

"Electronic reproduction" rights, on the other hand, are becoming more important than ever. My favorite contractual clause was one that reserved to my publisher the right to publish my work in any media or technology currently existing, or yet to be invented, in this universe, or any other universe yet to be discovered. (The loophole in that clause, I remember thinking, would not be easy to find.) In any case, publishers are intent on holding on to these electronic rights now, because they want to be able to publish your book in some downloadable form for devices like Rocket Books—or any other such tool yet to be invented. For electronic "version" rights, which refer to enhanced CD-ROMs and such stuff, where all kinds of bells and whistles and interactive elements have been added, they're less greedy. They've figured out in many instances that they don't actually know what to do with these rights, or how to exploit them, so they don't fight as hard to hold on to them.

"Audio" rights can be worth a lot of money if your book is a best-seller, but even midlist titles now stir audio interest. (It's all those people stuck in their cars, for those endless hours of the daily commute.) You generally keep 50 percent of the dough.

The movie rights, like the merchandising rights, are usually left entirely to the author. I guess that even professional publishers have decided the ways of Hollywood are too baffling and incomprehensible to decipher.

When it comes to "Permissions"—the right, for instance, for someone to quote from your book in their own—the publisher retains these rights, and splits with you the nominal sums that may come in. My biggest take from these rights, I think, was $50, out of the total $100, when part of a book I wrote was used in a college textbook. (If your head wasn't already spinning from all these heady figures, then surely it is now!)

In most contracts, the next thing you'll come across is some stuff about "Royalty Statements" (basically, twice a year, for the life of the book), "Copyright" (the publisher will make sure your claim is registered and the proper notice is printed in the front of the book), and "Author Copies." As the author, you'll receive ten, twenty, maybe even thirty, free copies of your book; after that, even though you wrote it, you will have to pay for them. In most cases, however, there is an author's discount of, say, 40 to 50 percent off the "Publisher's Suggested Retail Price." These copies, the contract will make clear, are for personal use and are not for resale. In other words, don't even think about buying thousands of copies and then marketing them to bookstores yourself at just 20 percent off the suggested retail price. The publishers have already thought of that, and they're way ahead of you.

You might also see a clause about the "Use of Author's Name and Likeness," and unless you're as averse to personal publicity as J. D. Salinger, you're not going to have any problem with this. Are you willing to have your name and your face emblazoned on billboards across the land to promote your book? Of course you are. In preparation, you might start looking for a decent photo or two right now, something that might look good on your book jacket. Writers tend not to have eight-by-ten glossies around the house, but you don't need anything that slick. A nice, smiling photo—of recent vintage—will do.

You'll also come to some sad paragraphs detailing what happens when your book goes out of print. There's always the chance that what you've written is a classic, a book that will endure forever as part of the canon of Western literature. But on the off chance that it's not, at some point in the future it will indeed no longer behoove the publisher to keep it in print, or even around the warehouse. When that time comes, they're supposed to let you know so you can determine how many more copies of your book to buy up before it disappears from the planet. At this juncture, you're entitled to buy copies of the remaining stock at the estimated remainder price plus freight. That remainder price is usually about 15 percent above the manufacturing cost—which means that, as we mentioned earlier, a hardcover will run you a few dollars, and a paperback even less. The hard part is deciding how many copies to stock up on.

Reasonable people will tell you to buy a dozen copies, maybe two dozen. And that's because they're reasonable people. Personally, I vote for whatever your basement and your bank account will allow. Yes, yes, I've got boxes and crates full of my old books, and there's just about no one left in my address book that I can even palm one off on as a Christmas present or birthday gift. Still, it's a solace to me to know that if I ever need another copy of one of my books, I've got it—with plenty yet to spare. In fact, there's only one novel I wrote of which I'm now short of copies, and I'm always on the lookout to buy any stray copies I can find in used or out-of-the-way bookstores. Fortunately, a friend

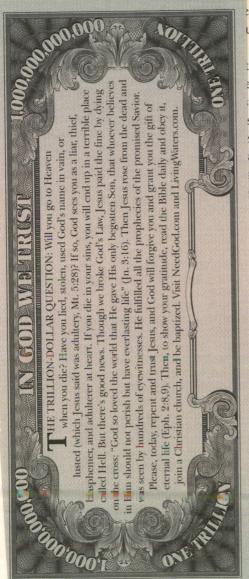

ed a couple of copies in a "Dollar
utlet, and I raced right over to get

t contracts, you'll find the "Option
e publisher generally wants from
specially if it's in the same category
stance, if you wrote *Lentil Health!*
e that first book has been officially
ee your proposal for *Bean There,*
aragraphs *obligates* you to sell your
sher; all you're *obligated* to do is
nd give them a certain amount of
o negotiate a deal for it with you.
rely free agent and can approach
has done well for them, or they
mes out, then they won't want to
ime around, they'll undoubtedly
ey go to $35,000 this time.

ou're feeling your oats (or beans,
k is worth more than that in the
m their offer, and instruct your
get. And let's say she does; let's
's willing to pay you $40,000.
act with the previous publisher,
er and forge ahead, or—and this
l to go back to that previous pub-
match the new and higher offer.
raise their bid by that extra five
k. All this haggling is one way to

clude a few terrifying paragraphs
and these are there, not surpris-
ingly, to put you on notice that nothing in your book had better be
libelous, unsubstantiated, or plagiarized. If you were quoting living
people, whom you interviewed for the book, have tapes or transcripts
available. If you claim that a national shoe-store chain sells shoddy

merchandise, have some serious evidence to back it up. And under no circumstances use portions of another writer's work unless it's in quotes, attributed, and of a certain minimal length. Yes, your publisher will be vetting your manuscript in-house, but as the author, you are still the one chiefly responsible for guaranteeing that your nonfiction book is true, and that your novel is original. The insurance and indemnification clauses outline your and your publisher's respective duties to each other, who's covered and for how much, by the publisher's policy (or your own?), and how—in the unhappy event of legal action—you will share the costs of a defense, or adverse judgment. If you're anything like me or most writers, the very sound of legal language will send you running for the hills, so the best advice I can give you is to be careful, diligent, and original as you write—so none of this stuff will ever come into play. In truth, it very seldom does.

Nor does the last thing—I promise—that I'll mention here. There's always the remote possibility that between the time your book is con-tracted for, and the publication date, the publisher will go under. The contract will say that you get your book back, but since copyrights (taken out in your name by the company) are considered assets of the now defunct company, there's a chance that you'd have to go to court to reclaim your copyright. Again, this happens almost never, but in keep-ing with my policy of sharing any and all possible bad news, I thought I should say something about it.

A contract, as you have undoubtedly guessed by now, never makes for pleasant or light reading. But fortunately, it falls more to your agent than you to thread carefully through all the mind-numbing verbiage, making all those little changes and adjustments that work to your advan-tage. When she's done, and the contract is about as good and as favor-able to you as she is able to get it—or perhaps I should say as favorable to you as the publisher will allow—she will send you several copies of the final agreement, and you'll have to sign or initial the pages at all the places she's marked with little colored Post-it notes. There might be as many as a dozen such spots. After you've signed wherever you have to, the contracts are then returned one last time to the publisher for countersigning, and the *final* final copy, with everybody's signatures on it, emerges some time later. By then, if you haven't already reached this point, you will never want to lay eyes on this document, or read a legal clause, again, for the rest of your life.

But be of good cheer. Really. With the contract done, the path is cleared for the cutting of your first check.

The Editor Idealized

Over the years, I've had all kinds of editors—good ones, bad ones, invisible ones. The invisible one must have worked on one of my first book projects, which was done for a company that made its real money in comic books and novelty sales. On that deal, I pretty much turned my work in, on a piecemeal basis, to a jovial businessman in his airy office high in a downtown skyscraper. He paid me promptly, never said one word about the material itself, and five minutes after the project was over, offered me the opportunity to write witty and whimsical copy for a roll of toilet paper that his company planned to sell—a different quotation or bon mot for every square of tissue.

That's when I knew there must be a bigger and brighter world of publishing that still awaited me . . . somewhere else.

On subsequent books, I learned gradually what editors can actually do for you, what separates the able ones from the rest, what you should expect from them, and what's beyond their grasp. The ideal editor serves many functions: she's your partner in crime, your most dedicated reader, your mole within the company walls, your advocate, your standard-bearer. And that's why, when a writer finds an editor he really clicks with, he's reluctant to go anywhere else.

Once your book deal has been successfully negotiated and every-body's on board, it's customary to have a celebratory lunch with your new editor. (After writing a number of books for his editor Robert

Gottlieb, John le Carré actually had it inserted into the next contract that Gottlieb had to take him out for at least one decent meal.) This free lunch is one of the big advantages to living in or near the city where your editor works, and in nine cases out of ten, that means the meal will be enjoyed in New York City. Yes, there are reputable publishing outposts in all kinds of places, from San Francisco to Chicago, but the bulk of the publishing business is still conducted between midtown and downtown Manhattan.

At this lunch, you and your editor will get better acquainted. You'll discuss your views on the nascent book, eat and drink well at the company's expense (if ever you wanted to try caviar on a blini, here's your chance), and outline your working strategy—addressing, most notably, how often the two of you are going to touch base while the book is being written.

Some writers want to be in steady contact with their editor, they want to feel *connected* during the writing process, they want to consult and discuss and reconsider each issue as it comes up. ("Should the heroine give up on both men and strike out on her own?" "Should the book be broken into shorter chapters?" "Should the narrative voice switch from first to third?") And if this is what the author wants, most editors will respond (within reason) and offer all kinds of editorial supervision and assistance while the book is getting done. If you happen to be one of those writers who might otherwise be inclined to canvas your friends and family for this kind of input, then by all means turn to your editor, instead. After all, she's the one who, ultimately, you're going to want to please, anyway.

It's also, I need hardly mention, her job. A good editor is someone who will help you make your book the best possible version of itself that it can possibly be. She will be supportive at all times, but critical when she needs to be; she'll do her best to help you steer the right course without actually altering where you plan to go; she'll let you write *your* book, *your* way. The last one is the true mark of a professional editor. She's someone who isn't striving to write her own book, under your name. She's there to help *you* say what you want to say, in the voice and manner *you* wish to say it. If there's anything that gives me the willies, it's when an editor starts confessing to me all about how she always wanted to be a writer herself. Suddenly, I start to feel guilty, and ask her about her own books, and why they didn't get done or published. And I know that unless I'm careful, she's going to try to write my book, too. The worst editors I've met are the failed writers. They're the ones who, out of frustration, unacknowledged envy, or the irresistible urge to create, have to meddle in their authors' books and make them into something the authors didn't necessarily want them to be. While a good editor holds your hand, a bad one holds your pen.

Personally, I'm the kind of writer who prefers pretty much to be left alone. At that celebratory lunch, first meeting, or, in some cases, first phone call with my editor, I try as gracefully as I can to indicate that the only way I know how to write a book is to dig a hole, crawl into it, and pull a rock over me to hide where I am. (My wife always knows where the hole is, just in case someone really needs to reach me.) I have to plow ahead under my own steam, guided only by my own lights, feeling my way forward like a blind man sometimes. (E. L. Doctorow once said, in effect, that writing a novel was like driving a car at night—you can only really see as far ahead as your headlights permit, but in the end, that's enough to get you where you're going.) One editor took umbrage at this idea that I was planning to go underground for the next five or six months.

"But how will I monitor your progress?"

"Well, on a day-to-day basis," I said, "you won't. You'll just have to trust me."

The look on his face said *Give me some other option.*

"How about if I call in every few weeks, just to let you know we're on track?"

"Will you send me pages?"

That was exactly what I was hoping to avoid. "I'll send you the pages," I replied, "but only if you promise not to read them."

He thought about that. "Okay," he said. "But if I really hate something in the pages I'm not reading, can I call you?"

"Absolutely, just so long as you never do."

He pursed his lips, then nodded to indicate that we had a deal. And strangely enough, it worked out fine.

Most editors, however, have been perfectly receptive to my disappearing act. And why not? For one thing, it means fewer frantic phone calls from one more needy author, and, assuming that the work comes in on time and in decent shape, less work for the editor.

It's really up to you what kind of a relationship you wish to forge with your editor. The only rules of the game to which you *must* adhere are the usual ones in life—remain courteous, respectful, and responsible. If she calls you, return the call promptly—just as you hope she'd return any call from you. If she has suggestions or even criticisms of the book, hear her out, no matter how painful it might be ("You think I should move the action from present-day Pittsburgh to seventeenth-century France?"). The one thing to keep in mind is that it is *your* book, and unless you and your editor have suddenly come to some terrible loggerheads, you are free to continue to write the book, regardless of what she has to say, the way you want to. You owe her a hearing—and you should always give serious consideration to anything she has to say—but the ultimate call is yours.

And that can be harder than it sounds. Sometimes, if you stick to doing it your own way, you'll wonder if you're just being stubborn. On the other hand, if you allow yourself to be swayed or redirected, you'll worry that you might be losing your convictions. Early in my own career, I had an appointment with one eminent editor at his stately town house on the Upper East Side. I had turned in half of the novel, which in this case I was obligated to do, and his secretary had called to tell me to go there on Sunday afternoon to meet with him. Putting a copy of the manuscript into my handsome fake-leather attaché, I walked up to his house and rang the bell. When the door opened, I got off on just the right foot by mistaking his wife for the maid. Once we got that little awkwardness cleared up (nobody had told me he'd married a beautiful foreigner five hundred years younger than he was), she showed me into what was once a baronial dining room but had now been turned into a kind of library/office. The editor, whom we'll call Gardiner, was one of those cultivated old WASPs with neatly brushed silver hair, manicured fingernails, and a low, diffident way of speaking—which might be why I might have missed his most important comment the first time he said it. I was still nodding my head, scribbling notes, trying to agree with everything he was telling me to do, when he said, "But that would change many things in the book. Are you comfortable with that?"

Finally, I had to look up and actually focus. "Comfortable?"

"Yes."

"With what, exactly?"

"With the idea that your character Richard is not gay, but straight, and that he embarks on an affair with Anna, your heroine."

I sat there like a rock, still trying to take it in. The whole book was built around this trio of characters, one of whom was gay. Loosely modeled on a friend of mine, who did happen to be gay, I had never imagined the character of Richard to be anything other than that, and it had allowed me, I thought, to make the book a little more real, a little less predictable. In short, it had permitted me to avoid the traditional love triangle; if he was gay, Richard would never vie with Joseph for Anna's love, and Anna wouldn't make her own hard decisions with an eye toward leaping from one man to the safe haven of another. That, at least, had been the game plan.

"I know it takes the book in a different direction," Gardiner was saying, "and perhaps it's a more traditional direction, but I think it would add some emotional involvement for the reader."

"Um, sure, that's definitely possible," I mumbled.

"Well, you think about it, and we can talk again next week."

We discussed a few other minor points, and walking home—a long walk, but boy did I need it—I kept turning over in my mind what this suggestion would do to the novel and its overall story line. For one thing, it would certainly change the second half of the book; now I would have to rig it so that Richard and Anna wound up together. For another, it would change the *first* half of the book, too—I would have to go back and start laying in all kinds of clues, and scenes, and lingering glances to set up the romance that would later blossom; it couldn't just come out of nowhere.

The more I thought about it, the more I hated it. It was going to mangle the book, it was going to make it a cheesy potboiler when I had been aiming for art, it would make my heroine, drawn into an affair with her husband's best friend, unlikable to the reader. I came up with a million-and-one objections to doing it, and I even got as far, the next day, as sitting down to write them all up in a letter to Gardiner.

But it was somewhere in the course of doing that, right around the point where I was explaining how some tiny plot point was going to make no sense whatsoever anymore, that I began to slow down. I'd been typing in a white heat, getting down all my problems and all the reasons I was resisting this change, when I sat back in my chair and took a long breath. Yes, there were all these problems that were now going to be created, and yes, the book would change drastically if I made this alteration, but what was it, really, that was still bothering me?

And that's when I knew, much as I did not want to acknowledge it, what it was.

I'd been fighting this triangle idea on all the high artistic grounds, or so I thought, but what was really gnawing at me was the idea of going back and rewriting, of reconstructing, so much of the book that I'd already done. I didn't want to have to stop writing and stop moving forward. And I definitely didn't want to have to go back and take things apart that I had already laboriously put together.

At the same time, I also knew that this wasn't a good enough reason to dismiss what Gardiner had suggested. The good of the book had to take precedence, even if it did mean more work for me, and when I looked at it that way, a lot of things started to become clearer.

For instance, I started to understand why some of my scenes were starting to bog down, why they were all right in terms of exposition or even dramatic event but were somehow lacking in heat. They were happening, but they weren't *unfolding*. My characters were going through their paces, but they weren't coming alive and interacting in all the rich, slightly unpredictable ways that real people do. And maybe, just maybe, it was because Gardiner was on to something; maybe they *were* just figures I was steering around the furniture, who didn't have enough emotional tension or connection among themselves to bring the story to life. Maybe what they needed, appalled and resistant as I had been to the notion, was to be enmeshed in a growing . . . love triangle.

Once I had decided to let the very idea in, once I'd let it slip past the gates of my ego and objections, I found that I could mull it over more calmly. I could see not only what it would cost me in terms of pages cut, chapters rewritten, internal monologues dropped, but what it would also gain me. It would give my characters more trouble among themselves (in real life, a bad thing, but in fiction, I need hardly remind you, priceless); it would give them individually more of an inner life, more repressed feelings, more thwarted desires, more guilt and doubt and self-recrimination. (I know, it sounds like a recipe for an encounter group, but in a novel you want to give your characters, no matter how much you might like them, psychological conflicts galore.) The longer, in fact, that I was able to coolly consider it, the more I came to believe that adding the triangle element would put some coal into the furnace, some gas in the tank. It would give some subtext to the actions the characters had to take, enhance their encounters and entanglements. In the end, after a long, hard wrestling match with myself, I had to admit that maybe Gardiner's gray hairs did indicate some hard-won wisdom, that maybe his forty years in the business had taught him a thing or two from which I, less than nine years out of college, might benefit.

I made the change.

Now, I'd like to end this little story by saying the book then cata-pulted to the top of the bestseller list, and became a major motion pic-ture release starring Julia Roberts as Anna, Rupert Everett as Richard, and Hugh Grant as Joseph (the role modeled on me). But it didn't. Was it better for the change? Yes, I still think it was. Artistically speaking, it was more solid, more charged. And commercially, who knows? Making the change might have accounted for that extra dozen copies that flew off the shelves.

Which isn't to say that I've gone along with what my editors have had to say every time. I can still dig in my heels. And just as you will have to do, I've judged the editorial advice by the source. On a subsequent novel, for instance, I had no contact with the editor throughout the entire process. In fact, he hadn't even been the editor who signed it up. That original editor had left the company, and her successor, whom we shall call Frederick, had called to introduce himself, and to tell me he was behind the book all the way. He also swore that he'd be in regular contact with me. Well, needless to say, I never called him, and he didn't call me, either. When I turned the finished manuscript in, I waited a few weeks, called my agent to see what was up, and then got a call from Frederick's assistant to set up a lunch date.

At the restaurant, we had a long and leisurely meal, talking about everything under the sun except the book, and by the time coffee and dessert had arrived, I figured we weren't going to be discussing the book at all. I thought the plan must be for us to finish lunch, and then repair to the office, just across the street, to have our editorial conference. In fact, I finally said something like, "I guess we can talk about the book back at your office."

Frederick looked surprised, and it wasn't just because the check was being placed at his elbow. "Oh, I thought we could do that here," he said.

"Well, sure," I said, glancing around the dining room, which at that point was occupied by only one other party, and even they looked as if they were planning to leave any second. "I suppose the waiters will let us stay awhile."

"It'll only take a minute," Frederick said, studying the check and computing the tip. "You know, first of all, that this really isn't my kind of book."

I almost brought up my éclair.

"I took it on only because your editor left," he added.

"But I thought you were," I said, trying to remember his exact words, "behind it all the way?"

"Doesn't sound like me. Anyway, it's done. Here's what I'd like to suggest." He paused to jot the tip in and sign the check, while I waited, hardly able to breathe, to hear whatever he was going to say next.

"You know your villain, the judge, what's his name?"

"Fitch."

"Right. Well, maybe you should bring him into the story sooner." He slipped the check into the American Express folder and closed it.

"How much sooner? Where?"

"I don't know. That's up to you. But I think it would help."

Then he got up; we collected our coats at the checkroom and walked out of the restaurant. Outside, he extended his hand to say good-bye.

"Is there any deadline that you need the changes by?" I said.

"No," he said, airily. "Take your time. The book isn't even scheduled yet."

Nor, did I think at that moment, it ever would be.

But this time, the more I thought about his suggestion, the more I figured I'd forget it. I mean, if the editor couldn't even be bothered to remember the name of my villain, a major character in the book, or suggest anything more specific than to bring him in sooner—*somewhere*—then he wasn't exactly invested in the book (heck, he'd told me so point-blank). Anything he had to say was suspect at best, and a bad idea at worst. I waited a decent interval—in this case two weeks—then had my agent turn in the book as "revised" and done. A month later, we got the acceptance check, and almost two years later, after delay after delay, the book was finally published. It looked fine, even if I did recognize the cover art as an outtake from a book they had published a couple of seasons earlier. And I never heard from Frederick again.

Am I suggesting that all editorial consultations are occasions to try the soul? Not at all. But many of us who write, and I have to count myself among this number, have some trouble when it comes to accepting criticism; we find it very hard to sit still and listen to comments, however intelligent or well meant, about the fruits of our labor. We get hurt—*You mean our baby isn't perfect?*—and even worse, we get defensive. We get so busy countering the criticisms and refuting the charges, as if we were having accusations hurled at us in a court of law, that we don't give ourselves time to calm down and think through what's being said. A good editor knows how to give her critique in a gentle, helpful manner.

But even the best and most diplomatic editor on earth can't make herself heard if we're determined not to listen.

Despite the problems I've had with some editors—and the problems you will no doubt have on your own—by and large I've found them to be very responsive, thoughtful, and attentive. In fact, there have been times when I've marveled at what I can't help but feel is selfless behavior on their part. I mean, I know why my book means so much to *me*—I wrote it and it's got my name on it—but I never fail to be impressed by the degree with which a dedicated editor also identifies with, and cares about, the success of the book. True, that's the editor's job, but the glory, if there's going to be any, always falls on the author. The editor's role is forever unsung.

Give me the sung part anytime.

The Editor in Practice

One of the most shocking moments in my publishing career came early on, when I visited the editor of one of my first books in her Manhattan office.

Yes, on an intellectual level I understood that my book was not her only concern, that she probably had others that she was editing, too. But it was still a devastating blow, as I folded up my wet umbrella in her office and she chatted with me about the rainstorm that was blowing outside, to survey the gray metal shelves that were packed—crammed to the gunwales!—with neat stacks of paper, some taller than others, and all bearing a little yellow tag that hung down just below each pile. Jotted on each tag, in green Magic Marker, was a title. And on one of them, no different from all the others, I could see *my* title.

It felt as if I'd arrived unexpectedly at a girlfriend's apartment and found a cigar stub smoldering in the ashtray. My editor had been cheating on me.

Amazingly, she seemed completely unaware of the extremely delicate situation we were in, and went right on talking, offering me a cup of hot coffee or tea, while I absorbed the emotional body blow . . . and strained to read the titles of her other suitors, ranged around those metal bookshelves.

To her credit, she did seem able to put them out of her mind for the duration of my visit. We talked about *my* book, which she swiveled in her chair to remove from the shelf, and my book alone, and she was very insightful and perceptive in all her comments. She had even typed up a summary of them, in a four-page memo, so I wouldn't have to be scribbling down what she was suggesting. And she was always careful to make clear that I was free to take her suggestions or not, that they were only her opinion and that if I felt strongly about something, I should either leave it the way it was, or that we should discuss the reasons for the suggested change and arrive at some mutually satisfactory solution. She was the soul of reason and tact.

But I never forgot sitting there, surrounded by all those other books in progress, and I've always felt that for me that afternoon conference was a kind of awakening. I realized that although my book was just about the single most absorbing, all-important thing in the world to me, for her, for any editor, it was ultimately a stack of paper on a metal shelf—elbowed by dozens of other similar stacks. While I was monogamous, even monomaniacal, my editor was promiscuous, involved with many authors at one time, all of whom might subconsciously feel that they had the sole claim on her time and her attentions. I think, as a result, I always dressed slightly better for future meetings.

While in an ideal world, your editor does nothing but think about and work on your book and your book alone, in the actual world she's got many books moving through the pipeline, and they're all in different stages of development. Some are in the messy first-draft stage, some are in galleys, some are just coming out in print. And perhaps the hardest part of her job is keeping abreast of all these projects, and stepping in whenever she has to, to do what needs to be done, at that particular moment, on that particular book.

In a practical sense, your editor's job kicks into high gear once you've completed the manuscript and turned it in. Yes, she's been there (we hope) as a sounding board and guiding light whenever you needed her to be, but now, with the book in hand, she has to burrow into it and see exactly what you've come up with. Usually, depending on her schedule and workload, this will take her from a week to a month to do. And even though I understand your nervousness and impatience, do not bug her. If you insist that she be bugged, let your agent be the one to do it.

When your editor reemerges, she will have in hand a couple of things. For starters, she'll have your manuscript, and on it she will either have penciled in changes, corrections, suggestions, or she'll have affixed Post-it notes to the pages with her comments written on them instead. This, I might as well warn you, can come as a dispiriting sight. It's as if you delivered a pristine little baby, with golden curls and rosy cheeks, and you get back a worn-out kid with dirty hair and a nasty scratch on his nose. But you'll get over it.

In most cases, your editor will also give you her overall comments and critique in a carefully crafted memo that runs anywhere from a couple of pages to a dozen. The first time you read through this document, you may experience a sinking sensation, but that's to be expected. If the manuscript were perfect, the memo would be four words long: "Don't change a thing!" Since it's not perfect—no one's ever is—the remarks are, perforce, critical. They can pinpoint anything from confusing punctuation you've been using—one editor just hated the liberties I took with dashes, just like these that I'm using right now—to more major issues of tone or characterization or pacing. It's the latter that are the ones you really have to scrutinize and ponder, because they will be the issues that require you to spend serious time on your revisions.

As will covering some of the points so obvious—at least to you—that you neglected to make them in the book. More times than I care to admit, I have had editors point out to me that I have somehow omitted something absolutely crucial to the book—an explanation of something, a description, a vital revelation—and I sit there, dumbfounded, wondering how I could have skipped it.

But I think, in fact, that I do know how it happens.

Sometimes, you are so aware of everything that's going on in the passage you're writing, you are seeing the action unfold so clearly in your mind's eye, you are moving so swiftly through your argument, caught up in the flow of what you are saying, that you forget to mention the one thing that is so plain, so obvious, so much in the foreground *to you*, that you forget that the reader doesn't know it, or see it, too. You forget that the reader is not inside your head, envisioning everything the way you do, hearing every nuance and emphasis and unspoken thought. When I got back the editor's comments on one novel I wrote, she told me she had forgotten that a certain critical character was present in an important scene until he finally spoke up. For me, he was always in the scene, the mute witness, the hub around which much of the action was turning, the eyes through which we were seeing and perceiving so much of what was going on. But when I read the scene over, I could see her point; for me, he was there all along, plain as day, but for a reader he was invisible most of the time.

In a nonfiction book, you can unwittingly overlook whole aspects of your subject, sometimes as an oversight, and sometimes because you've simply lost track of your reader. Ideally, your editor will perform the function of that reader and tell you what's missing. On a book I wrote about the TV industry, for instance, my editor brought up several points I had failed to make clear, or even address, in the book. I had written about how you find your next job in TV after the show you were working on has flopped, but the editor asked, "Does the fact that you were associated with a flop make getting your next job harder, or does it not matter?" It was a good question, and I had neglected to answer it. The same editor observed that most of the stories in the book revolved around men: "Are women underrepresented in the TV business, and if so why is that?" If you ask me, women are indeed underrepresented in the TV industry, but until the editor pointed out the omission, I hadn't thought of addressing that issue head-on in its own section of the book. There were three or four other catches like this, and I had to thank the editor for noticing the gaps and calling them to my attention. None of us likes to have to do more work, but if it's in the service of the book, if by doing the extra work, the book is going to turn out better, in the end we're glad to do it.

Strangely enough, on those occasions when the editor failed to do her duty—when my book was simply ferried straight through to production, or the job was foisted off on an ill-equipped and overburdened underling—I missed the extra work. No, I'm not crazy—I enjoyed the time off, but I knew in my heart that the book wasn't getting the attention and care that every book needs. I knew that it wasn't going to turn out as well as it could have, that it wasn't going to be trimmed and polished and groomed the way it should have been. It was also a signal, never pleasant to hear, that on some level the company wasn't really invested in the book. If they were giving it short shrift now, they were going to give it short shrift again when it got to publication day. If you get the feeling this is happening to you, that your book is moving to the back burner, or off the stove altogether, it's worth placing a call to your agent; she might still be able to set things right.

But once you have received your editor's reaction to your first draft, in whatever form she's elected to give it to you (a thousand Post-it notes, a formal critique, a lengthy luncheon discussion), it's time for you to go back under your rock, or into your room, and start work on your revisions. This part of the process is not only inevitable—so don't even *think* about getting out of it—it's essential. Writing, as I've been told a million times, is rewriting. It would be a wonderful thing if we could create and deliver perfect manuscripts, but that's just not realistic. The second draft, or revise, is when you fine-tune the motor to make sure your book runs smoothly, from the first word all the way to the last.

Revisionist Misery

When you're writing the first draft of a book, whether it's a deeply felt coming-of-age novel or a scholarly history of the Macedonian wars of conquest, there's a certain joy to the process, a sense of surprise and discovery as the words fall onto the page and you see your story, or your thesis, taking shape for the first time.

But when you're doing your revisions, most, if not all, of that is gone. Now your job is to make the necessary adjustments and corrections, the changes and emendations, and to read over your manuscript not with the wonder of a genuine reader but with the hard, cold eye of a professional writer. Now you're not looking to be pleased or delighted; you're looking for the holes, the problems, the nagging questions that your editor has pointed out, or that you've stumbled across on your own. And they're always there. Did you really mean to suggest, for example, that Alexander the Great was a cross-dresser? (Maybe you did.) Do you really want your heroine to embark upon an affair with her husband's best friend? (Quite possibly.) But whatever the problem, there's no putting it off any longer; in the revising stage, you must make up your mind, one way or the other, about every lingering question that remains. You must decide to fix what you will, and stand by the rest.

It's easy to say "be objective" about it all, but that's perhaps the hardest thing to do when it comes to your own work. You've got to read it all over, assimilate the notes and suggestions you may have received, and make a thousand and one final calls. Even though you'll get printed galleys down the line, and you'll be allowed to make a few small changes here and there, you must accept that this revision process is the last time you'll be able to make wholesale changes or major corrections to the manuscript without incurring significant costs to the publisher, and without getting them mad at you as a result. (In fact, you'll have to pay a surcharge if, later on, you want to make changes to the galleys that exceed 10 percent of the total production cost.)

The best way to ensure the artistic objectivity you seek would be to let the manuscript sit in a drawer for a year or two, then take it out and read it with an entirely fresh eye. But practical that's not. Depending on the speed with which your editor got back to you, you've probably had anywhere from a few weeks to a couple of months away from the book. If you were smart, you used that time to do something else—*anything else*, from writing a new proposal to fishing for trout in Montana—rather than reading over or brooding about your manuscript.

If you're anything like me, you know the rhythms of your own prose so well, the structure of your own sentences, the words you choose and the way you deploy them, that when you read over your work, the words have a hard time surprising you; you've almost got them memorized. That's why it's so crucial you get some time away from your book. You need to create a little separation, a little distance, so that you can come back to it with a clear head and a clean eye. Ideally, when it comes time to make your revisions, you should be far enough away from the book that you can read it with some kind of innocence, with some lack of awareness. Sure, you know how it turns out, but if you've been able to approach it with a new focus, you may be able to see, with a cold eye, where it loses momentum, or a scene becomes unglued, or the prose in a passage gets a little bit muddy.

In a way, your goal is to read it, as much as you can, as if you hadn't been the one who wrote it. Your goal is to pretend that you're an anonymous reader, someone who just happened to pick up the book from the "New Arrivals" table at your local bookstore and started leafing through it. Does it grab your attention? Does it hold it? Do the words flow unimpeded, or do you find yourself stopping to reread a sentence, a paragraph, a chapter, because something confused you, or bumped wrong?

It's a tough and often wearying task, but it's the last and critical step in making your book as good as it can be. So don't stint in your efforts.

I say all this from experience. On a couple of my own books, I got so tired, so distracted, so dispirited, for one reason or another, that when the time rolled around for me to sit back down and do my revisions, I just couldn't muster the requisite enthusiasm or energy to address the job properly. I let things slide. I let some sentences remain cloudy. I let some minor plot points remain insufficiently resolved (by telling myself that no one else would notice). And I can tell you now that I regret I didn't find the strength, the resolve, the industry, to make every single one of those corrections at the time. Even though it's true that most readers would probably never notice them, *I do*; every time I pick up one of those books, I know that something in there is not quite as good as I could have made it, and it makes me cringe. Yes, I'm crazy, that's a given, but if you're a writer, there's a good chance that you're crazy, too, and maybe even in the same way. So take my advice and make every single thing, from a scene to a sentence, from a climax to a coda, exactly the way you want it, and exactly the way you know in your heart it should be. Once it's printed, a book should go out into the world with as pure and unblemished a countenance as possible; it should never have to blush, and neither, for that matter, should you.

Blue Pencil, White Knuckles

Once you've made all the necessary revisions to your book—and that includes making a complete double-spaced copy, with everything in it from sequentially numbered pages to the bibliography (if it needs one)—it's time for the two of you to part for a while. To go your separate ways. Your editor has done all that she can do, you've done all that you can do, and what remains to be done lies chiefly in the hands of the most annoying person on earth—your copy editor.

Who is she? What does she look like? Where does she live? None of these things will you ever know. Personally, I've always imagined my copy editor to be a bespectacled lady with a helmet of iron gray hair, sitting with a mug of herbal tea at a kitchen table in Brooklyn. My defenseless manuscript is spread before her, under a blazing ceiling light, like some poor creature about to be dissected. In her hand, she clutches a blue pencil, sharpened to a point as deadly as any scalpel.

Her job? To find every last niggling problem, every hyphen that should be a dash, every unclear allusion and syntactical snafu, every trifling inconsistency ("Were Miranda's eyes brown with a fleck of emerald, or emerald with a hint of brown?"), and plant a flag on it. The big questions have, by and large, been dealt with by you and your editor, but the gazillion smaller ones, from punctuation to spelling to tiny errors of logic ("You say your character walks downtown along the east side of First Avenue, but doesn't that become impossible between Sixty-first and

Fifty-ninth Streets, because of the bridge entrances?"), are all hers to discover and point out. And trust me, she will. Copy editors can find a problem where nobody else can; like pigs rooting for a truffle, they can sniff it out, no matter how deep it lies.

When a copy editor finds a small problem, she uses her blue pencil to correct it on the spot, right on the manuscript. If it's big enough to call for an authorial response or consideration, she marks it, then attaches a Post-it note to the page with her query written on it. When you get your manuscript back from the copy editor, it may well have dozens of these little flags (in some color different from the one that your editor may have employed) fluttering from the pages. Let me tell you, it is a very disheartening sight.

What makes it even more so is the fact that good copy editors can see, as it were, right inside your head. To give the devil his or her due, I never fail to be amazed at the efficiency with which they are able to spot and question all the miniscule things that had been bothering me, on some barely acknowledged level, all along—stuff that I thought was so far beneath anyone else's notice that only I, the obsessive author, could possibly be aware of, much less troubled by, it. Copy editors find those little things every time—it's as if they've got radar—along with plenty of other things that I *hadn't* been bothered by, until they called them to my attention.

Anyway, one day you will go to get your mail—anywhere from a month to six weeks after you've turned in the final revised manuscript—and you'll find this copyedited manuscript waiting for your attention. Open the envelope, glance at some of the queries, clutch at your chest—don't worry, it's only a temporary fibrillation—then do whatever you normally do to relax. Go to the gym, catch a movie, take a walk along a wooded trail. Let yourself decompress. Then go back and deal with the problems.

Your job now—and you generally have a week or two to do it—is to address each and every one of those queries and come up with some suitable reply. Much as you might like to ignore them, you're not allowed to do that. If it's a question of fact, or consistency, you have to answer it. "Her eyes are brown, flecked with emerald." "He crossed the street at Fifty-ninth and proceeded along the west side." "The lentils are the only bean to provide this specific benefit." If you've said something contentious, or something that the copy editor for some reason thinks might be wrong, you can make the suggested change and move along to the next query. Or, if you feel you're right and want to leave it the way it is, you can simply write "stet" or "okay as it is" on the flag. As the author, you do still hold the ultimate veto power. But you must leave some sign that you've been there, that you've read and considered every one of the copy editor's queries, by scribbling some reply on the flag (generally in a colored pencil that differs from the blue one she is most probably using), and then putting your initials after your reply. On the cleanest manuscript I ever turned in, I had maybe two dozen queries from the copy editor; on the longest and most complicated, I don't even want to guess. In general, a nonfiction book will get more queries than a novel, if only because there are issues of fact to deal with, along with all the usual grammatical and tonal questions. But it also depends on your copy editor; while all of them are compulsive by nature—I once heard two of them in a magazine office arguing at the top of their lungs about the proper use of the semicolon—some are more compulsive than others. The one who will be copyediting this book, for instance, is undoubtedly one of the less driven, someone of sterling character and deep compassion, whose respect for the words I have written is equaled only by the reverence that I in turn accord the craft—nay, the art—of copyediting itself. (Remember me in your prayers, oh reader.)

Know, too, that another creature, even more fearsome than the copy editor, is also quite possibly scouring your manuscript right now; in fact, if it's nonfiction, it's almost guaranteed. Hold on to your chair—it's the attack of the legal reader.

As I'm sure I'm not the first one to tell you, it's an increasingly litigious world we live in, one where lots of people like to sue at the drop of a hat. And publishers make a very fat target. Traditionally, editors showed the same absolutely understandable resistance to lawyers as anyone else with a brain in his head. Lawyers were good for only one thing—they were supposed to cook up the obfuscatory boilerplate in the company's publishing contract, and then butt out. No editor wanted to have to submit the manuscripts he was working on to any sort of legal review. What good could come of that? By the time a lawyer was done with the book, it could read with the same clarity and grace as the publishing contract did.

But to a great extent, that attitude is changing now. More and more often, publishers are submitting their books to what is called a "legal read," which means that one of their in-house lawyers, or an outside lawyer to whom they submit it, will be reading through your book with a close legal eye, looking for any possible lawsuit material.

As far as I know, only one of my books was ever actually submitted for a legal read, and that was a nonfiction business book. The lawyer's job was to read through it and make sure that I hadn't said anything defamatory or libelous about anyone that I had written about.

"But I've changed all their names," I pointed out, "and I've even changed identifying details. If they're tall, I've said they're short. If they live in Las Vegas, I say they live in Seattle. If they're bachelors, I've said they're married, with three kids. Isn't that enough?"

"Not necessarily," the lawyer replied, before launching into some arcane explanations and reasoning that seemed expressly designed to prove, in the end, that even though I'd taken every precaution I could think of, a legal read was still in order. Why was I not surprised at this verdict?

Anyway, about a week later, the lawyer called me back and, while conceding that there was nothing really problematical in the book, he did have a few corrections that he suggested I make. None of them was of any magnitude; I made them all in about an hour and, much as I hate to admit it, I slept better that night, knowing that a trained attorney had read through the whole book and come to the same conclusions that my editors and I had—namely, that the book contained nothing that was likely to get any of us into any trouble whatsoever. The only mistake I made was when I said something to the attorney that suggested I was asking his opinion of the book itself.

"Are you asking me if I liked it?" he said.

"Well, not really, I was just saying that I hoped it wasn't too painful a chore to read through it," I mumbled.

"Oh," he said, thinking it over. "No. It wasn't too painful."

That was it. Lawyers, I'm beginning to believe, attend the same charm school as doctors.

But if you've successfully passed between Scylla and Charybdis—first the copy editor and now the member of the bar—you may breathe a huge sigh of relief. You are almost home.

The Cover Story

But no book is complete without its cover—and because sales catalogs have to be printed and bound, up to a year in advance of publication day, the publishers can't afford to dawdle when it comes to picking the cover design and cover copy.

Publishing houses vary in this regard—some may not wish to have your input at all, and others may be willing to listen to a little of what you have to say. Bestselling writers sometimes have cover consultation rights written into their contracts. But for the rest of us, it's not always easy to get the publishing house to listen at all. They have their own designers and copywriters on staff or on call, and they're the ones that the house will turn to when it comes time to get this work done. That's just the way it is, but it doesn't mean you should roll over and go along with any cover concept, or copy, the publisher floats past you. The earlier it is in the game, the more opportunity you have to steer things in another direction if the one that the publisher is planning on doesn't exactly bowl you over. (This is also your very last chance to tweak the title of your book, if it still seems to need tweaking.)

For instance, I usually ask if I can see the artist's thumbnails for the cover as soon as they come in to the publishing house. (I do not of course mean his actual thumbnails—I mean the very rough sketches he's making to suggest the artwork for the cover and how he'll be laying out the type.) There's not a lot of room on the front cover of a book, so the words that do appear there have to count; on most covers, all you get is the title, the author name, and a sell-line or two ("the most thrilling thriller ever to thrill you!"). If a big-shot writer was inveigled into giving a blurb, that might be there, too. (One publisher did get me a quote from one of their bestselling authors, but it was something along the lines of "Masello has done it again!" What I'd done, it didn't say—and I wondered if the bestselling author had ever so much as seen the book.)

But no matter what, if you can catch a glimpse of these thumbnail sketches, and the earlier the better, it's all to the good. You'll have a chance to get in on the game and maybe, if you see something that strikes you as wrong, bring it to the publisher's attention soon enough to have it corrected.

As a small example of that, I'll use a friend's young adult novel, which was all about a teenage girl who, though an outcast, excels at running and winds up being accepted in the end because she wins the big race for her school. When my friend got her cover art, it showed a beautiful blond girl racing across the finish line, her arms spread wide in victory.

The only problem was, the only beautiful blonde who appeared in the book was the villainess, a cold-hearted vixen who made the heroine's life a living hell.

And the heroine was a girl with short dark hair that, try as she might, she could never get the curl out of.

"What do I do?" my friend agonized. "The cover makes precisely the wrong point. The blonde doesn't even run in the race, and here they've got her winning it!"

"Call your editor," I said. "There may still be time to get it changed."

My friend did, and because her argument was so persuasive—I mean, the whole point of the book was that the best things in life don't always have to go to the beautiful blondes, that we all have our own talents and abilities to discover and develop—the cover art was changed. Not, to be honest, that successfully. I think the artist, annoyed that he was being forced to tamper with his gorgeous babe, just stuck a new head on her shoulders—a head with short, dark, curly hair—that didn't seem to fit quite as snugly as it should have (a flaw that, out of professional sympathy, I never mentioned to my friend the author.)

Many times, the cover art for a book is done in-house, by one of the artists that the publishing company keeps on staff to do just that; other times, the book is farmed out to one of an army of book-jacket free-lancers. Some of these people are brilliant artists and designers, and some of them are not, but very few of them have the time or the inclination to read through your whole book; instead, they have to rely upon the editor's brief summary of what it's about, or gather a sense of it from some jacket copy that's already been written. They're given some general direction—"It's a big-city cop story, and we want a sort of Joseph Wambaugh feel to the cover"—and then let loose to see what they come up with. A good cover has to do a lot of things, almost in the blink of an eye, and a good cover illustrator knows what they are.

First of all, a good cover has to catch your attention. You know as well as I do that when you scan the shelves and tables at your local book-store, there are more books there than you can possibly take in. Some of them you can rule out instantly—mountaineering adventures, say, aren't your cup of tea—but out of all the others that might appeal to your interests, only a few will leap out at you—enough, that is, to make you actually pick them up and read over the jacket copy. Sometimes it's the subject matter that really grabs you, sometimes it's the favorable reviews you've read that make you take a look, but more often than not, it's just the design of the cover—the bold colors, the striking artwork, the embossed typeface. Wes Craven's novel *The Fountain Society* featured a full-cover hologram on the front. Lots of paperbacks feature cutaways (where you look through a hole in the front cover to see a part of a bigger illustration beneath). Whatever it takes to snag your eye, a good cover will do. And it has to; studies of this arcane craft show that the average book buyer registers each book in some astonishing fraction of a second before his eye moves on to the next, and the next, and the next. If your book is going to grab the buyer, it has to make a clear, bold, intriguing statement with its cover, and it has to do it extremely fast.

In that regard, I've been pretty lucky so far; my covers have generally been good. In fact, the cover of my first novel was so great that I tried to buy the original artwork from the artist who'd done it. (The price, as I recall, was several thousand dollars, which I did not have at the time, so the cover now resides—if it still resides at all—in some trunk in the artist's attic.) Still, I remember being so astonished when I first saw it, a beautiful and very well wrought depiction of the book's main, and supernatural, antagonist, that I couldn't believe someone I'd never met had been able to interpret it so well. It was almost exactly as I'd pictured the creature myself.

The only problem I had, and this is a problem you may well face yourself one day, was with that same book's cover copy—the tag lines that trumpeted the virtues of the book. Most of it was fine, but there was one line that bothered me, or at least the way it was worded. In what appeared to be one consecutive thought, it read "A nightmare that never ends Robert Masello." Now some people might understand, or even agree with, that rather puzzling statement—was I the nightmare that never ends, or was I what the nightmare could not finish off?—but either way, it just didn't seem like something I wanted to advertise on my first novel's front cover. When I brought it up to the editor—"Don't you think it suggests that the author, rather than the story, is a nightmare that never ends?"—she paused, then said, "Yes, maybe it does."

"Can we change it?"

"Would a line break solve the problem for you?"

"Assuming that means we separate the phrase about the never-ending nightmare from my own name, and put it on two separate lines, it would."

And so it was done. I tell you this enthralling tale to make a small point: you *can* influence your cover, in at least some small ways, if you get there early and you're tactful about it. While authors, for good reason, are not considered to be experts in cover design, one thing we do know is what's in our books. That much, we know better than anybody. And that's why I pay special attention to the front cover copy—and even more important, the *back*—for all my books. The cover art may serve as the attention-grabber, but the real pitch for the book is made by what's written on the back cover, or jacket flap. Done wrong, it can cause the casual browser to drop the book back on the display table as if his fingers were on fire; done right, it can get him or her to carry the book straight to the cash register.

On one recent nonfiction book I wrote, for instance, the publisher sent me the back cover copy, and I could immediately tell that the copywriter who'd written the copy had completely misunderstood what the book was about, and what it actually had to say. I dropped everything else I was doing (washing the dog, balancing my checkbook, taping *The Sopranos* marathon) and, unbidden, quickly rewrote the back cover copy so that it indicated what the book truly had to offer. I also rewrote it to convey something else the original copy did not, and that was a sense of genuine *enthusiasm* about the book. This "hype," if you will, is sometimes the hardest thing for an author to write; we are, in most cases, a modest and circumspect lot. But the back cover of your book is nowhere to be self-effacing; this is your big chance to sell your book—you've got it into the customer's hand already—so don't hang back now. Go for it! Sing the praises of your book! Claim it's the definitive and groundbreaking book of its kind! Point to some of the things that make it so special, so valuable, such an indispensable part of any home library. (I once heard a newspaper writer compare his latest collection of columns—and not unfavorably—to the Bible.) Make that sucker—the book—stick to the customer's hand like it's coated with epoxy!

And don't be afraid to write a short—very short—author bio, letting the reader know what exciting and capable hands he's now in. Make sure your accompanying author photo also bolsters your case. You don't have an author photo? Then let me tell you right now to get one. Yes, you can hire a professional photographer to take a glamour shot, but most writers I know—myself included—simply use the most successful snapshot taken by a friend or loved one. If it's a sensitive novel, use a soulful photo of yourself standing in the woods. If it's a survey of encryption through the ages, get a shot where you're poring over some obscure document. Whatever you use, just make sure it enhances your image and reputation as the author of this particular book. (One friend wrote a very thorough and scholarly book about Asian art and culture, and used a photo of himself having a beer on what looked like a deck in Catalina. Not a good idea.)

Now, it's true that some publishers will resist your attempts to meddle in the cover copy, and many authors don't have the knack for writing this kind of hyperbolic prose. But if you don't think the cover copy, as written, serves your book well, then you should at the very least write a letter to your editor, explaining what you think is missing and how to fix it. Personally, I do like to offer my own alternative version, a technique that some publishers have welcomed and some have pretty much ignored. On that last book, for example, the editor not only heard my complaint but wound up using—word for word—the cover copy I myself suggested.

The good thing about that was that I got the book described exactly the way I wanted it. The bad thing was that if the book tanked, I couldn't blame the copywriter anymore.

Galley Slaves

Now that we've addressed the covers of the book, it's time we returned to what falls between them. By now, you've probably reached the stage where you can, with some confidence, submit the corrected, fully revised manuscript to the editor's office. When you do, you will probably be asked, if you haven't been asked already, to turn in the computer disk on which the text of the book is entered.

There's always a possibility, I suppose, that you've written your book *without* the use of a computer. Maybe you even wrote a draft in longhand, on a raft of legal pads, before typing it all up on your trusty old IBM Selectric. And that's okay. I wrote many books that way myself. But I do have to tell you, in case no one else has, that such behavior is increasingly odd, and in the final analysis, it will have cost you untold hours of extra work. Most publishers, too, will be surprised at your antiquated ways, and though they'll do their best to disguise it—"My, oh my, who'd have thought we were dealing with Charles Dickens!"—they may even be a tad annoyed.

If you're planning on writing another book, seriously consider doing it on a computer.

Assuming, for the moment, that you *have* a computer, you may wonder if the particular word-processing program you used will be compatible with the publisher's or typesetter's. If you're worried about it, don't be. Publishers have means of reading and retrieving almost any format. I turned in the text of my last book in WordPerfect 5.1, the present-day equivalent of Sanskrit, and I never heard a peep of protest.

A couple of months will now pass, in all likelihood, before you hear or see another word about your book. You will wonder if it was swallowed up whole into the bowels of the earth. You will be tempted to plaster fly-ers all over your neighborhood—"Lost! Brilliant First Novel Sure to Make a Fortune! Generous Reward Offered!"—but calm yourself. Your book is making its own slow and stately progress through the publishing machin-ery, and it will emerge eventually, like a butterfly from its cocoon, in a very altered state.

We call this state . . . galleys.

After all the work you've been doing on an actual typescript—a man-uscript that several people have now scrawled all over with colored pen-cils, that they've attached multicolored flags to, that they've passed around like a tray of canapés at a crowded party—it's an amazing thing to see your book, at long last, translated into galleys. It's like seeing the thing all scrubbed and clean, justified and printed—maybe even illustrated—and looking, for all the world, even though it's still unbound, suspiciously like a real live book. Your galleys are loose pages, on which all the text—edited, copyedited, massaged, the whole works— has been set in type. This is the first time you'll really be able to see what the pages of the printed book are going to look like—what the typeface will be, how the chapter headings will be set off, what little design devices (called dingbats) might have been added to separate blocks of copy (aka text) or to mark the start of new sections.

I always find it exhilarating to see my galleys for the first time, and at the risk of sounding like a name dropper, I can personally attest to the fact that the bestselling author and American icon James Michener felt the same way. We were once seated next to each other at a press dinner, and even though I'd heard of all his books, and he'd understandably heard of none of mine, we happily fell into shoptalk. He was a very per-sonable guy—who insisted for some reason on calling me "Skipper"— and when the subject of galleys came up, he volunteered that, in his view, this was one of the most exciting stages in the whole publishing process. "It's when it starts to look like the book that it's going to be,

Skipper," he said, and I could not have agreed more. Then the dessert cart was wheeled over, and we had to move on to the more crucial discussion of what to order.

Galleys also give you a good chance to read through the book one more, and ideally final, time.

"Again?" you may cry. "I have to read through the whole book again?" Well, yes, I'm afraid you do. But this time, all you're doing is looking for typos and itty-bitty, teensy-weensy mistakes that might somehow have slipped through your net, and everyone else's, so far. Believe it or not, there will be a few. There will also be some bloopers that have crept in during the typesetting stage—words that get dropped, sentences that get altered, occasionally a whole paragraph that gets skipped. (On one occasion, I had two entire sections of a book printed in reverse order.) You'll also find that reading through the book in galleys is far less onerous than plodding through the typescript. Now you're reading nice clear type, on clean white pages, and because it no longer looks anything like the pages that came out of your computer printer, you're capable of seeing it with a fresh eye.

You can use your colored pencil to mark any further corrections you wish to make, but you do have to understand that the time for big alterations is long gone. At this stage, as we've already discussed, it's expensive and time-consuming to make changes, and your publisher will take a very dim view of it if you try.

But if you've put in all the work I recommended on your first draft, and then once more on your revisions, the book should be awfully darn close to the way you wanted it. And now, for the first time, you'll also see just how many pages it came out to. One of the biggest surprises for many first-time authors is to see how much their manuscript has shrunk in the publishing process. Your galleys will almost invariably come out to a lower page count than your manuscript did, simply because a printed page in a book generally holds more words than your typed page does. For example, the last book I turned in came to 320 pages of typescript, but when I got it back in galleys it was 258. This is something to keep in mind as you write; you may think you have enough pages to make a respectable novel, when what you've really got is a novella. (All the more reason, as I suggested earlier, to keep track of your progress by periodically asking your computer for a word count. Computers don't lie, even when you want them to.)

If you're lucky, these galley pages may be bound into what are called uncorrected proofs, which the publisher sends out to reviewers with long lead times, or to booksellers it hopes to get excited about the forthcoming book. They're also used to solicit quotes and blurbs from bigtime writers, or other authorities on your subject matter. If it's a novel, the publisher may even slap on an early proof of the cover art.

In most cases, you'll have two weeks to read over your copy of the galleys before you have to return them to your editor. I know I've said this before, but this time I mean it: when you put the pages in an envelope and mail them back, you really are putting your baby to bed. You really are kissing the book good-bye. This is it. The next time you read your deathless prose, it's going to be neatly packaged and bound between two covers.

It's going to be . . . a book.

Part III

CELEBRITY

If you would not be forgotten, as soon as you are dead and rotten, either write things worth reading, or do things worth the writing.

—Benjamin Franklin,
Poor Richard's Almanack (1738)

Of Catalogs and Conferences

Just because the book is officially out of your hands right now doesn't mean it's sitting idle somewhere. *Au contraire*, my friend. While your work, with the return of your corrected galleys, may have temporarily abated, the work of your publishing house continues to chug along; all this time your publisher has been hard at work behind the scenes, performing a myriad of tasks necessary to the eventual publication and triumph of your book. Exhibit A? The sales catalog.

A seemingly innocuous document, the sales catalog can actually dispense many secrets—some you want to hear, and some you may wish you hadn't. In its simplest sense, the sales catalog is a pamphlet, maybe ten or twenty pages long, that lists all the books the publisher is bringing out on that particular seasonal list—all of its spring titles, for instance. Each book gets a brief description—maybe 150 words—that has been distilled from the tip sheet, a marketing/sales packet done many months before (and which authors never see). Your book, too, gets one of these capsule summaries. But you'll notice, from even the most cursory perusal of the catalog, that although the books are generally listed in chronological order of publication date, some of them get major play, and some of them don't.

Where, for example, is yours, and how is it featured?

At one publishing house, I was promised that my book was going to be "the A title" for the month in which it was to appear. In other words, it was going to be the book that the house really got behind and promoted like crazy. But no matter how many times I asked to see the catalog copy as it was being drawn up—a privilege to which every author is entitled—I never received it. And when I finally got their catalog itself (again, after asking three times), I couldn't help but notice that in the month in which my book was scheduled to appear, there were two other books also listed—and both of them came before mine, on full pages of their own. The first of these books was something like *All Natural Foods for Toddlers*, and the second was something like *Thirty Quick Remedies for Snakebite*. Then came my book, on a page it *shared* with a backlist book (one published several years before), along with a prominently displayed reminder to bookstore managers to place orders early to avoid shipping delays.

This, even to my relatively unpracticed eye, didn't bode well. Did the publisher really have more confidence in all-natural baby food and snakebite cures than he did in my breakthrough book, the one the house had claimed to be so enthusiastically behind, their "A title" for the month? Was my book really, in their estimation, less of a draw than those other two?

When I mustered the courage to call (a task, I now know, I should have left to my agent), my editor started out by claiming there was no particular meaning to the order in which the books were presented in the catalog. "Even though you all have pretty much the same pub date, I think the books just get listed alphabetically, by author name."

A quick check revealed the other author names to begin with a W and a Z. I mentioned this, and the editor regrouped.

"Maybe it's by the book title—yeah, that's it," he said.

That didn't work out in his favor, either.

"Well, all I can say is, all of us here at the house are one hundred percent behind your book."

"I'm sure of that. But just how *far* behind my book?"

"I'm afraid I don't follow."

"What about the half-page treatment? The other books got a full page each, with a colorful illustration showing their covers. I just got a title and a three-sentence summary."

"Let me check that," he said, and I could hear him flipping through the catalog pages. (There were a lot to flip through, as my book was nearly the last one listed.) "Yes, here it is." He read it silently. "That's a great summary," he said, "though I'd call it more of an editorial encapsulation. In fact, I wrote it."

Now I knew I'd gone too far. "Whatever we call it," I said, treading carefully, "it's unquestionably less extensive than the treatment the other books got. Wouldn't you agree?"

"Sometimes," he said, portentously, "less is more."

And sometimes, it's just less. In this case, the house did indeed pretty much bury my book. In retrospect, that "A" they kept mentioning must have stood for "Abandoned."

A sales catalog can give you some strong indication of how your book ranks in the publisher's hierarchy, and how much they're planning to push it. This catalog is what goes out to all the chain-store buyers and independent bookstore owners; it's what the publisher's sales reps carry with them when they make their sales calls. For all intents and purposes, it's the only advertising and promotion, in advance of the book's publication, that you're likely to get, and if it doesn't make a splashy statement on behalf of your book, if it doesn't make a convincing case for the importance and strong commercial prospects of your book, then it isn't doing the job for you.

This sales catalog will also be all over the place at the publisher's sales conferences—events that are held two or three times a year, and to which, needless to say, authors are very, very seldom invited. It'd be like keeping the patient awake during major surgery, and letting him listen in on your deliberations as critical complications arose; no one would benefit from that. At these sales conferences, usually held far from the main office at some resort hotel or corporate retreat center, the editors and publicists and sales staff all get together to socialize, get drunk, and consummate affairs that have been brewing for months. The hot tub is usually the most popular spot at a sales conference.

In the interstices, they discuss the upcoming books, how to sell them, and most importantly, get feedback from the field reps, who have been out there trying to drum up interest in the publishing house's list.

Your editor (*if* she's found time to go) is your advocate here: she's the one who will stand up and present your book to the rest of the company's militia; she's the one who should get them excited about what you've written; she's the one who should tantalize them with the huge sums of money they all are going to rake in from its much-deserved success; she's the one who must pitch not only the book, but you—what a fascinating and articulate talk-show guest you will be! How photogenic and cooperative (if *People* magazine wants you to pose in drag, hanging upside down from a window washer's scaffold, you're the kind of writer who will get right out there and do it). What a willing and tireless book-tour traveler you'll be (if, that is, the publishing house decides to spend the shekels touring you). In short, it's your editor's job to get the other branches of the publishing house as aware of, and excited about, your book as possible, to get the field reps psyched, and the national sales directors (the ones who service the big chains, such as Borders and Barnes & Noble) ready to put their considerable muscle to work on your behalf.

In this endeavor, she will soon get some help. She'll be aided and abetted by the in-house publicity person who gets assigned to your book. If, as is likely, you have never had a publicist before, enjoy it. This is how the stars live—with someone to trumpet their every good deed, and make some up if necessary—and you may well decide that it works for you, too.

The Song of Yourself

Once you've had a publicist, you'll never want to go back to being without one. There's something absolutely wonderful about having someone whose job it is to say nothing but good things about you. Even your mom may occasionally have her doubts, but your publicist? Never.

Not to mention, there's a very special *frisson* to be had the first time you drop into casual conversation something like, "Excuse me, but I've got to call my publicist back," or "If my publicist bugs me one more time about the 'Charlie Rose Show', I'll *scream*." Watch your friends squirm and look at you differently. *They* don't have publicists, but now *you* do. Score one for the home team.

But who exactly is this publicist of yours? More likely than not, she's a young woman of buoyant spirit and great energy, gifted with a good phone manner and a mind filled with the most recondite details of radio drive-time shows and audience demographics. She is a logician of the highest order, who, in another time and place, could have organized the Normandy invasion while simultaneously planning a society wedding in Newport. She is overworked, underpaid, and often harassed by authors less understanding and good-natured than you. She is there to help you, but you must also help her.

How?

First of all, by paying careful attention to what's known at most houses as your "Author Questionnaire." This document runs around five or six pages, and it's basically a list of questions about you and your book, with blank spaces where you can write in or type the answers. But since most of us work on computers now, you will probably find, as I do, that it's easier to just write the answers on the computer and then staple the printout to the questionnaire.

Since all of these questionnaires differ slightly, there's no point in trying to walk you through each and every step. Nor should there be any need to; if you have trouble answering questions about where you went to school or where you currently reside, then it's a miracle you were able to write a book at all.

And yet, there *are* some things to say and point out. For instance, you will probably be asked, somewhere near the top of this form, to provide a brief biographical sketch, including notable and unusual details of your life. This is not an invitation to write your autobiography. What the publicity department is fishing for here is material that they can use as a means of getting you interviewed by newspapers and magazines, or on a TV or radio talk show. In other words, your introduction to the world of sensual pleasure, no matter how memorable, is irrelevant here—unless, of course, that's what your book happens to be about. Then, and only then, is it relevant. If your book is about French cuisine, then the fact that you lived in France for three years, or that you worked in the kitchen of a famous French restaurant in New York, is what the folks in publicity want to know about. These are the things that provide "angles," ways that the media can use to get into, and shape stories around, your book.

You'll also be asked what qualifications you feel you had for writing this book. If it's a novel, you don't really need any. You had a story to tell, and you went ahead and told it. But if it's a nonfiction book, you may have plenty of pertinent credentials, and this is where you should lay them all out. Remember—you get no extra points for modesty, and no one, aside from your publicist, your editor, and some marketing folks, is going to see this questionnaire anyway. So go to town. If you worked in several three-star restaurants, then say so; if you invented the *Pample-mousse bombé de surprise*, say so; if you once made a birthday cake for Calista Flockhart, and she ate the whole thing in one sitting, say so!

(Celebrity stories are always like catnip to publicists, and in turn to the TV shows they have to pitch.) Include here anything you can think of to boost your stock and authority. For a publicist, information like this is like munitions to an artillery sergeant.

Most questionnaires will also ask you something like, "Who is your book written for or aimed at?" The obvious answer is, "Anyone who will buy it," but you should really try to be more specific. The publicist is trying to figure out who your most likely readers are, which will in turn help her to figure out how and where to reach them. Maybe your target audience is men and women who already know the basics of cooking, but who now want to experiment a bit with some traditional French dishes. If you tell that to your publicist, she knows a few places to look into, such as morning shows with a cooking segment, cooking schools, maybe even some French cultural outposts here in the U.S. All of these places may be amenable to promoting the book, hosting an event at which you lecture or cook, or maybe just selling a few copies of your book on their premises. A very dear friend of mine wrote a book designed to help petite women find chic and flattering clothes to wear, and even though the book sold well in bookstores, it sold like gangbusters in several boutiques that specialized in smaller sizes. Wherever those stores could be persuaded to stock some copies, their customers snatched the books up as fast as they came in.

The purpose of all this probing, as far as your publicist is concerned, is to find the places and venues where your book will come into natural contact with its most receptive audience—and that's why you'll also be asked if you're a member of any organizations, clubs, groups, societies, etc. The reasoning here is simple—where you're known, your book might also be bought. That is especially true if you're a member, say, of a large and prominent organization, such as a big university club; if a book party were to be held there, you might get a nice send-off and move a few dozen copies. If you're a member of a church congregation, maybe there would be some way to use that to advantage. (One of my college roommates became a minister, and, at the risk of being defrocked, he actually quoted from one of my books in a sermon he gave. I think he even went so far as to hold the book up to show its cover.) If you're the author of that book on French cuisine, and you regularly teach a master cooking class, the publicist may be able to suggest to a local newspaper reporter that she attend a session.

If you haven't gathered this already, when it comes to books, just about any angle or approach that allows for something *other* than a by-the-numbers book review is a welcome idea. Feature writers and show producers are looking for *active* ideas, things that you can be seen doing—cooking, fishing, taxidermy. They want to be able to focus on things that will help disguise the fact that what you *really* are is yet another author flogging his or her book.

To try another tack, is there, for the record, anything controversial about your book? Do you claim that space aliens are running, and purposely sabotaging, the NASA program? (Hmm . . . that's an idea I might be able to turn into a cheesy flick.) Do you believe that dogs should be able to run free in the streets, and all cats should be on leashes? Does your book prove that rich and fatty foods are actually healthier to eat than low-cal cuisine? If there's an argument that can be started based on something written in your book, then by all means tell your publicist about it. She knows that TV and radio shows like nothing better than controversy—and if she can give them the tinder for a ready-made conflagration, they'll love her (and you) for it.

Nor does this controversy have to be of earth-shaking proportions. When I wrote a book about love and romance, I appeared on dozens of shows just to address such age-old questions as why men say they'll call, and then don't. Or how to handle an attack of jealousy. Or where things presently stand in the so-called war between the sexes. My only credentials to be talking about this stuff were my chromosomes—as a certified man, I could at least speak from that experience—and my authoritative observations were based chiefly on countless hours of lonely introspection. But none of that mattered. What mattered is that I had opinions, some of them debatable, and I was willing to get out there and spout them.

It didn't hurt, of course, that what I'd written about in that book was chiefly of interest to women. It's generally accepted that most TV talk shows have a disproportionately large female audience, so anything you write that might appeal to, or simply intrigue, such viewers is a big plus.

Sad to say, if you write a book about ice hockey, you will have fewer opportunities to get on the air to promote it than you would if you'd written a book about estrogen replacement therapies. Your publicist, aware of this, will probably ask you if you see any ways in which your book would appeal specifically to female readers, so give it some thought.

In addition, and this may seem odd coming from your publicist, she'll ask you somewhere on the questionnaire if you know of any specialized media outlets that would help in promoting your book. *Isn't she supposed to know that stuff?* Well, yes she is, and she does, within reason. She knows all the mainstream newspapers and magazines, she knows the talk-show circuit, but no one, not even a professional publicist, can know every nook and cranny of the media landscape. If you've written a book about painting toy soldiers, you might know of a small publication or newsletter—*The Guys Who Never Grew Up Gazette*—aimed at toy soldier collectors like yourself. Your publicist may never have heard of the *Gazette*, but if you can supply her with the necessary information, she can contact them for you and maybe get your book reviewed there. The best way to sell copies of your book across the board is to find, and reach, the specialized audience to which your subject would most appeal.

When it comes to getting the word out, you might also have, among your friends and acquaintances, any number of people who could help. Your publicist will ask if you do. She'll ask if you know anyone in the media that she can get in touch with on your behalf. Most people are surprised, when they think about it, to realize how many contacts they do have. You may think you don't know anybody, but don't be too quick to dismiss the idea. Don't you work with someone who's married to a reporter for the local newspaper? Aren't you friends with someone at the university who arranges lecture series there? What about that guy whose brother works at a low-wattage local radio station? And say, doesn't that library across town hold a monthly "Meet-the-Author" tea? And didn't your college roommate go into journalism? Maybe he's now at a publication where he can either do something for the book himself, or pass it along to a writer or editor who can. Think hard, and be shameless. You'll be amazed at the number of direct, or tangential, contacts you can muster.

Think, too, about any names you can come up with who'd be good for a quote or a cover blurb. You know your subject better than anyone, and you know who the big names are in the field, or the well-known authorities who'd lend credence to your book. If it's a novel, ask yourself if you've ever met Judith Krantz, or Scott Turow, or Herman Melville. (Melville they can't check!) Can you get a quote from one of them? ("I'm well satisfied with my *Moby-Dick*, but it is nothing—a flickering wisp of St. Elmo's Fire—compared to this great achievement!") Your editor should be looking for these candidates, too, but your publicist will hope you can provide a few suggestions of your own.

Feel free, if there's something the Author Questionnaire has left out, to add it. This is an entirely fluid document, and its only purpose in life is to exploit every possible method of promoting, and selling, your book. Before you finish filling it out and return it to your publicist's office, make sure you've played every angle and explored every avenue. She'll do everything she can, but also keep in mind, she's got a whole bunch of other books and authors to work for. The average publicist at a book company has anywhere from twelve to thirty books at a time, all of which she's supposed to turn into a national sensation. She can do only so much for each one.

Her resources, too, are limited—chief among them, money. Publishers are notoriously cheap when it comes to publicity (Holt, the publisher of this book, being the universally acknowledged exception!), and they tend to throw what money they're willing to part with at just a few big books each year. When I'd finished my last one, for instance, and we were getting perilously close to the pub date, I called the publicist and asked what plans had been made to push the book. She seemed rather nervous.

"Why, have you heard of some plans?"

Now I was nervous. "No, I haven't heard a thing."

"Oh. Well, we were thinking about making a poster-size blow-up of the cover."

"Yes? That sounds good."

"And you could take it with you to anything you set up!"

The key word there was *you*—in other words, *they* hadn't set up anything, not a radio interview or a bookstore signing, and clearly weren't intending to. Publishing remains one of the most puzzling industries on earth—a business where they buy a property, develop it, produce it in some semirespectable quantity—and then at the last minute, toss it into the street as if they'd never seen it before. Books, like unwanted pets, are abandoned in droves.

Perhaps that's why some authors (a few of them my friends) actually dig into their own pockets to pay for an independent publicist. The cost? Again, it can vary, but my friends have forked over fees ranging from $750 to $5,000. When my cousin Chuck wrote a scathing novel set in the advertising industry, his privately hired publicist got him onto a couple of radio shows, not to talk about the novel per se (remember, fiction is of almost no interest to the media), but to talk about the current state of the American advertising business, where it was going, how it was changing, etc. News of his novel was wedged in sideways. My friend Alicia also hires private publicists to promote her books—but then Alicia is the heir to a manufacturing fortune. Since we're good friends and pretty open with each other (I've always told her the size of my book advances, she's told me how to choose a money manager—should I ever have money to manage), I was able to ask her what the added publicity help had run her.

"Five thousand dollars," she replied.

Wow, I thought. "May I ask what your publisher paid you for the book?"

She laughed. "Forty-five hundred. I know what you're thinking."

"What? I didn't say a thing."

"You know I'm lucky enough not to have to worry about the money. It's my literary legacy," she declared, in her best imitation of what we imagine Edith Wharton sounded like, "that concerns me."

We should all be so lucky—and because Alicia is aware of her own good fortune, it makes the situation bearable for the rest of her plebeian friends. If you're fortunate enough to be in the same boat as Alicia, if you'll never miss the money, and you want to do it, then by all means go ahead and hire your own publicist. But if you have to think hard about it, if spending the money on a publicist means you'll have to go without something else (from rent to warm socks), then in that case I would be hard pressed to recommend it.

Those of us who must rely solely upon the good offices of the in-house publicity staff must simply give them all the information and leads that we can, and hope that they're able to capitalize on them (with whatever resources their overlords have allocated to our little project). That's why, when the time comes, and our book is actually available in stores, we must also be prepared to get out there and do a lot of this legwork ourselves. I know that I drive people to distraction repeating this message, but it remains true, so I'll say it again: the proactive author, the one who gets out there and does whatever he can, whenever he can, to push his own book, stands a far better chance of getting it noticed than the one who waits patiently, politely, by the phone. If you're expecting the world to come knocking on your door, you could have a very long wait ahead of you.

The New Arrival

If you've ever wondered what eternity feels like, wonder no more. The time between the day you send the galleys back to the publishing house and the day you finally receive a finished book will seem, no matter what the calendar says, like forever. If it was three months, it will seem like six. If it was six, it will seem like a year. Longer than that, and it will seem as if this book were written in some previous lifetime, by a person you barely knew. An author waiting to see a finished, bound copy of his book is like a lottery-ticket holder, waiting for that one last number he needs to become an instant millionaire. The wait can seem forever.

But take it from me, that day will come—usually, when you least expect it. Some day when you go to get the mail, and you're not even thinking about your book, when your mind is somewhere else entirely, you'll find a padded envelope waiting for you, and the return address will be your publisher's. Sit down immediately, catch your breath, do not open the envelope (or box—sometimes, if it's all of your free author's copies at once, they'll be in a box) until you get back inside. You might want to be alone, or you might want to have a loved one present—that's up to you. Either way, this is a big moment in your life.

Only another writer will understand this, but the first time you lay eyes on your book—printed, bound, with your name on the front, and a price on the jacket flap or back cover—it can be an emotionally complicated experience. There's a lot of things going on. When I hold a copy of one of my books in my hand for the first time, there's satisfaction (at a job well done), relief (at a job that got done at all), and, last but not least, exultation—particularly if the book looks and feels as good as I'd hoped it would. You hold it in your hand, weighing its heft, its scale, its sheer *bookishness*. You flip through it, glancing at all the words cascading across all the pages, and if you're anything like me, you wonder for a split second *who* could have written all these words. Looking at them now, it seems a miracle that you were ever able to select them all, set them down, even *type* them, one after the other after the other. If it's a hardcover, you might prop it open on a table so that you can admire it from a distance. *Is that what it will look like when Oprah's cameraman focuses on the cover*? If it's a softcover or a mass-market paperback, you can still try this stunt, but the book'll fall over. (Take my word for it.) You may put the book down to make lunch, take a phone call, feed the cat, but you'll keep returning to it, like a talisman that you need to touch, to hold, to admire once again. Don't be ashamed; all of this is a normal reaction. You worked a long time, and now, finally, you have the goods to show for it. Enjoy yourself. (If, however, the condition persists beyond a week or two, to the point where you're forgetting to shower, change your clothes, or leave the house, then do consult your primary care physician.)

There's something else, too, that you're liable to feel, though this is harder to get a handle on: you're holding a little piece of your own mortality. I say that not only because of the time it took out of your life for you to produce this book, or because of the spiritual and artistic investment you've made in it. Sure, that's all there. But in an even simpler sense, this book, unlike nearly everything else you presently possess, will be with you, in this very form, all the way to the end. Think about it. What else, frankly, can you say that of? Look around your house—at your sofa, your curtains, your CDs, your new clothes. How many of these things, honestly, do you think will still be with you in ten years, much less twenty or thirty? Heck, those clothes will be lucky to make it into next year. (*A purple pashmina shawl? What were you thinking?*) But this book, printed and packaged in exactly the way that you now hold it, will be on your shelf, or in your bookcase—at the very least in a trunk under your bed—for the rest of your life. No matter how many editions the book may go through, from paperback to leather-bound Harvard Classic, I guarantee that you'll never let go of this first copy, this first fruit. Everything else, even a spouse, may come or go in this life. Everything will undoubtedly change—growing worn, or faded, or stale. And even this first edition, no matter how lovingly tended, may one day start to fall apart, the glue in the binding giving way, the pages threatening to come loose. But unlike nearly everything else, you won't throw this book away. You'll keep it, in whatever condition, for the long haul.

And that's why I've droned on and on about making it the best book it can be. It's a piece of your life, a thing that you have made with your hands, and your own talents, and your own thoughts, and you should be proud not only of the book itself, but of the fact that you made it at all. You know how many people talk about writing a book, and never do it? You know how many writers get started, but never see it through? Or how many do write the whole book, only to find that no one will publish it? But you've done it all—you've written one, *and* you've gotten it published. It's a very real accomplishment, and if you don't feel the full sense of your achievement right now, when you're holding that first copy in your hands, a full month or two before the rest of the world can line up to buy it, then you are not giving yourself anywhere near the credit that you're due. There'll be plenty of time later on for modesty and self-effacement (when you're being interviewed for a cover story in the *New York Review of Books*). For now, celebrate!

Publication Day

Although it may seem strange to you, the publication date of your book is not formally recognized as a national holiday. There's even a possibility that the occasion will go unnoticed by the general public and, I'm sorry to say, by the otherwise vigilant news media.

Hard to believe, isn't it?

Usually, your pub date falls about a month or so after you've received that first printed copy of the book, the first one off the press. If you happen to live in New York, or whatever other city your publisher might be located in, there's a chance—a small one, mind you, but a chance—that they'll throw a little party or press event to draw attention to the book. But unlike the bashes you read about in the paper, where Michael Crichton or John Grisham or Jackie Collins are surrounded by hundreds of ardent admirers at a posh restaurant or nightclub, your own party is more than likely going to be thrown at a somewhat less exalted venue—the conference room of the publishing company, perhaps. The publisher might spring for some pinot grigio, cheese, and crackers. And if they've really decided to pull out all the stops, there might even be a customized cake made to look like the cover of the book. Make sure you take a picture of the cake before somebody starts cutting into it.

Once all this wild party hoopla's over and your book is now officially published, your real work as an author begins. Forget about all that writing stuff—that was just laying the groundwork for the serious work to come. Now it's time to scour every bookstore in a hundred-mile radius and look for copies of your book. Where are they? In the front of the store? On a table in the back? Are they placed on the shelves so that the front cover is displayed, or are they just stuck in the rack with only their spines showing? If you're like every other author I know, your job is to make sure every copy is as prominently displayed as possible, even if that means breaking into a store at night and gluing a copy of your book to the front window. (Just *kidding*.)

When I was living in New York, there was a specialty bookstore a few blocks from my apartment, and almost every day I would go in there and take a copy of my latest novel and place it so that the cover faced out flat on the shelf. This, of course, obscured several copies of some other guy's book, whose last name—because titles were arranged alphabetically by author—was quite close to my own. Anyway, after doing this for about a week, I came in one day and found my own book slotted back in the shelf, and this other guy's book flat out, covering up mine. Of course, I quickly corrected the situation, but when I came back the next day, my book was once again back in the shelf, and his was on show again.

I decided to take action.

I called Information and asked if this guy had a listing in Manhattan. He did, only six blocks away from where I lived. The pieces were coming together. I called him. Once I'd identified myself, he said, "You."

"So, you know why I'm calling?"

"Because you obviously go to the same bookstore I do. And you keep covering up my books with yours."

"And now you're covering up mine with yours."

"So, what do you think we should do about it?" he said.

We both pondered that one for a moment. "I mean, we're both killing each other to sell three extra copies of our books," I pointed out, "while Stephen King is cleaning up all over the store."

"That's for sure," he said.

We pondered the impasse some more, then simultaneously came to the same conclusion. "How about if you put your books where they'll cover up somebody else's instead of mine?" the guy said.

"I will if you'll do the same," I said. We had a deal.

The next day, I found his books face out on the shelf above, obscuring an author whose sales were so huge he'd never miss one or two more, and I dutifully placed mine, cover out, on the shelf below. All of this subterfuge no doubt resulted in a total increased sale of five copies between us, but it's the kind of thing that authors do. We can't help ourselves.

Unfortunately, bookstore clerks and owners are trained to *undo* our little handiwork. It's as if they can spot an unauthorized placement from three aisles away, and before you can say, "Aw, come on, I'm just trying to make a living here," your book has been reshelved in the proper (and shamefully obscure) spot it was in before. They're particularly good at catching you if you try to stick your book in the racks, or even on the counter, up front by the cash registers. If they actually spot an author doing it, they've been known to graze him with a warning shot.

And they're not just being ornery.

Publishers—and I doubt you're going to be surprised to hear this—*pay* for the privilege of being displayed in such choice spots. Supermarkets aren't the only place where an "impulse buy" is encouraged, and though the publishing industry may be oddly antiquated in many ways, it *has* heard of product placement. If you're lucky, yours is one of the books they've paid a premium to have displayed up front, in the first-class section.

But if not, you're back on the shelves with the rest of us. In coach.

Don't be surprised, either, if the stores have only one or two copies of your book in stock. I hope for your sake that it's more, but many stores order sparingly. They have only so much room, and they figure they can always order more if they sell out of what they have. At least, that's their reasoning. In my own experience, unfortunately, they don't always do that (particularly in the big chain stores). At one such store in Los Angeles, I noticed that they'd had maybe a dozen copies of one of my books on sale, and when I came back a few weeks later there were none. I asked the store manager if they'd been reshelved somewhere else, but a quick check of the computer records revealed that in fact they'd all been sold.

"That's terrific," I said. "So how many more do you think you'll be ordering?"

"Well, I don't think we'll be ordering any more at all. Why would we?" he said.

"Because you sold a dozen copies in just a few weeks. I'm sure you could sell another dozen if you had it back in stock."

He shrugged. "Our book orders come from the main headquarters. We don't really worry about it very much."

Then he excused himself to help with the next customer. He was simply relieved, I think, to be rid of the copies he'd had on hand, and there was no way he was going to go out on a limb and risk being stuck with any more. Short of an angry mob descending on the store, demanding that he restock it, there wasn't much chance of seeing the book back on his shelves ever again.

It's a sad fact of life that the fate of your book is determined, to a large extent, the moment the print order is decided upon. The sales reps have gone forth, they have solicited orders from their customers, large and small, and that information has been used to figure out just how many copies to print. That number, in turn, determines how hard the company pushes the book, and whether they decide to throw some promotional dollars at it. I remember the first time I pressed an editor to tell me just how many copies of my paperback novel they were planning to print. After some hemming and hawing, she said, "About sixty thousand copies."

I was ecstatic until I relayed that number to my agent, who seemed unimpressed. "If they print anything less than a hundred thousand copies of a mass-market paperback, they're not really serious. It can't make enough of an impression on the marketplace."

Sixty thousand copies were too few? I was stunned. But since then, I've learned a couple of things. For one thing, she was right about that: a mass-market paperback has a shelf life of a few weeks, at best, so unless there's a zillion copies out there, it's very tough for the book to take off. When it comes to hardcovers—serious mainstream novels, for instance—a first run of 10,000 to 15,000 copies is more than respectable, and if 8,000 or 10,000 copies sell, the publisher's happy. With a trade paperback, much depends on the subject matter, but most of these books get print runs of 7,500 to 15,000 copies, and a 50 percent sell-through is pretty good.

What's galling, from the author's point of view, is that the publishers are so reluctant even to admit what the size of the print run is. It's like trying to pry a state secret out of them. Perhaps they don't want us authors to know the truth for fear we'll get obstreperous and demand more; perhaps they don't want their company's publishing plans to leak out into the general marketplace. Whatever the reason, they hate to be pinned down, and even when you do get them to cough up a number, don't bank on it. It may bear no more than a remote connection to the truth.

The only copies you know for a fact were printed are the ones you see yourself in the stores, and since we're on the subject, this might be as good a time as any to dispel another enduring myth among authors. Once upon a time, assuming that the legends are true, if a copy of a book was signed by the author, then it could not be returned to the publisher for full credit. As a result, authors were always trying to find and autograph copies of their books as fast as they could; a signed copy, it was naively believed, was as good as a sold copy. In some quarters, the belief persists to this day, but when I asked a publishing executive if it was true, he looked at me over the top of his glasses and said, "What do you think?"

"I'd like to think it's true," I said, having signed so many copies of my own books that friends used to call me up and tell me in amazement when they'd come across a rare *unsigned* copy in any local store.

"Well, you might like to believe it, but let's look at it rationally, shall we?" he said. "Who do you think the publishers are more interested in keeping up a good relationship with? Barnes & Noble, or you?"

I gave it some serious thought. "Me?"

"Wrong again. If a bookstore, big or small, wants to return an unsold book to us, autographed or not, we take it. They're the ones we're doing business with, and they're the ones we want to keep happy. With an author, we have what might be called a fling. But we're married to the bookstores."

Not that this has stopped me or my autographing pen; I'll still sign any copy that a store will let me sign. And if the store manager can find those little "AUTOGRAPHED BY THE AUTHOR" stickers (don't ask me why, but often, they can't), I try to persuade him to slap them on the front cover; some bookshop customers actually look for, and accordingly prize, the stickered books. And when the time comes to take the book off the shelves and send the leftover copies back to the publisher for credit—when its sales have slowed down, or stopped altogether—I still believe that the clerk or store manager might be just a little less inclined to return a book that's been autographed than one that hasn't. A book that has a hopeful little signature from a struggling author, scrawled across the title page. Wouldn't you be?

"You Want Me to *Buy* a Copy?"

Among the more surprising things you'll learn after you publish your first book is that no one you know—family, friends, coworkers—believes that books are actually sold. For money. In stores.

Everyone you know will expect you to *give* them a copy. Autographed. As soon as possible. It seems to be a commonly held belief that authors receive, from their generous and openhanded publishers, an indefinite supply of free copies to hand out to their friends and loved ones. And when you tell your buddies that it isn't true, that in fact you get fifteen, maybe twenty, free copies, and that after that, even you have to pay for them, they'll look at you as if you must be kidding. That, or you're just being stingy. If you openly suggest that they buy a copy, you risk losing their friendship and trust forever.

I remember one old friend of mine, gainfully employed in the Broadway theater business, slowly assimilating this shocking news. If she wanted to read the book, she was struggling to understand, she would have to *purchase* it? "But where would I do that?" she finally declared.

"At a bookstore. Pretty much any bookstore."

From her expression, you'd think that I had just advised her to climb to the top of Mount McKinley, nude.

"There are several good ones—bookstores, that is—right around the corner from where you work," I said. "On Fifth Avenue."

She nodded her head slowly, taking this in. *So that's why those windows had all those books in them!* (Not that she ever, to my knowledge, went into one of them to buy my book.)

Family is no better, and maybe worse, than your friends. Family *definitely* thinks you owe them. For instance, I always send my aunt and uncle in New Jersey, whom I love dearly, a free copy of every book I write. And I know they think they're flattering me when they tell me how the whole family is all lined up to read it, and how frustrating it is because Lynnie's got it in the tub right when Robbie wants to take it to the beach, or my uncle's reading it at work just when my aunt had planned to dip into it during her lunch break at the office. I know that it simply never occurs to them that, now that six people have bookmarks stuck in one dog-eared and soggy copy ("That Lynnie! She dropped it in the tub *again*!"), it might be time to drive to the mall and spring for a second copy. A copy that's completely dry.

Once, I tried to draw the line. My aunt, so proud of my latest novel, told me that she'd promised three neighbors that they could borrow her copy—"but only for one week each!"—as soon as everyone in her extended family (and I mean all the way back to Sicily) had finished with it.

"You know," I pointed out as diplomatically as I could, "I only make money when copies of the book are sold. It would actually help me out if some of these neighbors went to the store and bought their own."

Well, I might as well have suggested that we steal a bicycle from the garage next door. My aunt looked at me aghast. "These are friends of ours," she said. "I couldn't ask them to do that."

She was right, of course. What was I thinking? The next time I came for a visit, I handed my aunt a box of chocolates, a bottle of wine, and another free copy hot off the press. For peace in the family, it's a small price to pay.

The Critical Consensus

Just in case you were thinking of asking your publisher if they're planning to take out any print ads for your new book, let me save you the trouble—they're not.

"Print advertising doesn't sell," they will tell you. (I've heard it many times already.) "We're hoping instead to get some good reviews and capitalize on those."

But getting reviews—and good ones, yet—can be tough. Again, there are a lot of new books out there, and not much reviewing space in newspapers and magazines. Your publisher will be sending out bound galleys and finished books, with press releases attached, to try to get some review action going, but with the space devoted to book reviews shrinking all the time, it's an uphill battle. So let me tell you to cherish every notice that you do manage to get.

As far as the publishing industry itself is concerned, there are a few advance reviews that can count for a lot. These notices are published maybe a month or two before the official pub date of the book, and sometimes they're no more than a hundred words long. But they appear in such industry publications as *Publishers Weekly, Kirkus, Library Journal,* and *Booklist.* Just getting noticed by these trade publications is a coup, because they are inundated with all the books that every publishing company is producing, and they can pay attention to only so many titles each week. By the time they've gotten done with the big books that they know they *have* to review—if Mary Higgins Clark brings out another surefire bestseller, for instance—there's not much space left over for books by newcomers and relative unknowns. But they do select as many as they can, and if your book is one of them, you're lucky.

True, your friends and family are very unlikely even to see these trade publication reviews (unless you make copies and mail them out), but the people who *do* see them are the ones who really count—they're bookstore buyers and proprietors, editors and publishing executives. In other words, they're the people who can directly influence your sales and, to some extent, the course of your career. Even if this is your first published book, you've got other books still in you, and the readers of these professional journals are the very people who can offer you a contract for your next book, or order extra copies of this one to stock in their stores. A rave review in *Publishers Weekly* may seem less splashy than a favorable notice in a major newspaper, but it's probably more important.

But is it as much fun? Nah, I wouldn't go that far. It's one thing to be lauded by your peers in a professional forum, but let's face it—the real fun is in seeing your name and your book reviewed in the general media, in the newspapers and magazines that your friends and neighbors are likely to see. I once got a favorable squib about one of my books in *USA Today*, and I must have heard from half a dozen friends all over the country who'd seen it that day. Another book I wrote was "picked" (as opposed to "panned") by *People* magazine. And then I've had assorted reviews in newspapers, large and small, all over the place. Your publisher will no doubt subscribe to a national clipping service of some kind, so even if you don't happen to live in Topeka or St. Paul, you'll eventually get a copy of any review that might have run there.

That said, there are certain books that stand a far better chance of getting reviewed than others. If you've written a sensitive coming-of-age novel that's being published in hardcover, you'll probably land a few reviews, but not a lot. If you've written a serious nonfiction book—especially one that has a strong narrative pull and a relatively hot topic (a new kind of virus, discovered by a team of young scientists, which threatens to overwhelm the globe)—your prospects are definitely better. If your book is a hardcover that falls into a sort of genre, then you may get lumped in with some other related novels, in, say, the "Crime and Mystery" column of various book sections. Mass-market paperbacks almost never garner any reviews, and practical nonfiction books—sort of like this one—are most likely to get reviewed, if they get reviewed at all, in magazines aimed at their target audiences. (If I'm lucky, for instance, I'll see reviews of this book in writers' periodicals and digests.)

Now, there's always the chance—and you have to brace yourself for this—that a review you get will not be *entirely* positive. In fact, if I can be frank, almost no review is ever entirely positive. They're not supposed to be. I've worked as a freelance book reviewer myself, and I know from experience that if I had turned in a review that contained nothing but unqualified praise, the editor would have looked at me cockeyed. And the review would have been regarded as highly suspect. If a review doesn't contain at least a few critical caveats, it winds up sounding too much like a press release. It's the reviewer's job to read the book and make a careful and evenhanded assessment of its virtues and its flaws, and all but the most exultant, or excoriating, reviews will have a healthy mix of both. So don't take a critical word or two too much to heart; the reviewer's just doing his or her job (and usually, by the way, for next to no money).

Now, of course, I'm the least likely person in the world to say, "Don't worry about a few negative words." My skin is as thin as Saran Wrap and my feelings can stay hurt for decades. I don't care if the front page of *The New York Times Book Review* has compared my book to *Madame Bovary* (and to Flaubert's disadvantage). What I need is unanimous, and unqualified, praise, and if there's even one unfavorable comment about me or my book printed in the Omaha Library Association's monthly newsletter, then that's the comment I'll be obsessed with, and consumed by, for weeks to come. Once, I wrote a book of lighthearted essays that a reviewer had nothing but nice things to say about—it was warm, it was witty, it was deep—before concluding, however, that the book (a trade paperback) was overpriced at $6.95. $6.95? How much cheaper could we make all that warmth and wit?

Nor can you expect to have any control over who reviews your book, or where. (Or even when—sometimes a place like *The New York Times Book Review* won't get around to publishing a review of your book until the poor thing is gasping for air.) The one place, for instance, where I had always wanted to get noticed was the *Evanston Review*, the weekly publication that everybody in my hometown of Evanston, Illinois, read religiously. Along with news of school sports and downtown zoning decisions, it also carried stuff like news of gallery openings and reviews of plays at Northwestern University. But what mattered to me was simple: it was the one place where I could be sure, if a review appeared, that friends of mine from high school would hear about it. Even if they'd moved away by now, their *parents* might still be in Evanston and their moms could cut it out and send it along—most notably, to any girl from my high school that I'd wanted to date, but considered out of my reach at the time. ("Dear Jenny, Here's a clipping from the *Evanston Review*. Wasn't this the boy who used to paste all those dreadful little love poems on your locker at school?")

Yeah, guilty as charged. But come on, already, if you can't let your high school classmates know that you've made good, then what's the point of writing a book, or, for that matter, accomplishing anything in this life?

As far as the *Evanston Review* went, however, no matter how much press I got elsewhere, they were not about to be cowed. They remained the one place that ignored me utterly. I'd have the publicists send them press releases, with HOMETOWN BOY MAKES GOOD! scrawled on the top, and we'd hear nothing. I'd write personal letters to the columnists, offering exclusive interview rights, and I'd get no reply. I'd call the place up when I was back in town to visit my family, and I'd get nowhere that way, either. This lasted for years, until I'd long since given up. And of course, then, and only then, did I get a tiny mention in a book review column—and trust me, it wasn't exactly the kind of mention I'd been hoping for. Some brief description of one of my books appeared in a roundup, and the comments weren't exactly adulatory. Now I can only hope that the parents of those girls are *not* subscribing to the *Evanston Review* anymore.

Still, unless the notice your book gets is an out-and-out pan, any attention is worth it (I guess). It's so hard to break through, to get your work noticed at all, that any publicity is good publicity. Not only that, there's almost always at least one line that you can lift and use as a blurb your next time out. (Often, this line is something you wrote yourself for the intro or flap copy, and the critic has simply appropriated it.) In that way, even a review that is, on the whole, unfriendly can be turned to your advantage.

And sometimes, let's not forget, the reviewer can be your best friend. In one particularly bizarre twist of fate, a pal of mine was actually asked to review a novel that he himself had written under a pseudonym. The book was about a painter in New York, and my friend Barry was a painter who occasionally wrote short pieces about the gallery scene for local publications. Anyway, that's how he came to get the call from the book review editor, asking him if he'd like to review this new novel that happened to be set in the downtown art world that Barry knew and wrote about so well.

"That's incredible," I said, laughing. "What did the editor say when you told him you were the author of the book?"

"Nothing," Barry replied. "I didn't tell him."

"You took the assignment?" I said, incredulously.

"You bet. I mean, it's not as if I don't know the material."

Anyway, about ten days later, the review appeared, and I know what you're thinking—you're thinking it was a rave. But it wasn't. It read like a perfectly honest, ordinary review: Barry knew that an authentic review was a mixed one, and he went out of his way to point out some of the minor flaws in the book. Who knew better than Barry what didn't really work? Of course, he did offer a great deal of praise, and he did wind up his assessment by recommending that everyone rush out and buy a copy of the book. But honestly, is there an author alive who could have resisted the chance to do that? (Note: I have a comment from the editor of this book, the one you're holding, on the manuscript page where I wrote this anecdote, and she tells me that this behavior is "highly unethical" and that a reviewer is always expected to reveal any relationship he has—friendly or hostile—with the author of the book under review. If he's the very *author* of the book he's been asked to review, this, of course, would make him totally ineligible. So, let me state for the record, that I am shocked—shocked, I say—by my friend Barry's conduct and in no way endorse or recommend it. In fact, when Barry and I have lunch next Tuesday, I intend to give him a very stern lecture.)

Still, the odds that you will be asked to write a review of your own book are so slim as to be nonexistent. So it's best to prepare yourself for anything. Write your own reviews in your head—"The Great American Novel Emerges at Last!" "Move Over, Hemingway, There's a New Kid in Town," "Bestseller Meets Classic in a New Work of Breathtaking Excellence"—but remember that in real life, most reviews you get will be a little less declamatory and exuberant than that.

Especially the ones you are bound to receive, whether you want them or not, from your friends and family members. "Hey, hold on there," you might say, "my friends and family are my biggest fans. I have nothing to fear from *them*."

Oh, if only I could say that was true. Some of the most memorable jabs I've ever gotten came from my nearest and dearest. It's come to the point now where, whenever a friend says to me, "Hey, I just read your new book!" my immediate reply is, "Thanks *so much*! Can you *believe* this weather we're having?" Anything to change the subject, as quickly as possible. To move *away* from the book and onto neutral ground. Everybody's a critic—your friends included—and no matter how well their comments may start out, they won't stay that way. There's a worm in the apple, a thorn in the rose, and if you let your pals talk long enough, you're going to encounter that nettlesome little surprise. The very fact that you've written a book—a book that's been published, yet—sets off all kinds of alarm bells in the heads of those who know you, alarm bells that sometimes even they do not consciously hear. There's envy, of course—you've gone and done the thing that some of them have been talking about doing forever. There's that competitive instinct—you're two steps ahead right now, but they don't want you thinking you've won the race altogether. There's also some strange, primordial urge to show you just how honest and true their friendship really is. What better way could there be to do that than to be completely straight with you about your book? Sure, they're your friend and booster, but that doesn't mean they've taken leave of their finely tuned critical instincts; if they criticize your work, you're expected to understand that it's just because they know how good you can be, and they don't want your next book to trip up in the same ways as this one did. Hey, isn't that what friends—real friends—are *for*?

Recently, for instance, a nonfiction book I wrote was published, and several friends called in with their congratulations and praise. The first started out by saying how hilarious the book was and how informative, and even as I was doing my best to change the topic, she went on to add, "Of course, by the end, you'd abandoned all pretense to being an authority. By then, it was nothing but a bunch of your old stories."

Thank you so much.

The next caller—all the way from Miami, yet!—wanted to let me know that she didn't think I came off as "all *that* dweeby. I mean, you could have edited out some of the self-effacing stuff—we'd have liked you, anyway—and the book would still have worked."

I'll keep that in mind, too.

The coup de grace was the last call, which employed an ingenious technique I'm sure you, too, will run into. I think of it as using one book to bash another. The caller, someone I've known since high school, said, "I always knew you had it in you to write a book that would make me laugh out loud. All your other books, I mean, they were fine, but anybody could have written them. This is the kind of thing you should have been writing all along. It's just too bad it took so long, you could have been a star by now."

Wow—what a shame I'm not.

I know that you're thinking this is just my problem, that I've got a defective bunch of friends. You're sure that you have chosen your own friends much more wisely and that *they* would never utter a word of anything but unadulterated praise. Okay, go ahead and think that way. But when your book is published and your own friends call you up to offer their compliments and congratulations, don't say I didn't warn you . . . to duck.

If This Is Tuesday . . .

Among the many perks a publisher can offer its authors, perhaps the most coveted is the book tour. It is also, however, among the most endangered. Sending an author out on tour—to appear on local TV and radio shows, to do in-store readings and signings—is expensive and logistically challenging, and as a result, publishers are doing less of it than they used to. Why buy an airplane ticket to send some schnook all the way to Decatur when you can just sit him in a room in New York and satellite-feed him anywhere? Why pay for a hotel room in Kalamazoo when you can set up a live chat with your author on the Internet?

Only certain authors really rate when it comes to book tours; if you're one of the publishing pantheon, a bestselling writer with a track record, your publisher will, of course, set up anything you're willing to do. If Bob Woodward or Patricia Cornwell is prepared to travel to Minneapolis, you can bet a ticket will be promptly provided—and the shows will be lining up to have them on.

So where does this leave the rest of us? Are we destined to stay at home and never meet our eager public in person?

Not at all. Even regular writers sometimes get to tour. But if you do want to go out on one, you've got to understand that there are certain prerequisites that will either put you in contention or disqualify you right off the bat. For instance, if you're hoping to go on a book tour one day, if that's your fondest dream, then the worst thing you can do is write a serious and literary novel.

Novelists, by and large, are anathema to TV shows. They tend to be too lofty, too cerebral, too much at home with solitude and too off-kilter under the bright lights of a TV studio. That's part of the problem. But even the most articulate and personable novelists are tough for a TV or radio host to interview. Why? Because the interview would presuppose that the host had read the book, which in almost every instance will not be the case. To some extent, you can understand it. Even a TV host has only so much time to prepare for each segment—and if he hasn't read the book, then how are you going to talk about the plot and the characters, and if you can't talk about that, then what on earth *are* the two of you going to talk about on the air?

Not to mention the fact that novels are just plain hard to discuss under even the best of circumstances. People listening to the radio on their way to work, or watching TV while making lunch for three kids, aren't really in the right state of mind to hear about your artfully constructed story, your lapidary literary style, your thematic motifs and heart-rending denouements. If they want to read a novel at all, they'll read the one that Oprah tells them to. Otherwise, they'd much rather hear about the latest anti-aging discovery.

Still, even the most battle-hardened novelists dream of breaking through, of crawling into the limelight for just a few precious moments. My pal Manny, for example, has been writing highly praised novels for many years, but he hasn't exactly been swept up into America's embrace. So he decided to take matters into his own hands; after he'd written a comic novel called *Field of Greens*, about a down-on-his-luck farmer who resorts to some unorthodox crop-rotation ideas, he decided to hire his own publicist out of his own pocket. The one thing she managed to do for him was book him on a late-night radio talk show in New York, where I, too, was living at the time. He called to tell me to be sure to tune in, and of course I did.

"My guest tonight," the host intoned, "has written a wonderful new book called *Field of Greens*, and from what I hear, it's just filled to bursting with great and healthful ideas for salads, veggies, all the things we should be eating more of, but don't." Then she introduced Manny to her listening audience, and as I waited for him to correct her—to tell her that it wasn't a cookbook at all, that it was a novel, about a free-thinking Midwestern farmer—Manny simply said, "Thanks, it's great to be here."

"So, Manny, tell us—what first got you interested in food?"

"My mom," Manny replied. "She was a terrific cook. And she knew how to make delicious low-calorie food long before anyone else was even thinking about it."

"What were some of your favorites?"

And as I listened dumbfounded, Manny went on, for one solid hour, to describe the perfect recipe for hummus, the virtues of a vegetarian diet, the secrets to making a light, soft-on-the-inside, crispy-on-the-outside blintz—"a baked blintz will always be lighter than a fried one"—without once mentioning that what he'd really written was fiction, a story that had not one thing to do with any of this. He talked about canola oil and arugula and bok choy, and when the time was up, the host thanked him and the show went off the air.

I waited about half an hour, which was just enough time for Manny to get from the radio station back to his apartment, and then I called him up. "What were you doing?" I said. "Why didn't you correct that dope? Why didn't you tell her you'd written a novel?"

I could all but hear Manny shrug on the other end of the line. "It'll sell more as a cookbook than it ever would have as a novel."

His answer caught me so off-guard that I fell silent. Could he be right? Was I being too hasty?

"But how'd I sound?" he asked. "Was I good?"

"Yes. You were very good," I had to admit. "In fact, if you don't mind my saying so, I'd like to try your blintzes sometime."

With a nonfiction book, your chances of going on tour are a lot better—though much still depends on the topic of your book. Baroque art is probably not going to get you far. But something newsworthy and at the same time a little bit squishy—how teens and their parents can communicate better, why we're working harder but feeling less satisfied with our lives, what we can do to retire by forty—those are the kinds of things TV and radio shows like to focus on. By no means let that determine what kind of book you write . . . but if you *do* happen to write one that meets the media requirements, congratulations. You're halfway to *Good Morning, Shreveport!*

Now, the question becomes this: Are you the kind of author a publishing house will want to get behind? Do you have what it takes, in their view, to go out on the road and make their expenditure worthwhile?

Since they can afford to send only a few authors out on tour at any one time, publishers do undertake a cruel but necessary winnowing process. The authors they choose are the most articulate, the most animated, the ones that the publisher feels will make the best impression on the air. It doesn't hurt if you're gorgeous, or a celebrity in your own right, but barring that, the best thing you can do for yourself is convince your publisher that you're comfortable in front of an audience, that you're capable of speaking in catchy sound bites, and that your grooming is impeccable. I have a very talented friend who wrote a health-oriented book, and she did a stellar job on it, but her publisher did not opt to do much publicity for it, and they never even considered sending her out on tour. How come? They told her there just wasn't any money left in the budget, but I have this terrible, sneaking suspicion that they felt the author—a bit overweight, and (okay, let's be honest) in pressing need of a makeover—would not make the best advertisement for the book. If Gwyneth Paltrow had written it, trust me, they'd have found the dough to send her all the way to Honolulu.

And if the problem had only been one of presentation—if my friend's only drawbacks had been that she didn't speak as clearly as she needed to, or didn't know how to edit her thoughts into tasty sound bites—then the publisher might have provided her with some quick media training. Some publishers do this now, if they think the author's message is one that will appeal to a lot of shows, but they're still not convinced the author knows how to deliver it. On TV especially, it's important to make your points quickly and clearly, while holding your head high, your gaze steady, and your hands still. If your publisher decides you're worth it, you'll be sent to a media trainer who will tape sample interviews with you, then play them back so you can see just what problems need to be corrected.

But let's assume that you and your book are admirably suited to the airwaves, and that your publisher, seeing all the personal virtues in you that I do—your spontaneous wit, your photogenic kisser, your succinct delivery—decides to do the right thing. What happens next?

Your publicist and your editor confer, and a few weeks before your official publication date, you get a copy of your book tour schedule. What you will see is a well-orchestrated itinerary—perhaps four or five cities—and under each one, a list of shows you'll be doing, the hotel you'll be staying in, the name and phone number of your local escort (which I'll get into later). The first time I went out on a book tour, more years ago now than I care to say, I remember getting my schedule, and reeling when I realized it listed twenty-six cities, to be covered in a period of thirty-four days. I quickly called my friend Larry, who'd done book tours of his own, and when I told him the news, he said, "Whew. Twenty-six cities?"

"Yes," I said, "from Toronto to Houston, L.A., D.C., San Francisco, Chicago, and all major stops in between."

"I only did nine cities."

"So this is good then? They're really getting me out there."

"Yeah, it's good. But twenty-six cities? Your brain is gonna turn to jelly."

Not exactly the rousing send-off I'd been hoping for, but, as I would learn weeks later, and for reasons I'll explain, pretty much on target.

When you go out on a tour, especially one as unusually extensive as my first one (which I have never since repeated or equaled, by the way), you become a bookselling machine. Your itinerary has not been organized in such a way as to give you time to relax or dawdle or see any local sights; your schedule has been set up to maximize the publisher's investment in you. They're not paying for your airfares and hotel room bills so you can have a good time, see America, and drop in on old friends. They're paying for you to hit as many media outlets and bookstore branches as you can, in the shortest span of time possible. On the twenty-six-city tour, for instance, I appeared on fifty-eight shows, gave twenty-nine interviews with local newspapers, and did at least a dozen autograph sessions. I went to bed in a different city nearly every night, and yes, after a while it did begin to feel as if my brain had turned to jelly.

It isn't the constant shuttling through airports and time zones that

does you in (though that certainly has its effects); it's the relentless bar-
rage of questions—almost invariably the same questions you've been
asked a hundred times before—coming at you from an interchange-
able contingent of local TV hosts with blow-dried hair, gleaming smiles,
and a priceless ability to simulate interest. Your brain becomes a cas-
sette deck, into which you slip the tape with your prerecorded answers,
and when the red light on the camera goes on, you just try to deliver
these canned replies with a semblance of excitement and spontaneity—
something that becomes harder and harder to do as the days, and the
cities, pile up.

Which is why it's so critically important that you simplify your touring life in every other way that you can. When I go out on the road, for
instance, I bring nothing but identical outfits—two blue blazers, several
pale blue Oxford cloth shirts, a couple of pairs of chinos. The last thing
you want to have to do, when you wake up at 6 A.M. in some anonymous
hotel room, is start mixing and matching clothing items. The folks in
Denver aren't going to know that you wore this same outfit in Detroit the
day before, so why should you care? All you're looking for is a simple,
presentable outfit that you look good in, and that the camera will like.
Yeah, yeah, television reception has gotten much better over the years,
but unless you've written a book about making a bold fashion statement,
you're still making a mistake if you wear loud colors, plaids, stripes, or
anything else that might not transmit so well.

Another advantage to wearing the same ensemble over and over
again is that you're always able to tell your escort how to find you in the
lobby the next morning. ("I'll be the sleepy-looking guy wearing a blue
blazer and khaki pants.")

Your escort, you'll find, is your best friend on the road. In every city,
he or she (though "she" is more common) will be your guide and porter,
your wheels and your general factotum. Escorts come from all walks of
life—in Boston, I had a sculptor; in Detroit, an ex-cop; in L.A., an aspiring actress (big surprise)—and they're essentially stringers for the big
publishing houses. For maybe a hundred dollars a day, plus expenses
(but don't sweat it—the publisher pays), they're there to hold your hand
while you're making the rounds of their town. They have a good sense
of direction, a reliable automobile (*generally*, that is—my escort in

Cleveland had a coughing and wheezing Volkswagen bug with a gaping hole in the floor), and they know where all the local bookstores and TV and radio stations are. They also have a copy of your schedule in their hand so they know where you have to be, when you have to be there, and what time they have to get you back to the airport for the next leg of your journey.

They're also there to deal with any emergency that might arise, anything from lost luggage (though if you're traveling with more than a carry-on bag or two, you're doing things wrong) to the inevitable conniption fit you'll have when you get to the bookstores and find out that your book hasn't even arrived in town yet.

"But I've just been on four local TV shows! Thousands of people are leaping into their cars right now to race to their nearest bookstore and buy a copy. If they can't find one, things could get really ugly."

Your escort will talk you down off the ledge, hand you her cell phone, and let you make an irate call to your publisher's office, where the voice mail will take the brunt of your anger. If it's any help, let me tell you, the "no-books-in-town-yet" syndrome affects us all.

On one stop of a book tour, the publisher had actually arranged with the local afternoon talk show to shoot my segment live, right outside a huge bookstore in the local mall. I was scheduled to do a signing in there right afterward. When I arrived, the stage was set up, the lights were glaring, the mikes were on, and there must have been a couple of hundred people milling around, soaking up the show-biz excitement and hoping to catch a glimpse of the show's host. I got up there, did my spot, and, I must say, it went unusually well—the crowd loved it, and when it was done, the host obligingly pointed everyone toward the bookstore just a few yards away. Like the Pied Piper, I led the happy multitudes into the store . . . where there was no display of my books, no table for me to sit down and sign them at, no indication anywhere that we were even expected.

On seeing the crowd, the twenty-something manager did come up, nervously scratching his goatee, and ask me what was up.

"I'm the author who was supposed to sign copies of my book in here after the TV interview we just did outside."

He looked at me blankly. "What's your name again?"

I told him.

"And you've written a book? That's cool. What's it called?"

I could feel the crowd starting to disperse.

I gave him the title, and he looked just as blank. "Let me look it up on the computer."

As he did so, I watched another dozen people or so drift toward the door.

"Yeah, it's right here on the screen. We should get a couple of copies in by next week."

"A couple of copies? Next week? There were supposed to be dozens of copies here right now, for me to sign."

"I don't know," he said. "Nobody told me."

The escort stepped to my side and took my elbow. "We should be leaving now," she said, in a gentle voice. "We have a radio show to do across town."

"That's not for hours."

"I know," she said, ushering me toward the door. "But there's a bar around the corner where we can relax for a while."

The two or three remaining customers smiled as I passed, and the last thing I heard was one of them, making the most of finding himself in a bookstore by asking the manager where he could find the discounted calendars.

After all the interviews are over, and any copies of your book that you can lay your hands on have been signed, the escort performs her last duty, which is to get you to the airport in time for your next flight. There, you leap from her still-moving car, with carry-on bag in hand, a crumpled copy of your itinerary wedged into your pocket, and less than fifteen minutes before you're due to take off for your next port of call. Still, this will give you just enough time, as you race for the boarding gate, to perform the one irresistible duty of an author on tour—a quick check of the airport book racks to see if they're carrying your opus.

Talking Head

If they could, most TV and radio shows would book nothing but movie stars, TV celebrities, and Britney Spears. But they can't. Even Britney needs some downtime, and many of these famous faces have trouble stringing three words together in a row.

Who, then, can come to the rescue and fill up some of that precious airtime?

Authors, known first and foremost for their ability to put three, even four, words together in a row.

Authors are also known for their ready availability. No author in his right mind ever turned down the opportunity to get out of his grubby little office and go on the air to sing the praises of his new book. On one occasion, when I was invited to appear on a big national talk show to discuss a book of humorous essays I'd written, I personally paid for my own cross-country airfare and hotel. (If you're wondering why my publisher didn't ante up, you haven't been paying attention: publishers hate to spend money.) But since this was such a popular show at the time, I figured it was worth the investment.

Anyway, I walked out on the stage, sat down in the main guest chair (which had just been vacated by a beautiful actress of foreign extraction), and about fifteen seconds into the interview, the affable host said, "In one of these essays, you say that it's actually okay for a woman to ask a man out these days. Has that ever happened to you?"

"I wish I could say that it had," I replied, but before I could finish the thought, the beautiful actress, who had been moved down one spot to the adjoining sofa, took great umbrage at the very notion and jumped in with, "That is a terrible idea. No, no, no, a woman should never ask a man out. A woman must always be a mystery, she must always let the man come to her first," and so on and so forth, for what amounted to pretty much the rest of my entire segment. As I politely sat there, waiting for her to catch her breath or finish her semicoherent ramblings, I prayed that the host would jump back in and somehow save me—but he didn't. Perhaps he knew that his audience would rather be watching the actress than the essayist, and I suppose he was right. A few minutes later, we cut to a commercial, the host leaned across his desk, shook my hand, and thanked me for the great interview—*what interview?*—and before you could say "waste of money," I was back in a gypsy cab, on my way to the standard room I'd booked for the night at the nearby Ramada Inn.

From that misfire, and others like it, I learned, above all else, to be prepared—loaded for bear and ready for anything—for all my future spots. I learned that it wasn't enough to be well groomed and attired (along the lines we have discussed earlier)—it was also important, as much as possible, to *control* the interview. To be so well primed that, if necessary, I could take over the interview process and do it single-handedly—which, in most cases, isn't as hard as it sounds. Most talk-show hosts have spent more time combing their hair than they have preparing for your interview.

Chances are, your host/interviewer hasn't actually lifted a finger himself. Instead, he'll be relying upon some sketchy notes he received from some overworked, half-dead intern who barely had time himself to read your jacket copy. I remember one nationally known anchorman strolling into the makeup room just as I was having some color sponged into my face. (Never, ever turn this service down, by the way. You may think you don't need it, but everybody else on the show will have had makeup applied, and if you decline, you'll be the only one on the air who winds up looking like Tony Perkins's mom in *Psycho*.) Anyway, the anchorman shook my hand and held up a copy of my magazine column—no more than six hundred words long, from start to finish—that we were going to discuss that morning on the air. "I didn't have a chance to read your whole column," he said, and I could see that about three sentences had been outlined for him in yellow marker, "but what I did read was very provocative."

Gee, I thought, *those must have been three of my most provoking sentences*. I wondered which ones they were. (Even after the interview was over, I wasn't quite sure.)

But that guy comes across as a Talmudic scholar compared to the other show hosts, who will blithely shake your hand, tell you how much they enjoyed your new movie, and then swivel to start reading their "off-the-cuff remarks" from the teleprompter.

That's why I've decided that it's best, strange as this may sound, to conduct an interview with yourself first. You can give this ready-made Q&A to your publicist, who can use it to get you booked on shows, and you can also carry it along to the TV studios with you; there, you can simply hand over this list of the top ten questions that *you* think they should be asking you, and relax. Some poor schnook, probably that overburdened intern, will have been assigned to do the pre-interview with you—in other words, to find out why on earth the booker booked you in the first place—but you cannot imagine the look of relief that will cross this kid's face when you hand over your prefab questions.

Questions that come with a snippet of the pithy but punchy answer that you're going to give to each one.

The intern will get your questions transferred to the teleprompter posthaste, and the host, when he reads them, will do his best to give the impression that he's thinking of these questions right then and there. It's your job to react as if he is.

To give you a better idea of how this ingenious system works, let's say, for argument's sake, that your book is called *365 Ways to Cut Your Own Hair*. Here's what you might hand over:

Q: *"What a great idea for a book! How did you come up with it?"*
A: "Well, it's funny you should ask that, Gary." (Always use the host's name at least once, in a friendly, familiar manner. The shows actually like it when you do that because it implies that you're familiar with their Gary, host for the past eleven years now of *What's Up, Utica!* I mean, isn't *everyone* in

America a fan of Gary's?) "I was cutting my hair, as I do every day before going to work, when it occurred to me, *Hey, wait one darn minute here . . .*"

Q: *"What first got you interested in cutting hair?"*
A: "My family, when I was growing up, lived above a barbershop, and I couldn't wait to get home from school each day to play in the piles of dead hair that they'd throw out back in the alley."

Q: *"But cutting your own hair? What gave you that idea?"*
A: "For years, I'd been looking for a way to take control of my life. I think that's important to a lot of people today." (This is a clever ploy to demonstrate how your story no doubt resonates, on many levels, with countless Utica viewers.) "Then, one day, I just happened to pick up an old machete my great-uncle had brought back from Guadalcanal, and . . ."

Well, by now, you get the idea. Make sure your questions have short, interesting answers, which ideally will lead you into the next question on the list. What you're creating here is the illusion of a real conversation.

And don't be surprised if, during your TV interviews, you never make it past the halfway point on your list. With rare exceptions, your TV interviews will be bracketed by commercial breaks and weather reports, and last no more than four or five minutes; if you get eight or ten minutes, you're doing swell. That's why it's so important to stay focused—get your message across—and stay still.

Stay still?

Another case in point: my first national TV spot was on the *Today Show*, back when a young Jane Pauley was one of the hosts. Just before going on the air, I was taken out to the set and seated behind a semicircular desk on a blue, fabric-covered swivel chair. When Jane came out to conduct the interview about my new book, I was pleasantly surprised to see that, as attractive as she was on TV, in person she was even prettier. I felt my temperature, already high, rise another degree or two. She sat down in an identical chair next to mine, we exchanged a few friendly words, the red light on the camera went on, and we were off and running.

I was so thrilled to be on TV, and so excited to find myself trading remarks with such a lovely and famous woman, that I lost any fears I might have had and just let fly. Never, I thought, had I been so brilliant, so spontaneous, so animated and witty. In fact, at one point about midway through the interview, I was absolutely stunned to see Jane's hand creep out under the cover of the desk and rest gently, but firmly, on my right thigh. She spread her fingers and squeezed me.

She wants me! Jane Pauley wants me! I could not believe it. My life had just changed completely.

Somehow, I was able to control myself enough to get through the rest of the interview, still speaking English and mostly making sense. But when it was over, I was surprised to see Jane get up from her chair, as if nothing had transpired between us, and casually mosey off to another part of the studio for her next setup.

Oh, I get it, I thought. *She doesn't want her coworkers to know what's going on. She wants to keep this thing under wraps until we can get together again, in private, away from all those prying eyes.*

I nodded and threw her an understanding smile as I left the studio—she looked slightly puzzled—and when I got home, I called my mother to see how my first network television appearance had gone over in the Midwest.

"You were fine, Punky," she said, but without quite as much enthusiasm as I'd hoped. "Very interesting."

"I hope so—the book went on sale last week." I waited for another compliment. None was forthcoming. I went fishing. "You know, Jane Pauley and I were really getting along," I said. "Did that come across?"

"Oh yes. You were clearly very excited."

"I was?"

"Yes. In fact, you were swiveling back and forth in your chair so much, it was a wonder she didn't get seasick sitting next to you."

"Really?" My heart was already sinking in my chest.

"But only at first," my mother rushed to reassure me. "About halfway through the interview, you seemed to settle down and sit still." Right around the time, I suspected, that Jane had reached out and gripped my thigh. Not, I realized now, out of barely restrained passion, but in a desperate attempt to make me behave and stop squirming in my chair like a nervous third-grader.

No wonder she never called me.

One more thing to keep in mind: although most shows are pretty well run and organized, some of them are not—which means you must never show up for an interview without a copy of your book in your hand. Yes, I know that your publicist has sent a copy on ahead, but you would be amazed at the number of times that the advance copy will have disappeared somehow and you'll be about to go on the air with no copy of your book for the camera to focus on. Make sure you have one with you—and that if you're going straight on to another show right afterward, you retrieve it before you go. One glimpse of the cover is worth several mentions of the title.

Which, by the way, is something you should do sparingly—interviewers hate it when you keep blatantly plugging your book. It's okay to say, "as I point out in my book" now and then, but your segment is supposed to appear newsworthy, and not as a promotional spot, so leave it to the host to mention the title of your book—ideally at the beginning, and again at the end, of your appearance. In TV, as has already been noted, these plugs will come only minutes apart, anyway. Before you know it, a sound guy will be unclipping the microphone from your tie or lapel, and a PA (production assistant) will guide you by the elbow back to the green room, where you can pick up your bag or briefcase and leave, as quickly as possible. Don't even try to snag a last sweet roll from the hospitality table—just go. There is nothing in this world, you'll discover, so unwanted as a TV guest who has already done his spot.

When it comes to radio, you'll probably get more time on the air, but that's because radio time is cheaper, and everything about the experience, from the cold coffee in your styrofoam cup to the dismal state of the station's rest room, will bring that home to you.

Nor are your interviewers likely to be as attractive as their TV counterparts. If they were, they'd *be* on TV.

Although a radio host will be no more likely than a TV guy to have read your book, at least he'll have one big advantage: he'll be able to leaf through it, unseen by his audience, while the interview is actually going on. (I guess my friend Manny's host found even that to be too much trouble.) It's like an open book test; the host can literally pick up on something right then and there—"I see, in chapter three, that you believe it's better to use a scissors than a knife when cutting your own hair?"—and then launch into his next question.

On a few programs—most notably those on National Public Radio (NPR)—your airtime will be much better spent; whether you're being interviewed or simply reading from your book, you can be assured that you'll be treated with greater respect, and that your words are reaching a book-buying audience. NPR is like the Holy Grail for writers.

But on most radio shows—the morning drive-time shows, the late-night marathon talkers—don't be surprised if the questions you're asked seem unnecessarily argumentative, or even confrontational. Be forewarned, radio hosts like to tangle with their guests. They think it passes for intellectual discourse. It brings controversy, electricity, to the airwaves, and it stimulates listeners to call in with their own two cents worth, which in turn means that the radio host can simply take calls from the switchboard and do even less of the work.

When the radio host gives out the station phone number and invites his audience to call in with their questions and comments, he's *hoping* for some trouble to ensue. The worst thing that can happen in radio land is a dead switchboard. Your callers will range, in most cases, from the clinically depressed to the outright lunatic, but as long as you don't give out your home phone number or address, you'll be okay. Just throw yourself into the hurly-burly, act engaged and challenged and invigorated, and don't be afraid to fight back—nobody takes it personally (least of all DJs like Don Imus), and neither should you. It's all in a worthy cause, remember—selling your book.

An even more direct method is the Internet. What better place could you be to sell your book than on the Web sites for Amazon.com or Barnes&Noble.com? If someone is inspired to buy your book, all he or she has to do is click a button! More and more, publicists are arranging for their authors to do these online chats and forums. For my own last book, I was the honored guest in the writer's corner of a major Web server, where every other night, for several weeks, I would log on to answer questions from their subscribers about television writing and getting ahead in Hollywood. I know for a fact that one woman actually bought a copy of my book—she quoted a couple of lines back to me— but I have no idea how many others, if any, followed suit. Most of the time, I spent answering the same basic questions—"What script software do you recommend?" "How do you get an agent?" "How much money do you get for a feature script?"—over and over again, while fending off the attacks—flames, I guess you'd call them—of a bitter, frustrated guy who was wildly incensed by my typos. As a working author, yes, I'll do anything to get the word out, but while I was online, I was not only unsure of who I was talking to, but I found the one-on-one intimacy, the back-and-forth with people calling themselves things like Super Dude or Bella Donna, curiously unnerving.

Perhaps that's what accounted for all the typos.

Still Talking

TV and radio appearances are all well and good—the more of them you can get, the better—but in many cases you can't get them. The publisher's not really behind your book, the topic isn't sufficiently sexy, you have no celebrity status, whatever. Does that mean you have to go to your room and not come out again until the book has been remaindered?

Not by a long shot.

As long as you have a telephone, and you live within range of some bookstores, you can get on the phone and start setting up your own in-store appearances, to read from your book and sign copies afterward. And this is one method that works as well in the boondocks as it does in the big cities, maybe even better. If you call a Manhattan bookstore to set up a reading, you can hear them yawn. They've already got Susan Sontag, Norman Mailer, and Tom Wolfe reading that month. There have been times when I was in a New York City bookstore and I'd have bet my bottom dollar that there were more authors patrolling the aisles, looking for their own books, than there were regular customers.

But if you call up a bookstore in your local hometown, someplace a little less sophisticated, they'll be thrilled to hear a real live author on the line, and happy to arrange some kind of in-store event. If it's a small store, you'll be talking to the owner or manager; if it's one of the chain outlets, you'll probably have to go through what is called the Community Relations Coordinator (or CRC). Either way, your job is to convince this person that you'll be a lively speaker/reader/signer, and that the topic of your book will bring in some interested customers. Some stores will even want to know if you have a mailing list of your own, people that you'll personally be notifying of the event. If you do, great; if you don't, you might immediately consider putting one together.

To make sure there's time for the word to get out—and time for the store to stock up on copies of your book—your event will probably be scheduled a month or so away. If there's anything you can do in the interim to advertise it—such as distributing flyers at your weekly reading club, or phoning interested friends, or putting up a notice on a bulletin board at work—do it. The store is going out on a bit of a limb for you—setting up the event, ordering the books—and you want to do everything in your power to make it a success. That means the biggest audience possible, and as a result the most copies sold.

Now, there are a couple of ways you can go with the event itself. The simplest and least time-consuming is to do nothing more than a signing. Some stores, particularly those that are pressed for space or not especially adept at these things, will arrange for not much more than a card table with a stack of your books on it, and perhaps a homemade poster in the window. Then you're pretty much left on your own, to sink or swim.

Once, when I was out promoting one of my darkest and most adult novels, I arrived at a local bookstore to find that I had been stationed in the Kid's Corner, where I was surrounded by tykes and their moms and big cardboard blowups from Sesame Street. I felt like some deviant, lacking only a raincoat and fedora. Another time, making the rounds for a book I'd written about love and romance, I was positioned between Computer books and Astronomy. This kind of thing happens all the time—sometimes I think that people who go into the book trade are absolutely lacking in the mercantile gene—but if you politely mention that there might be a better or more appropriate location in the store, you can generally get your little display table moved there. If you can't be right up front in the store, where there's the most foot traffic, at least try to be in the section where people who are interested in your topic will naturally gravitate.

And don't be shy. Most people who see you sitting at your little table will steer clear, afraid they'll be snookered into buying something (and they may have a point). Others will just think you're a clerk of some sort. If I told you the number of times I've been asked things like, "Where can I find the *Chicken Soup for the Soul* books?" "What time does the store close?" or "Do you have the men's room key?" you would weep with me. Ever helpful, I answer such questions as best I can, before gently pointing out that the stacks of identical books, all artfully arranged on the table I'm sitting at, were written by me, and that now would be a perfect time to procure a rare and *autographed* copy. You would not believe the number of people who greet this news with unfeigned astonishment. "You wrote this book?"

"Yes, this very one."

"Huh." A pause. Apparently, the news that a person—much less you—wrote this book is almost impossible to process. Then, "So, I wonder, how long's it take to write a book like this?"

Now, my friend, you are about to be taken down the path of no return. Since you are kind of marooned there, tethered to your table for the next hour or so, you are a sitting duck—and let me tell you, there is no shortage of would-be writers out there who are always up for a free tutorial. Once they realize they've got a real live author sitting there, they'll happily quiz you on everything from where you get your ideas to how much money you make per annum. The only thing that is almost guaranteed is that, after they've bent your ear for an hour, while absent-mindedly bending the spine of a copy of your book, they'll conclude by putting the slightly damaged copy back on the stack, wishing you luck, and moving off to the magazine rack. I don't know what it is about these encounters, but I know from the get-go that they're not going to result in a sale. Personally, I'd be too embarrassed to subject a writer to a lengthy interrogation, and then mosey off without even buying his book, but this is not a problem that afflicts many bookstore browsers. One guy, not long ago, ended our lengthy session, during which I had answered no less than a dozen of his questions in great detail, with "Thanks. I'm not gonna buy the book, but I'm sure you'll understand."

"Sure," I said. "Millions of people, all across America, aren't buying this book. You're just one more."

That's why I recommend you step up the action—a signing, where you're just sitting there, hoping some reasonable person with a few bucks in his pocket stops by for an autographed copy, is too passive. If the store is amenable, tell them right up front that you'd like to do a short reading or talk before sitting down to sign. Not only does this turn it into more of a destination event—people might come for a free lecture, who wouldn't come just to spend money—but it gives you a chance to make contact with the customers, a chance to woo them a bit with your stories and your expertise.

If you're going to do a reading from your book, keep a couple of things in mind. The section should be relatively brief—not more than fifteen or twenty minutes' worth—because even the best writing gets boring to listen to after a while. The printed word and the spoken word are two different things, and even the most artful prose—in fact, it's exactly the most artful prose—often sounds stilted when it's read out loud. What you want to do is give your audience a taste of the book—a tempting sample, which will make them want to buy the book to get even more—and you want to give it to them in a self-explanatory chunk. In other words, if you're reading from a novel—and novels are usually better to read from than nonfiction books—don't read a dense and com-plicated scene with a lot of different characters in it. Pick something where the action is somewhat self-contained and, unless you're a pretty fair actor, too, the dramatis personae are limited. Most authors aren't so hot at doing voices. Rehearse the section ahead of time, too, so that you feel comfortable looking up from the page now and then. You want to make eye contact with the people who've come to hear you.

Because that is the essential point—these people have come to hear you. If all they wanted was to read the book, they could have come in anytime and bought a copy. No, what they've come for is to see and lis-ten to the author, to meet some other people, to have some human inter-action. That's why I think it's so important that you also make yourself available to your audience after you've read from your book. I think what most of them come for is to ask questions, to hear other people ask questions, to be a part of a social event. By entering into some dialogue with the customers, you're not only fulfilling your end of the bargain, you're also, quite frankly, moving them closer to the point where they'll actually spring for a copy. The more they feel they've come to know you, even if it's only been for an hour, the more likely it is that they'll come forward at the end of your presentation and ask you to sign a copy of your book.

How many copies will you sell at most of these readings? There's no telling, but the numbers are sometimes pretty low—on my worst nights I've sold none, on my best a couple of dozen. So, if you're looking at this in strictly business terms, signings and such are not what you'd call cost-effective; you'd make more money baby-sitting than you will on the royalties. But there are other benefits, too, from doing them. For one thing, the stores themselves will often do a bit of advertising for you and your book; the small bookshops do their best to get a mention in the current events column of the paper, the big chain stores will usually write you up in their monthly newsletter—a newsletter which, in many cases, they also mail out to a couple of hundred customers. In the weeks before you do your stuff, the stores will prominently display a poster for the upcoming event and copies of your book will be placed in a much better spot than they normally would have been.

But there's even a better reason for doing these presentations wherever and whenever you can. While writing the book, any book, you had several goals in mind—and one of them, aside from striking it rich, was telling the world something. A story. A theory. An argument. You wanted to get the word out, whatever it was, and a reading or signing is just one more opportunity to do that—in person, this time. A book is your baby, and refusing to do everything you can to publicize and promote it would be like abandoning the infant on the church steps. Who could bear to do that? Certainly not you—and me, neither. So, if a store is willing to have you come in and sign your book, or read from it, or talk about it with however many people show up to hear—and again, I've had crowds of two to maybe twenty-five people—then, of course, you do it. It's the grassroots style of building your book, but grassroots campaigns have been known to win in the end.

Hollywood Calling

In every book contract, among the list of rights to be divided between the author and the publisher, there's a clause or two about motion picture and television rights—and unless your agent was asleep at the wheel, she drew a neat, but decisive, line right through that section. As a result, you, the author, retain those rights, and any money that they may fetch.

Somewhere deep in his or her heart, almost every author nurses a secret hope that Hollywood will call. Who cares what happened to F. Scott Fitzgerald out there? We can learn from his experience. And wouldn't it be great to land a movie project. Or even a TV deal.

There's always a chance that you will, too. The Hollywood machine needs constant feeding—it's a vast, insatiable maw, into which hundreds of books are thrown each year, chomped and chewed and churned around, and ultimately turned into everything from feature films to MOWs (aka movies of the week). If your book has any potential for the big screen or the small, someone in the huge entertainment complex will probably take note of it, and with some luck—actually, a pretty big share of luck—the project will make it through all the hurdles and wind up getting made.

But the first step, no matter what, is getting the book noticed.

If your book deal was handled by one of the big literary and talent agencies, such as ICM or William Morris, then you're already one step ahead. Those agencies have branches in Los Angeles, and they also have agents on staff whose job it is solely to market their clients' books to the studios and production companies that are always on the lookout for new material.

But even if you're with a smaller agency—one woman in a rocking chair, sitting in a studio apartment with an iMac and a file cabinet—the agency's probably got a contact or two in the TV and film business. Strictly in the interest of self-preservation, most agents have formed some kind of an alliance with a West Coast counterpart (where the vast majority of these deals are done), and when the agent comes across a property that seems to lend itself to the screen, she forwards it to her comrade-in-arms and together they try to make something happen.

The time to do this, oddly enough, is often before the book is officially published. While the book is in bound galleys, it's an unknown, even mysterious, quantity. If the agent's really doing her job, it can also be positioned as a hot property. She can stir things up a bit and get the Hollywood players, a notoriously insecure lot, worrying that this is the next big thing and they're about to miss it. Nothing works more effectively in Hollywood than the fear that the other guy might have gotten something you want.

But even with the most likely properties—the ones that positively scream "I'm a movie imprisoned in the body of a book!"—it's an uphill battle. In Hollywood, there are just too many variables, too much money at stake, too much politicking, too many layers of bureaucracy. Unless your book has taken off and now sits securely on the bestseller list, you're going to be offered what's often referred to as a "step deal." The first step is the option, and the producer acquires it by paying you a fee, generally under a few thousand dollars. In return, he holds the rights to the project while he shops it around town, trying to get all the pieces (financing, stars, distribution rights, etc.) put together.

An option can be anything you want it to be, but in most cases it will grant the producer six months or a year in which to set things up. If he doesn't manage it, then the option lapses and the rights to your book return to you. If he does, then he has to proceed to the next step, and pay you the money—usually, a lot more than the option—to keep going with the project for another set period of time. When and if the picture gets made, you're due some more. Usually, this money is due when the cameras first roll (in the contract it's sometimes called "on the start of principal photography") and if it's a feature film, you may even have been given what are called "points." These represent a share of the movie's total proceeds after it's been released. But the fact that these points are often referred to as "monkey points" should tell you something about their true value. Even if the movie goes on to set box-office records all over the world, it may never show a profit. Hollywood's book-keeping practices are famously fungible, and authors, I'm sorry to say, are always among the first to be funged.

Still, in search of the elusive film or TV deal, your agent will send out copies of your book to her connections at movie studios, TV production companies, and networks—wherever she thinks it will get read and "covered." By "covered," I refer to the distillation process that most material goes through in Hollywood; since the movers and shakers don't have time to read through all the properties that come in each week, all this material is slogged through by readers—underpaid, overworked young people looking to get a foothold in the business. These readers write one- or two-page reports, called "coverage," summarizing what the books are about and giving them, depending on the studio or company, a score of some kind. Most important of all is the bottom line that says "Pass" or "Consider." A "Pass" pretty much means you're out of the game, at least at that company, but a "Consider" moves you up the ladder to the next rung. Another set of eyes, one invested with more authority, will now read through the material and make another judgment about its screen potential.

With one novel I wrote, I happened to get hold of the inside coverage done by the major movie studio to which it had been submitted. And I've got to say, it was very interesting to read—the novel was essentially stripped down to its main plotline, the characters were sketched in by their ethnic background and age (they all happened to be young, which helped a lot), and then there was a little grading chart for things like "Plot," "Characterization," "Tone." All my grades were either "good" or "excellent," and the box at the bottom was checked "Consider." My agent at the time was sure we'd get a sale. In fact, the day after I'd turned the manuscript in to her, she'd called me up to tell me, "Anybody who doesn't see a movie in this isn't even looking."

Well, that one studio looked, and then decided that they would indeed pursue the project. A few weeks later, I got a call from another agent, the one who was handling the movie deal, and he didn't sound too pleased. "They've made their offer," he said, with a noticeable lack of enthusiasm.

"They have?" I shouted.

"Calm down. It's not all that great." Then he proceeded to tell me the details—something like a $10,000 option payment, a $20,000 production fee, and a consulting deal on the project worth about another $10,000. "The grand total for you is going to come in at around $40,000," he said.

To say I was hyperventilating is to sadly understate the case. "And the bad news would be what?"

"Well, they want to do it as a TV movie—not a feature. We think we can do better elsewhere."

"You do?" My brain was racing. $40,000 in the hand? That was already way more than I'd been paid for the book in the first place. It was probably more than anyone in this lifetime would ever again offer me for anything, including a kidney. I told the agent that, while I was happy to be guided by his judgment in this matter, I was more than happy to collect the forty grand and have my book turned into a mere television spectacle.

"If you say so," he said, as if he didn't know what to make of such a pushover. "But I'll see if there's any way we can sweeten the deal."

That night, and for many thereafter, I went to sleep with visions of movie deals—even if they were only *TV* movie deals—dancing in my head. But no sooner had the project apparently cleared all the hurdles at the big Hollywood studio than there was, as the agent reported to me, a massive purge. "All the people who were enthusiastic about your book are gone," he said. "We have to start over."

He did, and once again we got a bunch of "yes" votes from the new regime. But by the time it happened, months had passed, and these people were themselves in jeopardy now. My god, they had been on the job since spring and hadn't produced a single hit! They were fired, too, and once more my project was dead in the water. As the agent explained to me, "the execs who are coming in now don't want anything to do with any project that's already been sitting around there."

"So, let's put a new title on it and submit it all over again!"

The agent seemed to think that was a bad idea, and I could sense his diminishing interest in the book altogether. My Hollywood dreams were dying before my eyes.

"I'll see what I can do," the agent replied, and as it is now eleven years later, I think it's safe to say the deal is off.

Not that the story ends completely right there. That same book has bobbed to the surface like a cork almost every year since, and each time it has secured a small option fee—ranging from $1 to $1,500—from one production company or another. Everybody seems to see a movie in it, or even a TV series, but no one has ever been able to make it happen. The reasons for this are many and varied, but as the author, I have very little say in the matter.

In Hollywood, you must understand, authors are highly suspect.

After all, we write books, those big thick piles of pages covered with words (so many words!), and who in his right mind would do that all day? It's also assumed that we do not know the first thing about how to convert our work into a movie script or TV show. Screenwriting, it's true, is a very different discipline, but the accepted wisdom is that book authors can't master it and shouldn't even be asked. And even though, in my own case, I have since written a pretty fair amount for TV, I am still not in contention when it comes to turning my books into feature films. That, I am repeatedly told, is a job for the professional screenwriters. Recently, when one of my novels was under discussion as a dramatic series for TV, I was allowed, as a courtesy, to sit in at the meetings, but the agent presiding warned me not to say anything.

Nor did I, for the first half hour. I sat there, dutifully silent, while the would-be TV producer, who held the option on my book, proceeded to "pitch" (that is, try to sell) the project, but in such a bumbling, confused fashion that no one in the room could even begin to follow it anymore. When he had so garbled the plotline that even I, the guy who'd concocted it in the first place, was lost, I jumped in. I couldn't stop myself. I tried to explain what the book was about in a simple and dramatically appealing fashion, and I could sort of feel the studio execs rousing themselves and catching on. But then I got a warning glance from the agent—

the meeting, I guess, had already dragged on too long—and we hastily took our leave. Exiting the room, we knew it was a "no sale."

As soon as we got to the hallway outside, I got an impromptu and stereophonic lecture from the agent and the producer, reminding me I was only there as a favor, and that if I was ever permitted in the room again (which seemed doubtful), I was to keep quiet. Authors, they made quite clear, never knew how to stay in their place.

And even though I've done my best, ever since, to mind my manners, I still haven't seen any deals come through as a result.

All in all, it's best to put Hollywood out of your mind when you're writing a book. I've had several writer friends sit down to write books they were sure would be catnip to Hollywood, but I have yet to see one of these books turned into a movie. The one time I tried it myself, I learned too late that by making the hero a man of Eurasian descent, I had ruined its movie potential from the start. As my agents belatedly informed me, what bankable, big-time movie star—Tom Cruise? Nicolas Cage? Harrison Ford?—would or could play a Eurasian? Oops, my mistake.

It's hard enough to write a book as a book—but if you're trying to write one that also reads like a movie-script-in-waiting, you're going to wind up with a hybrid that does neither thing very well. Books are all about words and language; movies are all about action and visuals. Not to mention the fact that any time you try to guess what Hollywood is looking for, you skirt the shores of insanity. My advice is not to try. Books, by their very nature, take a fairly long time to write and get published, and if you're trying to catch the Hollywood wave, the one thing you can be sure of is that the wave you see today, while you're writing, will be long, long gone by the time your book is done. A much better idea is to concentrate your fire. Write a book so good, so powerful, and so original, that it creates a wave of its own.

Other Paths to Glory

Even as I'm writing this book, I'm feeling like a dinosaur—and one that's just stepped into the tar pits, no less. You can't pick up a newspaper these days without reading one more article about the demise of print, the obsolescence of books as we know them, the stupendous rise of e-books, e-commerce, e-life. When Stephen King "published" his short story *Riding the Bullet* on the Internet, so many people logged on to read it that the system was swamped. And another friend of mine, who's written maybe half a dozen novels that were printed the old-fashioned way, is writing his new one in installments on the Web. Have I followed suit? No. But then, to me, the iMac I'm working on right now seems as miraculously high tech as the Mars probe.

Still, even I can see an asteroid when it's about to hit me. More and more books are going to be published online, others are going to be printed "on demand" (one at a time) when a bookstore customer puts in a request. Lots of books are going to get read exclusively on computer monitors, or with portable handheld devices. Instead of appearing in print, they're going to be translated into code, and show up in glowing type on all kinds and sizes of screens. And what will all of this mean to you, the budding twenty-first-century author?

Not that much, really.

Sure, your work will appear in different formats and venues, and your agent will have to iron out all kinds of clauses and rights that she hasn't had to fret over in the past, but as far as your actual labor is concerned—the writing of words, one at a time, according to a carefully constructed narrative plan—nothing much will have changed. Some writers, I know, wish with all their hearts that they would; with the advent of the super-speedy Internet, they divine an equally speedy, and easy, route to publication. And in one regard—the time it takes for a finished work to get out into the marketplace—that may well be true. If physical books don't have to be printed, bound, boxed up, and shipped to stores, then a text can certainly get out into the public arena in a much shorter time.

But the real heavy lifting—the conceptualizing, the outlining, the fundamental task of *writing* a book—is still going to follow the general steps we've already covered. Even the editing, though it may move along faster, will still have to be done by somebody who diligently attends to your words, and does her best to make sure that they convey exactly what you want them to. Nor is the traditional book—a bunch of printed pages, bound between two covers—in any imminent danger of disappearing. The book is a miraculously economical, transportable, and efficient means of information storage and transmission, to be blunt about it, and it will never wither away. It took too long to get here.

Of course, what many writers perceive in the Internet is chiefly an alternative means to get published. Several companies are already establishing themselves as online commercial publishers. I'd mention their names, but who knows which ones will still be around when this book is published (the antediluvian way)? When or if these companies make money—and how much—remains to be seen, but in the meantime, they are providing another platform for writers, another way to bring the books to market.

The Internet also offers a chance for writers who can't find a commercial publisher, online or off. More and more often, I meet people who tell me they've published dozens of short stories, or even novels, and when I ask them what houses brought them out, they tell me their work was published (though *posted*, I guess, might be more accurate) on the Web—and in almost every case, for no money. Now, there's nothing wrong with this—in fact, there's something rather noble in the desire to get your words and stories out there, without any immediate thought of monetary recompense—and if that's a route you want to take, you have my blessing, whether you want it or not.

Self-publishing on the Web is in perfect keeping, too, with my general philosophy: your goal is to get your work out there and into the world, in as many different venues and to as many different readers as possible. Yes, at present I'd advise going the more traditional routes first, but if Random House and Simon & Schuster don't seem interested, then why shouldn't you try something else? In fact, who's to say some old fuddy-duddy print editor in New York might not come across your book on the Internet, swoon (print editors still do that) over your prose, and offer you a deal to bring the book out in one of those delightfully antiquated paper editions?

The one problem with Internet publishing, if I may be allowed to say so, is that there does remain something suspect, even solipsistic, about most of it. When anything and everything can be published on the Web, by anyone who chooses to post it there, it becomes impossible to know what might have demonstrated real merit, and what is just there because somebody (undoubtedly its author) wanted it to be. Yes, we can always read through it all, and then judge for ourselves, but don't we also have lives to lead and better things to do? The one painful drawback to the publishing industry, as it now stands, may be that it presents such an insuperable barrier to so many would-be authors, but that same stringency is its greatest strength. If a reputable house, or an impressive imprint, brings out a book, that book benefits from the connection. Readers know that it has achieved a certain level of literary accomplishment.

Publishers aren't always the most perceptive lot. A lot of great books (several of them *mine*) get rejected many times before finding a receptive house. But quality really will tell; a good book will eventually find an editor who recognizes its virtues, and champions it through the process. And when we go into a bookstore, or even shop for books at one of the online bookstores, we are, whether we like it or not, relying upon that; we assume that the books we are considering have all measured up to some standard, that they have all been vetted for us by someone, somewhere, whose job it is to see that they were worth publishing in the first place. We may feel bad about all the struggling authors shut out by this exclusionary approach, but if we *didn't* have it, the bookstores would be the size of football fields (though some, I guess, already are), and it would be impossible for any of us to wade through all the indiscriminate chaff to find those few lean blades of wheat. It isn't fair, but then, as I can't be the first one to tell you, neither is life.

The other option, readily available to any author who feels like laying his own money down, is self-publishing. But self-publishing the old-fashioned way—making books and then selling them, one way or another, on his own. For the better part of publishing history, self-publishing was better known as "vanity press" publishing, and its core group of authors was weekend poets and retired army colonels who wanted to publish their memoirs. It had an unmistakable stigma about it; any book printed by a vanity press was automatically excluded from most stores, and book columnists would never deign to review it.

But some of that has changed. While a self-published book is still not accorded the same respect and consideration that a commercially published book gets, there have now been enough big success stories, enough books that started out as self-published volumes and later went on to sell zillions of copies (such as *The Christmas Box*) that everybody, from editors to readers, is now paying more attention. James Redfield started out selling *The Celestine Prophecy* from the back of his car. And when a big-cheese New York editor, who happens to be a friend of mine, recently visited Los Angles, one of her first stops was to a Latina author who had written a book that she was selling all by herself, with great success, at all kinds of local festivals and street fairs. Word of the book had actually traveled as far as Manhattan, and my editor friend wasted no time scooping it up for the big house where she worked—and for a six-figure sum. Miracles like this can happen.

However, like all miracles, they are rare. Your best bet, if you want your book to sweep the nation, is still to find a commercial publisher to take it on. What the big publishing houses have, and you don't, is the massive infrastructure—the editors, the publicists, the network of contacts, the clout, and most of all, the distribution capabilities. They can get your book into stores all over the country; they can track the sales;

they can push it, and you, to the media. Yes, you can do a lot of these things on your own now, with a humble PC, a Web site, and some spare garage space to store all the books you've had printed up, but few of us are very good at all that. It's a costly and time-consuming job, and if you're busy fulfilling orders and running to the post office, then you're not writing your follow-up blockbuster. (If you do self-publish, then let me advise you to keep careful records of your sales figures. When and if a publishing house comes sniffing around your project, they like to see, with some substantiation, just how many copies you've been able to move under nothing but your own power.)

No matter what method you use to get your book out there, through Penguin Putnam or printing up copies in the basement, the Internet can still be used to your advantage in a big way.

If you self-publish, the Internet affords you a cheap and powerful way to advertise and market your book.

And if you go with one of the big publishing houses? Then the Internet can help your book to have a much more fruitful life than it ever would have in the past. For those of us who are considered midlist authors (or less), the Internet keeps our books alive and available a lot longer than they used to be. For most of my publishing career, for instance, my books have been available, in limited numbers, for a relatively short period of time—maybe a few months. After that, if somebody actually wanted a copy, he had to place an order, wait a week or two, then return to the store, when they called to say it was in, to pick it up. You can imagine how well, and how often, this worked out.

But all that has changed now. If somebody actually wants to buy a copy of one of my books and can't find it at the local bookstore, he can log onto Amazon.com, or Barnes&Noble.com, and get a copy delivered to his door, sometimes in a few days, with a couple of clicks. And that has made a mighty big difference for me and many other midlist writers. In the past, I've got to admit, I often found it hard to go out and promote certain books I'd written; I knew they were already off-sale, and that no matter how many lectures or classes I gave, my audience would have trouble buying a copy. It made the whole endeavor feel pretty pointless. But now, even if it's a year or two after the publication date, I can still go out to pitch and promote a book because I know that, if the corner store doesn't have it in stock anymore, the Internet stores do—and anybody I can convince to buy a copy can go right home and do it. Publishers take note of this sales activity, too; if a book is continuing to sell, even in modest numbers, they're a whole lot less inclined to pull the plug on it and destroy their remaining inventory.

All of which, as you can see, once again rewards the motivated author, the one who's willing to do whatever he can to keep his book alive and before the public. I would hope that you are one of those motivated authors; the fact that you picked up this book is a strong indication that you are. If I've been able to make even one thing clear in all the previous chapters, it's that you have to work hard, all along the way, to make your book a success. Your publisher is your partner, but nobody cares more about the fortunes of your book than you do. Your publisher has probably got dozens of titles on the same spring list that yours is on, and while they'd love to see your book do well, they'd be equally pleased to see any other book of theirs ascend into bestsellerdom. To them, it doesn't really matter which book brings in the bucks, as long as the bucks come in.

You, of course, are not so cavalier about it; you want the big book of the season to be yours. And why shouldn't you? Authors, I'll grant, do tend to have big egos—but we have them for a reason. Without them, how would we ever find the willpower and tenacity to sit there for months scribbling down what we think the world needs to hear? We've gone to a lot of trouble, and done an awful lot of work, in our lonely little room under the eaves, so what's wrong with expecting a few accolades when we finally come downstairs?

"And Now for My Next Trick . . ."

Eventually, of course, the publication of your book becomes old news. All the hoopla—if hoopla there was—starts to die down. Friends stop calling to say they've actually spotted a copy at their local bookstore (usually in the same tone of voice you'd reserve for having spotted Bigfoot). Your publicist no longer leaves you breathless messages to let you know she's found a library group— "just thirty or forty miles from your house!"—that would be happy to have you come and deliver a free speech. Your significant other discreetly takes the book off the mantelpiece and puts the candelabra back where it used to be.

These are the times that try the soul.

It's a common problem among authors—this deeply embedded, if unconscious, ineffable, and atavistic belief that somehow the publication of your book is going to change your life. That once the book is between covers and out there in the world, it will bring you fame, fortune, the love of supermodels, and the adulation of the masses. I've seen it a million times among my writer friends who have just published their best attempt at a blockbuster novel, and even among my friends who've just published books that, under the best of circumstances, would compile only a modest sale. One woman I know, who wrote a nice little book about doll collecting, published by a nice little house, got so excited when the book came out that I thought she was going to need to be shot with a tranquilizer gun. For a week or two there, she actually got awfully hard to take. Her publisher had told her they had really high hopes for the book—which in their specialized world probably meant a couple of thousand copies would be sold—but somehow my friend got it into her head that all of America had been waiting, all this time, for a book about her doll collection, and she started to swan around like Joan Collins, freely dispensing all kinds of advice to me and her other writer pals about the marketplace, how to break through, how to persevere when the going got tough, etc. I'm not saying we wished her any ill—we're all too familiar with this strange euphoria to pass any judgment—but I will say it was a relief when a few months had passed and she had safely returned to Earth.

With only the rarest exceptions (a novel like *Cold Mountain*, a memoir like *Angela's Ashes*) do books, especially first books, make such a significant splash that their authors' lives are changed forever. Most books come in somewhere in the middle, between catastrophe and wide acclaim, and that's where most publishers expect them to come in. (I was very disappointed with the sales of one of my early books until the publisher accidentally stapled somebody else's royalty statement to the back of mine. This other guy's book had proven to be so lame, it made mine look like Secretariat!)

But let us say, and I do hope this comes true, that your book has done well, that it has sold out all or most of its printing. What do you do next? Why, you follow up on its success, of course. If the book has made a bit of noise, your publisher will want you to do another, your agent will want you to do another, and most important of all, *you'll* want to do another. There's nothing like success to whet the appetite for more of the same.

Which is, to be blunt, what you might be wise to do—provide a little more of the same. If your first book, for instance, was a nonfiction look at the current music scene, then you would be well advised to follow it up with another take on the musical front—this time concentrating, say, on a particular megaband, or on some aspect of the music business that you didn't really cover the first time. What you're trying to do here is get people who bought one of your books to buy another. You know they were interested in music before—maybe they still are.

It also doesn't hurt to establish yourself as something of an authority in the field, the one that people turn to for information and expertise on this subject. Back when I was making a living writing books and articles on love and sex (yes, yes, I know how absurd that very notion is), I got a request, through my agent, to write a blurb for somebody else's book on the same general topic. I was appalled.

"Why would I give this guy a nice blurb for his book jacket?" I asked my agent. "I want people to buy my book, not his."

My agent sighed, then explained, "You should do it because this sets you up as the authority. You're the guy that other writers turn to for a plug."

"But what about my book?"

"It doesn't do anything to your book other than advertise it on his book. Look at it this way—you're just hitching a ride in this guy's car."

Seen from that perspective—as a totally self-serving act that essentially cost me nothing—I could certainly warm to the task. I sat right down, and after a few false starts—the first versions were too wishy-washy, I was still having trouble getting to the point where I didn't see this other book as competition—I eventually managed to turn out something that sounded enough like unqualified praise to pass muster. At least I know it must have been acceptable because a few months later it showed up on his book jacket.

If it's a successful novel you've written, there's less chance that you'll be setting up shop soon as an authority. It could take you several novels before you do that. (One of the things I most admire about Stephen King is his willingness to boost the stock of other horror writers with blurbs, quotes, and enthusiastic praise.) But even a novel has *some* follow-up potential that you should seriously consider exploiting. Whatever area your novel fell into—romance, horror, literary mainstream—there's something to be gained from writing one more book in the same general vein. You've found an audience, however modest it may be, and these same people may be very inclined to board your bus, as it were, for another excursion. Readers tend to return to certain kinds of books, and if they've identified you as one of the writers who provide them with the kind of story they enjoy, they'll be only too happy to give you another shot. Do well that next time out, and you may have launched a serious, and highly lucrative, career.

There is, in fact, no greater pot of gold than the one that awaits authors who manage to create not only an ongoing world, but one that happens to be inhabited by repeat characters. Did Ian Fleming ever have to look back after creating James Bond? Did Sue Grafton ever regret giving birth to Kinsey Millhone? Is Tom Clancy not grateful every day for his dashing protagonist Jack Ryan? If you are lucky enough to write a murder mystery, an international thriller, a torrid romance, whatever, in which you have a lead character who captures the imagination of your audience, and who could conceivably go on to other, and equally gripping, adventures, then you're crazy if you don't pursue that. Creating a memorable and multifaceted character, one that can not only hold your audience's attention, but grow and change and display different colorations in new stories, is one of the hardest things for a novelist to pull off, and if you've done it, if you've created such a marvelous and fully realized being, you should make the most of it. I have friends, very talented writers, who have been trying, without success, to do it for years.

Hollywood also knows just how hard this is, and as a result they are always on the lookout for just such a creation. With the exorbitant cost of making movies these days, producers keep an eye out for anything that can become a franchise. If audiences had not fallen in love with Mel Gibson as the suicidal cop in *Lethal Weapon*, we might have been spared all the sequels. Anyway, if you can create a strong, charismatic protagonist— one who could be played by, say, Keanu Reeves, or Julia Roberts, or Matt Damon—then you stand a very good chance of finding yourself on Easy Street for life. (If you do, give me a call—I'd like to rent the apartment over your garage.) And let's not forget TV—they're always scouting, too, for a character and a milieu that might lend themselves to a series. Of course, they'd then be looking at stars of mainly TV magnitude—Ted Danson, or Tony Danza, or Amy Brenneman. But I really don't see how that would be a problem for you.

A problem is writing a book that, like most books that get published, does *not* stir up any attention, a book that seems to have been published in the dead of night, distributed under the tightest security, and publicized at a pitch that only dogs can hear. Most of us who write books are used to this; they wash in, and wash out again, like a tide—and get just about as much notice. And even if you do all the things we've discussed, from contacting local bookstores to sending out flyers, the world is a noisy place and it's very hard to make yourself heard above the din.

But does this mean you should just throw in the towel?

Absolutely not. What you can't forget in all this is the essential fact that you've written a book. You've shown you have it in you. You've made it all the way from that idea you first had in the tub to a finished, published book. You know what the odds of that are? You know how many people think they're going to write a book, talk about writing a book, plan on writing a book, and then never actually write a book? Well, I don't know the exact number, either, but it's a lot. So, if you've done it, then that alone should give you an overwhelming sense of accomplishment.

And if your book hasn't exactly set the world on fire, so what? Look at it this way—you are now free to write any other kind of book you want. The world—including your publisher and agent and editor—isn't going to be badgering you to turn out a quickie sequel or volume two. As far as the world is concerned, you can try any other path you want. You always had that option, of course, but now there'll be nobody trying to steer, or stop, you. If your first book was a gardening guide, then maybe now you'll want to try writing a novel of suburban skullduggery. If your first book was a period romance, then now you might want to try a memoir. The great thing about writing is that it's a fresh roll of the dice every time, and you never know what'll turn up.

For some of us, there's no way we'll stop playing, anyway. We happy, and generally impoverished, few can't think of anything that beats seeing our name on the front cover of a book. For that, we'll go through countless hours of solitary work, of private angst, of doubt and worry and sometimes, in the end, disappointment. For us, there's still something *sacred*—and I mean to give that word its full import—about a book, even if it's just a little detective novel, a biography of an obscure artist, or a memoir set in our old hometown. If books are in your blood, as they are in mine, you have about as much chance of changing that as you do your fingerprints.

But then, why would you want to?

Index

Index

239

About the Author

Robert Masello is an award-winning journalist, the author of thirteen previous books, and a successful television writer.

His articles, essays, and reviews have appeared in such diverse publications as *The Washington Post, Newsday, New York* magazine, *Mademoiselle, Redbook, Travel and Leisure, Harper's Bazaar, Town & Country, TV Guide*, and *Elle*.

His books include several novels, published both here and abroad, and nonfiction works ranging from histories of the occult (*Fallen Angels* and *Raising Hell*) to a guide to writing for television (*A Friend in the Business*). His books have been translated into eight languages, from Swedish to Korean.

In addition to various talk shows and specials, he has written for such television series as *Charmed, Early Edition, Sliders*, and *Poltergeist: the Legacy*.

A graduate of Princeton University, where he studied writing under Robert Stone and Geoffrey Wolff, he has also taught and lectured on writing at New York University, Pace University, Brooklyn College, UCLA Extension, and the Columbia University School of Journalism, where he served as an adjunct professor for five years.

He now lives and works in Santa Monica, California.